Art in Los Angeles   Seventeen Artists in the Sixties

This exhibition was made possible by a grant from The James Irvine Foundation.

Los Angeles County Museum of Art

Maurice Tuchman

Art in Los Angeles

Seventeen Artists in the Sixties

Library of Congress
Cataloging in Publication Data

Art in Los Angeles.

Includes bibliographies.
1. Art, American—California—Los Angeles—Exhibitions. 2. Art, Modern—20th century—California—Los Angeles—Exhibitions. I. Tuchman, Maurice. II. Los Angeles County Museum of Art.
N6535.L6A7 709'.794'94074019493 81-6003
ISBN 0-87587-101-1 AACR2

Published by the
Los Angeles County Museum of Art
5905 Wilshire Boulevard
Los Angeles, California 90036

Curatorial liaison for the publication:
Stella Paul

Edited by Jeanne D'Andrea,
Stephen West, and Aleida Rodríguez

Designed in Los Angeles
by Louis Danziger

Text set in Century Schoolbook typefaces
by RSTypographics, Los Angeles

Printed in an edition of 11,000 on
Lustro Offset Enamel Book and Warren's
No. 66 Antique Bulking papers by
George Rice & Sons, Los Angeles

Exhibition Itinerary

Los Angeles County Museum of Art
July 21–October 4, 1981

San Antonio Museum of Art
November 20, 1981–January 31, 1982

Contents

Lenders to the Exhibition

Artist Studio, Venice, California
Betty Asher
Asher/Faure Gallery, Los Angeles
Larry Bell
Mrs. Kathleen Bleiweiss
The Brooklyn Museum, New York
Dartmouth College Museum and Galleries, Hanover, New Hampshire
Ronald Davis
Betty and Monte Factor Family Collection
Lynn Factor, Brentwood, California
Sir John Foster
Sam Francis
Mr. and Mrs. Philip Gersh
Gilman Paper Company Collection
Dr. and Mrs. Merle S. Glick
Hal Glicksman
Milly and Arnold Glimcher, New York
Dr. and Mrs. Charles Hendrickson
Walter Hopps, Washington, D.C.
Robert Irwin
Judge Kurtz Kauffman
Vivian Kauffman
Lyn Kienholz
Mr. and Mrs. Gilbert H. Kinney
La Jolla Museum of Contemporary Art, California
Collection of Frances and Norman Lear
Sydney and Frances Lewis Collection
Los Angeles County Museum of Art
Milwaukee Art Center, Wisconsin
Edward Moses
Museum of Fine Arts, Boston
The Oakland Museum, California
Mr. and Mrs. Richard Jerome O'Neill
Giuseppe Panza di Biumo, Milan
Mr. and Mrs. Morris S. Pynoos
Mr. and Mrs. Jack Quinn
Hanna Renneker
Robert Rowan
Edward Ruscha
Santa Barbara Museum of Art, California
Mr. and Mrs. Henry Shapiro, Chicago
Mr. and Mrs. Stanley K. Sheinbaum
Becky and Peter Smith
Dean Stockwell
The Times Mirror Company, Los Angeles
Dr. Leopold S. Tuchman
University Art Museum, University of California, Berkeley
Whitney Museum of American Art, New York
Laura-Lee and Bob Woods
Edward and Melinda Wortz
Anonymous lenders

Foreword

This year marks almost two decades since Los Angeles began to emerge as a major center of contemporary art. It also marks the Los Angeles Bicentennial, an occasion that prompts the Museum to present this two-part exhibition: *Art in Los Angeles—Seventeen Artists in the Sixties* and *The Museum as Site: Sixteen Projects*. The first is a fresh approach to group shows that reveals the extraordinary achievement of seventeen recognized painters and sculptors who worked in Los Angeles in the sixties. For the second exhibition, sixteen Los Angeles artists who have achieved recognition in the last decade were invited to create works specifically for this Museum's sites—both conventional and nonconventional.

During the sixties an unprecedented number of artists began to mature in Los Angeles, bringing to the city a creative impulse that has permanently defined the community's cultural stance. The exhibition *Seventeen Artists in the Sixties* calls attention to the rich diversity of artistic activity that characterized this period. The occasion of the city's bicentennial, with two decades of perspective on this fertile period, is an especially appropriate time to present a selected retrospective of some of Los Angeles' major artistic talents.

To date, this most fascinating period in our history remains inadequately documented. With the exhibition and its accompanying catalog, the Museum attempts to address this need. The Museum has collaborated with the West Coast Area Center of the Archives of American Art in commissioning a number of interviews with artists and other members of the art community as part of the Archives' California Oral History Project. These documents constitute an invaluable resource for both scholars and the general public. The Archives' role in collecting and microfilming artists' papers is certain to become increasingly important to students of art on the West Coast.

This exhibition could never have occurred without the generosity and support of the lenders. We wish to thank the fifty-two individuals, museums, corporations, and galleries who have contributed to the realization of the show. As always, the Museum's Modern and Contemporary Art Council has supported this project from its inception.

We are especially pleased that the San Antonio Museum of Art is participating in this exhibition, and are appreciative of the enthusiasm and support of its new director, Kevin Consey.

For the commitment shown by the James Irvine Foundation, which has made this exhibition possible as a centerpiece of the bicentennial year, we are especially grateful.

Earl A. Powell III
Director

Acknowledgments

Several people who were active in the Los Angeles art community during the late fifties and sixties generously shared their experiences with me. Discussions with Betty Asher, Irving Blum, James Elliott, and Nicholas Wilder were especially valuable. Christopher Knight's comments about this project were also an asset in the planning stage.

I would like to thank those people in the Museum who were exceptionally involved with this project. Curatorial Assistant Stella Paul was my principal assistant, coordinating all matters of organization of the exhibition and catalog, displaying initiative and exceptional efficiency. Stephanie Barron, Curator of Modern Art, was always available for consultation. Katherine Hart, Assistant Curator, helped us with the myriad details involved with the final stages of the project. Donna Wong, secretary, performed diligently and tactfully. Museum Service Council volunteer Grace Spencer was again indispensable to us in providing archival research materials. I would like also to cite the Photography Department, under the direction of Larry Reynolds, for its special resourcefulness. I am also grateful to Lucille Epstein, docent, for helping us assemble a research library for this project. Laura Revness, Deanna de Mayo, and Robert Pincus gave generously of their time.

Museum Director Earl A. Powell III has been a constant enthusiast and supporter of this project.

I am personally grateful to the Modern and Contemporary Art Council for the unfailing support they have provided the Department of Modern Art once again in the course of organizing this exhibition.

Maurice Tuchman

Introduction

Although numerous exhibitions have surveyed the new art that emerged in Los Angeles in the late fifties, beginning with the Whitney Museum's *Fifty California Artists* of 1962, this presentation is the first to highlight what actually did occur rather than what seemed to be developing.

Given a necessarily restricted gallery space, two basic procedures were possible: an exhibition of, say, one hundred works by the same number of artists—or by fifty, or thirty—as an attempt to document diverse statements; or a show that would focus on the fewer, outstanding figures of the decade, exhibiting their work in depth. I have chosen the second method. Further, I have emphasized the individuality of the selection by showing work that falls for the most part into a single, specific phase of each artist's development in the sixties. By bringing together, for example, a group of sprayed paintings by Billy Al Bengston or the "two-lined" abstract paintings of Robert Irwin, greater insight into the singular achievement of each artist may be afforded than would be possible by a scattered view of their diverse modes throughout the sixties. Such a method of organization allows the viewer, in walking through the exhibition, to encounter singly, in roughly chronological order, artists such as John McLaughlin, Peter Voulkos, and Wallace Berman at the outset of the decade, through a dozen artists of the mid-sixties, to Richard Diebenkorn and Bruce Nauman at the end of the decade. A sense of progression and change is implied. Although there is, of course, nothing magical about the sixties as a discrete entity, it is nevertheless demonstrably true that the late fifties in Los Angeles witnessed a surge of artistic vigor which led some artists who matured in the sixties to attain world-class stature. Although these artists continued to create at a high and distinctive level in the seventies, the general parameters of their work were established by 1970. It is always difficult to omit serious artists of real value from any group exhibition, and certainly the exclusion of perhaps thirty artists whose achievements have already been cited by the Museum with solo shows and acquisitions is particularly felt on this occasion. Such omissions can only be justified by the successful organization of an exhibition of exceptional strength, by inclusion of artists whose work will have enduring interest and importance in art history.

All of the artists, or their representatives, participated in the selection process, often interceding with owners of their work to secure loans. The late Wallace Berman is represented by all his early extant collages and by the issues of *Semina* he produced from 1955 to 1964; these much admired collages fused the mystical and the topical and placed Berman, as Anne Ayres points out in her essay in this catalog, at one end of California's assemblage polarity, with Edward Kienholz at the opposite end. By the late fifties John McLaughlin's pristine canvases took on individual force and commanded respect, but at the turn of the decade a distinct fulsomeness and serene authority, reflected in the use of fewer and more symmetric forms and in a more frequent deployment of black and white alone, became the hallmarks of his style. Peter Voulkos, who influenced most of the artists in the Ferus group, both as sculptor and teacher, created ceramic sculpture of a monumentality and vigor almost unprecedented in the medium; indeed, even today the "crafts" connotation of the clay medium unfairly serves to diminish the importance of these works.

In this catalog, interpretation and appreciation of the work of Voulkos and of the younger ceramic sculptor Ken Price is insufficiently presented largely for the same reason. Although in 1978 I wrote on Price's monumental effort of the seventies, the series called Happy's Curios (*Ken Price: Happy's Curios,* exhibition catalog, Los Angeles County Museum of Art), I could not secure an independent art historical essay for the present catalog on the 1960s work of Voulkos and Price. I hope the interest generated by this exhibition will result in much-needed studies of these artists. Meanwhile, the reader's notice is called to John Coplan's 1966 catalog essay for *Abstract Expressionist Ceramics* at the Art Gallery of the University of California at Irvine.

Of the artists associated with the Ferus Gallery, Irwin, Price, Bengston, Moses, Kauffman, and Kienholz are each represented by a number of their early works. (They are also seen, as are the other participating artists who resided in Los Angeles in the late fifties, in the introductory section of this exhibition, represented by significant works made just prior to their maturity.) Kienholz developed the environmental sculpture format he titled "tableau" with the powerful recreation of a brothel called *Roxys*. The space built for each installation accommodates the furniture, props, and individual sculptures that comprise the work; later the artist would create a container-like space with immovable parts, as in *The Beanery* where we witness the baroque culmination of the assemblage movement. Although neither *Roxys* nor *The Beanery* could be brought to Los Angeles for this occasion, Kienholz is well represented by the notorious *The Back Seat Dodge '38* and *The Illegal Operation,* perhaps the strongest work the artist has made. Sculptor Ken Price has almost nothing in common with Kienholz, except for a shared wizardry of technique and masterly craftsmanship. It is this stylistic disparity that has successfully defeated efforts to label these artists. Price's egg-shaped sculptures of about 1962 appear as miraculously "right," vulnerable yet strong, cheerfully accessible as images yet uncannily mysterious. These are sculptor's sculptures, appropriately prized by artists and by cognoscenti. Robert Irwin's exquisite, cerebral, abstract painting is seen here in the series of "two-line" canvases of 1962, works that challenge the viewer's ability to see an entire field whole. Their creation led Irwin to undertake still more difficult artistic tasks later in the sixties and seventies. These paintings—justly celebrated now—anticipate Irwin's pioneering efforts in recent years to transform public spaces by seemingly simple alterations of the total field (whether by tapes, scrim, wire, or elementary structural additions). Bengston's early sprayed paintings announced a veritably new aesthetic. The chevron that instantly became famous and was for years the artist's trademark was both as unemotional as an industrial technique and as idiosyncratic as a personal symbol. This fusion of tough-minded artmaking with unabashed aestheticism holds for all the members of the Ferus Gallery group, including Craig Kauffman. From the outset one of the most virtuoso of the group, Kauffman is here represented by works made later in the decade, the Bubble series of 1966–67, in which plastic is made to appear colorfully lush and sensuous, with the forms hinting at an odd biological origin. Ed Moses, in a dazzling series of large floral drawings made in 1963, reflects his fellow artists' extraordinary commitment to craftsmanship, but in the most traditional of techniques—graphite on paper.

Larry Bell and Ed Ruscha came to the Ferus group in the early sixties. Bell was influenced by Irwin (and later affected Irwin's development) in his ready acceptance of total-field, geometric concerns, and in the making of sculptures—such as the seven cubes in this exhibition—that welcome pleasing illusions and reflections without abandoning a grave mien. Ruscha, along with his friend Joe Goode, struck a new note in the developing Los Angeles scene with works referring to the new urban idiom of commercial design. Ruscha redesigns, as it were, the styles and packages of a consumer society, filtering them through his ironic, bemused gaze. Joe Goode's work was more stark and emotional in the early sixties than Ruscha's, but equally object-oriented; later in the decade Goode's work such as the Vandalism series, or in this exhibition the Unmade Bed series, reveals an increasing interest in the devices of picture-making (torn canvases, the incorporation of glass and frame into the image) as well as in psychological implications that go beyond Pop art's usual parameters.

English artist David Hockney first came to Los Angeles in 1964, and it has frequently been his residence since that time. Los Angeles had a direct impact upon Hockney's works, as evident in the brilliant portraits and domestic scenes in this exhibition. In his essay on Los Angeles' version of Pop art, Christopher Knight points out that "things" in L.A. took hold of Hockney's imagination immediately after he arrived here; interestingly, Hockney's recent Los Angeles paintings may be seen as an effort to contend with the glaring light that has been so difficult for painters of nature. The quality of light in Southern California also played an important role in inducing Richard Diebenkorn to move to Los Angeles in 1966. His justly renowned Ocean Park series, named after a neighborhood in Santa Monica where his studios are located (an area that also provided subject matter for earlier artists, such as John Altoon and Robert Irwin), intently and lyrically addresses the particular color, humidity, temperature, air currents, and evanescent light conditions of the area. Sam Francis, like Diebenkorn, moved to Los Angeles as an established artist in 1967, thereby further contributing to the city's artistic vitality in the second half of the decade. Francis' "open" series of paintings, among the most adventurous abstract works created in the sixties, exhibited in a one-man show at this museum, is also a direct response to the West Los Angeles ambience. In this exhibition a less well-known series of Sam Francis from the late sixties is presented, characterized, as Susan Larsen writes, by "a heavier, firmer structure alive with fluid, glowing pigment."

Moving south to Los Angeles from San Francisco in the sixties were two exceptional, dissimilar talents: Ronald Davis and Bruce Nauman. Davis would inject new vitality into the tradition of painting *per se* by translating the neglected powers of perspective with new materials and techniques; Nauman would radically extend elements of body and performance art, videotape, and environmental concerns into a personal and influential artistic style and way of thinking. Davis is represented here by works from one outstanding series of the several he created in the sixties, the fiberglass Dodecagons. The exhibition concludes with Nauman's *Video Corridor: Live and Taped* (1969). As the sixties in Los Angeles began with a polar contrast—the painting of McLaughlin and the assemblage of Berman—it concluded with the reaffirmation of painting by Diebenkorn and Davis and the exploratory environments of Nauman.

The New York art world, stimulated each season beginning about 1960 by aesthetic upheavals, sought to locate a common denominator in the style of new artists emerging on the opposite coast. Within a few years the term "L.A. Look" came to be applied to the artists identified with the Ferus Gallery and later to artists who worked with glass and plastic materials integral to the impeccably crafted Los Angeles art works. Curiously, this interest in California developments on the part of New Yorkers did not include any great sympathy for the artists themselves. Simultaneously, however, European museums and collectors displayed an unprecedented interest in Los Angeles artists, clearly evident from exhibitions in London, Brussels, Eindhoven, and Amsterdam, and from collections such as that of Count Panza in Varese, near Milan.

To date, the most significant art writing on this period has been contributed by Los Angeles critics. These writers have been, as may be expected, involved with the artists in many personal ways, whether as friends, dealers, or spouses. Now, however, a new generation of art historians, professionally intrigued but personally detached from these artists, has begun to address basic issues of style and substance in a less biased manner. In this catalog Susan Larsen and Anne Ayres, dealing with abstract painting and assemblage art respectively, seek to characterize the salient qualities of each artist and the roots of his expression. Michele De Angelus and Christopher Knight each points to the connections between Los Angeles' "perceptualism" and its Pop art, and the nineteenth-century American Luminist movement; De Angelus and Knight are eager to dispel the "finish fetish" appellation applied to much Los Angeles work. Finally, Stella Paul has compiled a photographic chronology of the 1960s Los Angeles art world.

The Museum as Site: Sixteen Projects, to open July 21, 1981, is an exhibition that draws upon the talents of many artists who developed in the 1970s. Sixteen of these artists were approached by the organizer of this show, Curator of Modern Art Stephanie Barron, to create site-specific works throughout the Museum—interior gallery areas, the B. G. Cantor Sculpture Garden, the Frances and Armand Hammer Wing and Ahmanson Gallery building facades, the Atrium, and stairwells. I have no doubt this exhibition will reveal that the generation that emerged in Los Angeles during the seventies is one the city can be deeply proud of as it celebrates its two-hundredth birthday.

To the exhibiting artists, all of whom cooperated fully, to the catalog essayists, and to the generous lenders to the exhibition, who are listed individually, I am deeply grateful.

Berman and Kienholz: Progenitors of Los Angeles Assemblage

That's one of the reasons I like Los Angeles, because Los Angeles throws away an incredible amount of value every day. I mean, it's just discarded, shitcanned. From automobiles to desks, to clothes, to paint, to—you know, half-bags of concrete that are hardened up. I mean, whatever it is, there is an incredible waste in the city of Los Angeles, and if you're living on the edge of the economy like that, all the waste filters through your awareness and you take what you want. —Edward Kienholz[1]

It has been twenty years since the art of constructing objects from the preformed "stuff" of the actual world was baptized assemblage and given an official history grounded in twentieth-century modernism.[2] By the early sixties, artists of this alternative medium claimed a mixed heritage that included reality/illusion queries and anti-art gestures. Modernism's emphasis on the thing-as-such favored the found object; at the same time, its search for the "reality" beneath the gloss of civilization encouraged the incongruous juxtapositions of Surrealism. Assemblage was on the cutting edge of advanced art. But, always an ambiguous medium, it also was given legitimacy by modernism's embrace of the "primitive." Assemblage is an activity congenial to tribal and folk-art conventions, as well as to the art of autodidacts, children, and disintegrated personalities—to those, that is, who have not erected rigid boundaries between subject and object, reality and fantasy, life and art, plastic and literary means. Assemblage traditionally attracts the aesthetically rebellious, but also the academically untutored and the artist in pursuit of idiosyncratic vision.

In early American modernism, the investigation of mixed media that emerged from Duchamp-influenced New York Dada was cold by about 1920. Assemblage of the next two decades—in the work of its most noteworthy practitioners, Arthur Dove and Joseph Cornell—indeed appears idiosyncratic. Dove's work is a good example of assemblage's knotty history. Confined to the twenties, his assembled "things" reflect the influence of Dada shock as well as primitivistic aspects of modernism; they are related to usages of nineteenth-century folk art, the legacy of American pragmatism, and a peculiarly American nature mysticism. Cornell's "shadow boxes," introduced in the thirties, combine a nineteenth-century romantic and poetic sensibility with the discoveries of Surrealism; although plastic in means, they emphasize literary content and arcane associations. By the post-1945 period, however, mixed media experienced a resurgence within the mainstream of advanced art in New York. A susceptibility to junk ingratiated itself into Abstract Expressionism's play with "non-art" scraps (de Kooning, Pollock); it exploded in the next generation's freestanding junk constructions (Stankiewicz, Chamberlain, di Suvero) and breakdown of painting/sculpture boundaries (Rauschenberg, Johns, Kaprow, Dine). In San Francisco, the anti- "fine arts" Beatnik mystique joined gestural expressionism with a Surrealist sense of the magically banal (Lobdell, DeFeo, Hedrick, Conner). With the "affluent society" providing a bottomless wastebin fed by throw-away consumerism and mass-media overload, it was Los Angeles especially that made the art of assemblage a heaven-sent metaphor for Wallace Berman's "city of degenerate angels."[3]

Los Angeles in the late fifties and sixties had no monopoly on refuse, detritus, junk; it was, however, already the city of the smoggy future, the archetypal consumer society gagging on the boom of planned obsolescence and unplanned urban sprawl. Vulgar, extroverted, spontaneous, energetic, proudly unsophisticated—Los Angeles discouraged a civilized sense of art historical continuities. As Edward Kienholz had it, "Los Angeles was more of a virgin. When I first came to Los Angeles, it was virgin so far as art was concerned, as far as I could sense and feel it."[4]

Assemblage developed as a shadow side to the famous "L.A. Look" characterized by the cool, the elegant, and the highly crafted. As an idiosyncratic (and often autodidactic) alternative to the newfound professionalism, assemblage evolved as a complex medium for social protest and personal expression. It could be accessible in genre-like narrative content or exclusive in occult reference. The West Coast assemblage phenomenon took off from a Symbolist/Surrealist heritage that had a closer kinship to Beat poetry and underground films than to an understood history of Cubist innovation. Counterculture rebellion saw society as violent, repressive, hypocritical—and individual works of assemblage appeared to preach to the multitudes or speak in undertones to the initiates. Out of the San Francisco/Los Angeles nexus, assemblage developed as a vehicle compatible with the fashions of the period from occult mysticisms and non-Western thought systems to cosmologies of love and human-potential psychologies. The expanded consciousness of drug visions focused upon the isolated object, disconnected from familiar, identifying environments: the support system of comfortable associations disintegrated and novel relationships were suggested. Long and close attention paid to the formal qualities of the discarded, the banal, and the conventionally ugly revealed odd beauties and intense significances. Assemblage evolved as a language of subjectivity and absolutes, its artists seen as poet-visionaries or social critics. Los Angeles produced many serious assemblage artists.[5] Of these, Wallace Berman and Edward Kienholz represent, both formally and expressively, highly diverse approaches to the medium.

What is this, an art show? Where is the art?
—arresting officer at Berman's Ferus show[6]

I found the scene in the automobile and the house of prostitution repugnant. This kind of expression is not art in any sense as far as I am concerned. *—Warren Dorn*[7]

I'm a romantic. I preach. *—Edward Kienholz*[8]

Until recently, the art of Wallace Berman has been something of an underground phenomenon and local affair. Edward Kienholz, on the other hand, achieved an international reputation by the end of the sixties and is often considered *the* West Coast artist. Yet both occupy seminal positions. Berman traditionally is cited as the progenitor of Los Angeles assemblage and as a conduit of occult sources and private reveries. Tragically, Berman died in a car accident in 1976 at the age of fifty; although retrospectives followed, during his lifetime he had avoided the limelight of regular gallery shows and the pragmatic "moves" of art-as-career. Edward Kienholz is the towering figure—the artist of public engagement and baroque

Fig. 1
Wallace Berman
Veritas Panel (closed), 1949–57 (destroyed)
Mixed media

Fig. 2
Wallace Berman
Veritas Panel (open), 1949–57 (destroyed)
Mixed media

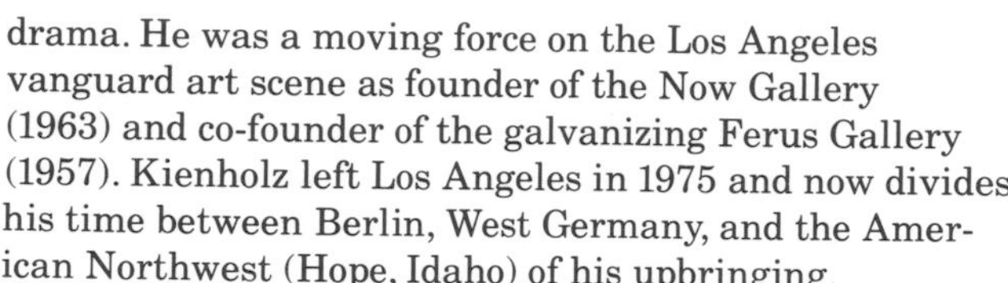

drama. He was a moving force on the Los Angeles vanguard art scene as founder of the Now Gallery (1963) and co-founder of the galvanizing Ferus Gallery (1957). Kienholz left Los Angeles in 1975 and now divides his time between Berlin, West Germany, and the American Northwest (Hope, Idaho) of his upbringing.

In the powder-keg environment of the sixties, both Berman and Kienholz experienced the fallout of outraged sensibilities. Although most postwar artists denied that shock was the intent, the medium of assemblage remained a magnet for controversy and was associated with neo-Dada menace. At the same time, with its stress on actuality and its sympathy for narrative associations, assemblage can be highly accessible to the viewer. Because it sheds high-art intimidation, assemblage frees the viewer to participate on his own terms and, in the process, invites untutored certainties. When—as in the cases of Berman and Kienholz—the subject matter is believed offensive, assemblage by its very form works to deny redeeming value. Berman's arrest in June 1957 at his first and only Ferus Gallery exhibition was precipitated by unidentified complaints concerning a sexually explicit image included in an assemblage. The arrest was an unobtrusive event generating no newspaper response and no art-community demonstration. The artist and the gallery were not well known; more nearly unknown in 1957 was the art of media exploitation and counterculture organization. Fined $150, Berman quietly moved to San Francisco and then to Marin County, returning to Los Angeles in 1961. In March 1962 an exhibition called *Edward Kienholz Presents a Tableau at the Ferus* introduced *Roxys,* a three-dimensional environment that recreated a house of prostitution. *Roxys* combined mannequin and doll fragments with other found objects in a realistic setting that included music and aromas. It was Kienholz's first tableau; his reinvention in stridently modernist terms of the traditional nineteenth-century genre scene fused nostalgia and nightmare. *Roxys* was a *succès d'estime* at the vanguard Ferus, but four years later it became a *succès de scandal* at the respectable Los Angeles County Museum of Art. *Roxys* and *The Back Seat Dodge '38,* (cat. no. 76) created a county-wide debate on such emotional issues as art versus pornography, government interference versus museum responsibility, and county stewardship of public morality versus professional art expertise.[9]

Fifteen years after Los Angeles County Museum's exhibition, several tableaux, including *The Back Seat Dodge '38*, return to Los Angeles as part of a civic celebration—their historic and aesthetic significance are beyond dispute. Less clamorous, however, is the sense of Wallace Berman's distinction within the Los Angeles art scene of the sixties. His large freestanding assemblages of the 1957 Ferus exhibition—*Veritas Panel, Temple, Factum Fidei* (or *Cross*)—are known only from photographs and memories. Berman is represented in the present exhibition by five of the twelve untitled "parchment" paintings (cat. nos. 32–36) that formed an important part of the original Ferus show, and by a complete set of *Semina* —nine small unbound albums of drawings, poetry, photographs, and collages produced on a hand press by Berman from 1955 to 1964 (cat. nos. 23–31). Thus, an understanding of Berman's importance as progenitor of a Los Angeles assemblage movement is best served by a discussion of the destroyed assemblages from the early Ferus exhibition. Although his mature oeuvre investigated numerous media,[10] its consistent symbolic resonance was established in the 1957 show. These assemblages did not form a tableau in the unified and narrative mode of Kienholz; nevertheless, the installation as a whole suggested a cohesive—if elusive and multivalent—thematic organization.

> I'm letting it come through from dead Poets.
>
> —*Wallace Berman*[11]

Berman's earliest extant sculpture, a work in wood titled *Homage to Hesse* (1949–54), exhibits a feel for the spaces and forms of Giacometti and Arp and for the textural sensuousness of Brancusi. Keyed by the title, its formal harmonies suggest a physical evocation of the magical activity and formula called the "Bead Game" that occupies the philosophical center of Herman Hesse's masterpiece *Magister Ludi*.[12] Translations of Hesse's work provided Berman—as it did for a later generation of youth in the sixties—with inspiration and a workable integration of Eastern and Western thought. The later editions of *Semina* included poetry by Berman, by his friends in Los Angeles, and by poets associated with the San Francisco renaissance. In the early editions, Berman's sense of a unifying stream of consciousness and of a magical confraternity was attracted to the French Symbolist and Surrealist tradition and to the visionary poetry of Blake, Tagore, and Yeats.[13] The existence of a secret brotherhood of minds stretching backward and forward in time is essential to Hesse's novels in which spiritual journeys of discovery parallel the mundane passage from birth to death. This brotherhood is deeply felt in Hesse's poem "The Bead Game," (included by Berman in *Semina 2* (1957):

> Music of the spheres, music of the masters
> We venerate and gladly harken to,
> To glorify with taintless celebration
> The spirits of the great of long ago
> ...
> And none of us can fall from out their courses
> If not toward the holy colophon.

Berman's personal colophon, his printer's mark, was announced in *Semina 2* by the motto "ART IS LOVE IS GOD." Although the tenet was made Berman's own, it is explicit in the work of Hesse. Included in the first edition of *Semina* (1955), Hesse's "To a Toccata by Bach" presents a grand equation: "And further the great creative urge swings back toward God.../ It is drive, it is spirit, it is struggle and joy./ It is love."[14] The quintessence of Berman's Ferus exhibition is this conscious cultivation of the sacred.

Fig. 3
Wallace Berman
Temple, 1957 (destroyed)
Mixed media

Fig. 4
Wallace Berman
Factum Fidei, 1956
Mixed media

Accompanying *Homage to Hesse* at the Ferus exhibition were three large, freestanding assemblages that incorporated disparate fragments from the worlds of nature and manufacture and from Berman's wholly personal repertoire of drawings, calligraphy, poetry, and photographs: *Veritas Panel* (apparently worked on from 1949 to 1957), *Temple* (1957), and *Factum Fidei,* (1956). *Veritas Panel* (fig. 1) is a container for highly subjective relics which, keying associations with ancient mystical paths, reveal the artist as a carrier of truth. The assemblage is dominated by Berman's photograph of his wife, Shirley Berman. Compassionate, accusatory, enigmatic, the large eyes evoke an iconic madonna, the High Priestess of the Tarot—or even an allusion to the Cabalist concept of *bina,* feminine understanding. The title of this "truth panel" derives from the inscription *(veritas)* that is painted on the photograph. It is scrawled with Latin-sounding neologisms suggesting mysteries of truth, confirmation, being, existence, ecstasy, and descent into watery depths in quest of rebirth; images of a free flying bird (panel closed) and of sunlight and human buoyancy (panel open) echo the calligraphy (fig. 2). Using letters and numbers, Berman alludes to ancient wisdoms —a kind of Judeo-Christian eclecticism that hints at possibilities but does not spell out certainties. The number 12, revealed only when the panel is open, may refer to the twelve "parchment" paintings (disciples or witnesses) that comprised an integral part of the Ferus exhibition. Painted with black ink, the chance configuration of Hebrew letters is made timeworn by being torn in eccentric patches from a larger sheet of paper, itself artificially aged by woodstain. Affixed to canvas, they create the allure of an archaeological conservation of venerable and incomprehensible teaching. Originally twenty-two pieces were planned[15]—perhaps related to the twenty-two letters of the Hebrew alphabet and the twenty-two major arcana of the Tarot deck. *Veritas Panel*'s elusive references are concentrated by the probing gaze of Shirley Berman; she challenges the viewer to the introspection offered by the mirror behind a small door.[16] This mirror is confronted only after passing through a scrap of Berman's handwriting. The implication is that the "characters" of a personal script create a parallel system to the "character" that is an individual's private truth. Such correspondence is consistent with Berman's method of symbolic linkages. The High Priestess, for instance, is signified in the Tarot by *beth,* the second letter of the Hebrew alphabet and the force that begins the creation of the world. Behind *beth* stands *aleph,* the source of the letters of the alphabet and of all sound—that which makes possible language and understanding. In the system of the Tarot, *aleph* expresses the unity of the Creator; moving through levels of being, it becomes the unity of the divine and the demonic, and the collective unity of mankind. It is the letter-sign of the Tarot's first arcanum, and its image is the Juggler. If Berman took *aleph* as his "soul-letter," he did so in partnership with *beth,* the High Priestess and mediator of *Veritas Panel.* His identity with mankind is expressed in the act of artmaking. He becomes the Juggler with his magician's wand who deals in images and letters and numbers and who manipulates the shapes and textures of the world in order to create a reliquary of mysteries.[17] Unlike Edward Kienholz, who feels that "art should be an easier experience" for the viewer, Berman is brother to Mallarmé— "Everything sacred, and which wishes to remain sacred, is enveloped in mystery. Religions shelter behind arcana unveiled only before initiates. Art too has its mysteries."[18]

Temple and *Factum Fidei* enlarge the theme. Literally a container, *Temple* (fig. 3) is a vertically upended, cratelike construction that is open on one side. It is the sanctum of a priestly contemplation. An apparition within the temple recalls the figural conventions of medieval art; it appears to float in an otherworldly space and is without corporality beneath hooded drapery. A large key hung about the figure's neck holds forth the promise of mysteries unlocked. On the walls of the temple a photograph of mentor Herman Hesse mediates between ancient and contemporary rituals in the forms of Berman's "parchment" painting and his photograph of a Rachel Rosenthal "Instant Theater" event.[19] On the floor of the assemblage the cover of the first edition of *Semina* reveals Berman's eerie photograph of the Los Angeles poet Cameron, an inspired sorceress within Berman's circle of like-spirited friends. Placed on an object that is both prayer stool and footlocker, she functions as guardian and transmitter of the secrets. Ultimately *Temple* is inspirited by the loose pages of *Semina* which, "seeded" randomly on the floor, form a germinant network of "dead poets" and living singers. This brotherhood is focused by the third assemblage, *Factum Fidei* (fig. 4). It presents a rough-hewn wooden cross firmly set upon a wooden crate or altar; from the transverse bar, attached by an iron chain, hangs a close-up photograph of sexual intercourse inscribed with the phrase "factum fidei." The assemblage is an icon; it expresses the "act of faith" of a prototypal heterodoxy. A correspondence is set up that unites the Christian resurrection theme with the creative forces of human sexuality. Formally, the sexual image echoes the composition of the cross; this correspondence is deepened, however, by visual and symbolic suggestions of a rose—perhaps an allusion to the rose of Rosicrucianism, an esoteric knowledge itself influenced by the Cabala. An explicit sexuality replaces the rose as the flower of Love and the center of Wisdom. In *Factum Fidei,* the rational, geometric, and synthetic structure of the cross is completed by the rose of sexuality—intuitive, organic, and god-animated. In Cabalistic terms, the act of intercourse structures the universe by uniting masculine and feminine principles, wisdom *(chochman)* and understanding *(bina).* In contemporary terms, the assemblage implies a surrender of the ego-centered self to dualism-destroying powers. Berman's assemblages obviously invite multiple interpretations that, in Cabala-like manipulation, pile association upon association to convey hidden levels of meaning. One starting point would see the Ferus Gallery installation as a coherent whole in which *Factum Fidei* evokes an icon of a unifying absolute,

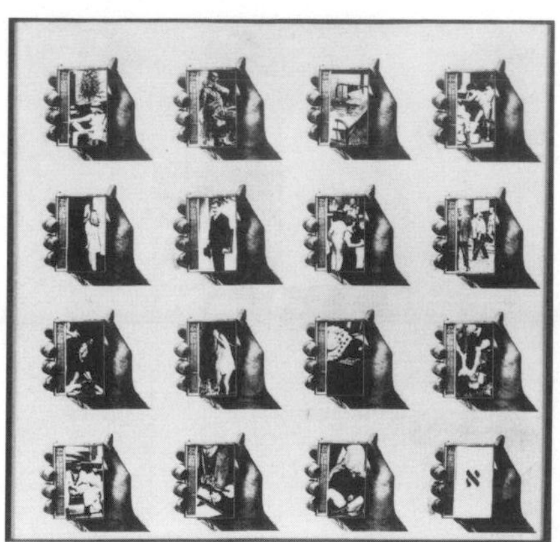

Fig. 5
Wallace Berman
Bouquet, 1964
Verifax collage
28 x 29⅜ in.
(71.1 x 74.6 cm.)
Los Angeles County
Museum of Art, Los Angeles
County Funds
65.20

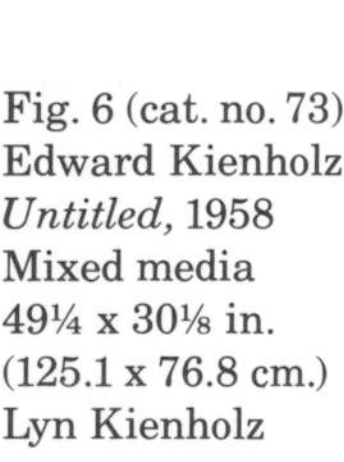

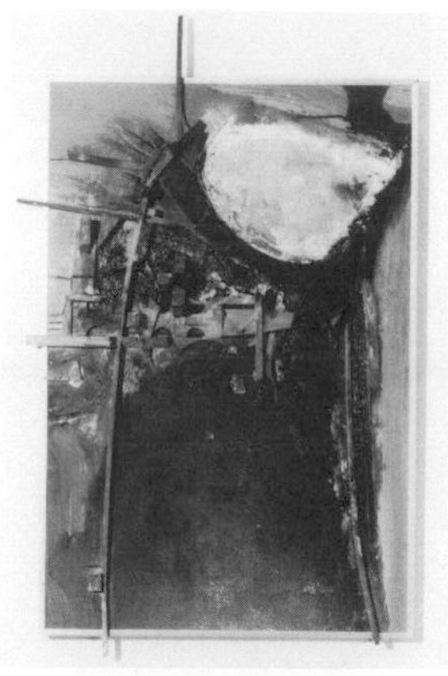

Fig. 6 (cat. no. 73)
Edward Kienholz
Untitled, 1958
Mixed media
49¼ x 30⅛ in.
(125.1 x 76.8 cm.)
Lyn Kienholz

Temple a community of belief and a seedbed of revelatory possibilities, and *Veritas Panel* the veiled autobiography of an individual initiate and spiritual traveler. In conjunction with the "parchment" paintings, this threefold unity turns the entire gallery into a temple and the act of artmaking into a sacred rite.[20]

As containers for spiritual accumulations, Berman's large three-dimensional assemblages[21] were superseded in his later Verifax collages by a flat grid format. In the Verifax collages (fig. 5), isolated "found" pictures are centered on the constant image of a small hand-held transistor radio. These individual units, mechanically reproduced on an old Verifax machine, are mounted on supports of varying sizes. The radio "ground" of the collage is a receiver of divinities and demons, a transmitter of talismans and secret codes: Hebrew letters, crosses of all types, locks and keys and doors; fragments of Greek and oriental sculpture, and newspaper photographs of contemporary religious leaders; female nudes, body parts, and star clusters; guns and snakes and birds and roses and mushrooms; press celebrities—the "angelheadedhipsters"—and, as George Herms put it, "the passing parade of angels in human disguise."[22] Throughout the series the same images are often repeated. Like a cinematic technique, their impact vibrates according to placement within a montage sequence. Equally, the images are a "deck" of symbols to be dealt out in the manner of a fortune-telling grid. A medieval sensibility takes the objects of the world as signs of Revelation. A process prefigured in the three-dimensional assemblages, each image of a Verifax collage functions as a starting point for breaking into a circle of mystery.[23]

In Berman's art, reality is not caught in an intellectually constructed net of order; rather, it is invited to reveal itself through random configurations and trial-and-error arrangements. Although the inventions of Surrealism remain crucial to Berman's art, they were less relevant to the ambience of the sixties than was the pervasive allure of arcane metaphors—the Tarot, astrology, white and black magic, palmistry—as well as the I Ching, Cabalistic and Christian esoteric lore, American Indian rituals. In popular psychology, too, Jungian thought suggested that, "All divinatory practices, from looking at tea-leaves to the complicated oracular methods of the I Ching, are based on the idea that random events are minor mysteries which can be used as pointers to the one central mystery."[24] Fascination with occult belief systems and with hallucinogenic drug experiences coalesced—on the West Coast especially—with earlier Beat sympathies for Symbolism and Surrealism. Further, counterculture withdrawal from the violence and hypocrisy of the "establishment" paralleled a spiritual tradition of anonymity. From this mix was created the underground artist-poet-seer; and the art of assemblage yielded the compatible medium.[25] Berman's assemblages of the 1957 Ferus exhibition presaged the Los Angeles assemblage explosion of the sixties, but it was his particular genius to fuse underground preoccupations with compelling images and inventive forms. An act of surrender to the Cabalist doctrine that heaven and earth mirror each other, Berman's revelatory art brought enigmatic messages for surviving in the world.[26]

> I would like my work to be understood for just exactly what it is: one man's attempt to understand himself better.
> —*Edward Kienholz*[27]

> They're fantasies. They're fantasies that are worked out in 3-D.
> —*Edward Kienholz*[28]

Edward Kienholz's rural and Protestant upbringing was often solitary within the context of a tight family unit. Born near the Idaho-Washington border, he absorbed from childhood the continuities of farming life—an intimacy with births and deaths and the rhythms of the seasons, a respect for nature's power and caprices and for the necessary competencies of man's survival. Physically strong and early trained in manual skills, Kienholz would channel into his art a satisfaction for working with his hands and a feel for efficient rather than abstruse solutions. With a variety of make-do jobs and some erratic college experience behind him, Kienholz was living in Los Angeles by 1953. The poet David Meltzer described the camaraderie that pervaded the artist's working space on Santa Monica Boulevard behind a fiberglass car-body shop:

> Kienholz, from the Northwest, expansive, gregarious, goateed, energized.... The door was always open and, whether Ed was working or not, there were usually people hanging out, talking, drinking. Kids in the neighborhood would sometimes come around to watch Ed hammer together his early constructions. An open house. It was my first introduction to working artists and some of the most interesting on the scene passed through Ed's: John Altoon, George Herms, John Kelly Reed, Craig Kauffman, Billy Al Bengston.... At Kienholz's studio I met Robert Alexander and Wallace Berman.[29]

Kienholz's early abstract "paintings" are low-relief constructions of scraps of wood nailed and glued to a panel support (fig. 6); they were painted densely and rapidly, usually with a house broom and "pouring" technique. Pragmatically, he fused his poverty situation with modernism's permission to exploit "non-art" materials. Independently of New York and San Francisco, he deaestheticized the art object while stressing the emotional force of abstraction and tactile body identification. These works gave way in about 1957 to painting constructions with centralized imagery, photo-figuration, and social commentary—works that increasingly invaded the viewer's space. By 1960 the wall-bound constructions of wood fragments, paint, and the occasional preformed "found" object were joined by fully three-dimensional "off-the-wall" assemblage.[30] *John Doe* and *Jane Doe* infused new life into the broken doll and mannequin imagery explored by Surrealist art of the thirties; at the same time they announced sixties sympathy for the representational object.[31] These companion pieces—"proto-tableaux"

Fig. 7
Edward Kienholz
Roxys, 1961
Furniture, bric-a-brac, live goldfish, disinfectant, perfume, juke box, clothing, etc.
Collection Reinhard Onnasch, Berlin, West Germany

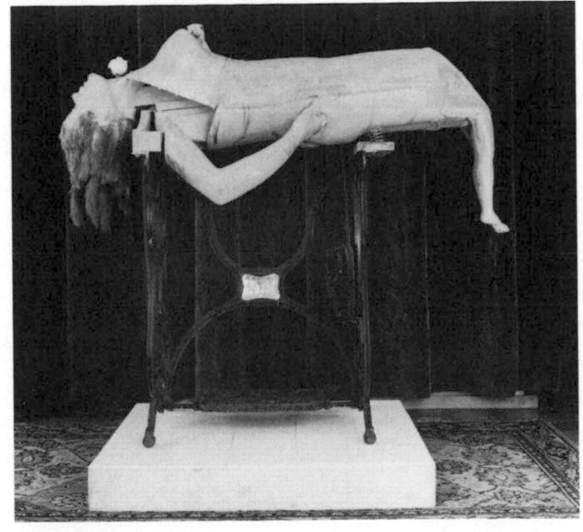

Fig. 8
Edward Kienholz
Five Dollar Billy
(from *Roxys),* 1961
Paints and fiberglass, sewing machine, mannequin parts, squirrel, nuts
40 x 45 x 22¼ in.
(101.6 x 114.3 x 56.5 cm.)
Collection Reinhard Onnasch, Berlin, West Germany

—continue to shock by the violation of the human figure, but they also ingratiate by a straightforward theme. Modern men and women are alienated from their emotions and body truths; behind the pretense of maturity lie psychological fragmentation and sexual anxiety.

Although *Roxys* (fig. 7) is Kienholz's first tableau, it was preceded by other assemblages from 1960 that use detached parts of mannequins to propose depersonalized, mechanized sexuality—an unapologetic focus upon women as sex objects. The impact of, for instance, *American Lady* and *American Girl* is disconcerting because the message is mixed. The artist's exploitation of the female image exists simultaneously with a felt sympathy for damaged, incomplete human beings. As sexual emblems, the trapped fragments are mindless (decapitated) and ineffectual (armless and legless); they are both victims and arousers of fantasy. In *Roxys* the subject matter of a house of prostitution forces home the tension. The doll as helpless plaything/sacrifice merges with the erotic challenge of sleek mannequin legs, only to be further cursed by images of inner decay and stupor. The squirrel gnawing through the chest of *Five Dollar Billy* (fig. 8) and the mindless grin—trapped under a burlap bag—of *Dianna Poole, Miss Universal* give only two examples from a nightmare of brilliantly shocking inventions. The prostitutes of *Roxys* were grounded in the artist's own innocence and apprehensions, but they remain icons of the violation of the human spirit. By laying out his personal fantasies, Kienholz unmasks shared cultural assumptions and makes confrontation unavoidable.[32]

"My work," Kienholz has commented, "is devised to show life stripped of sham and hypocrisy."[33] His tableaux of the sixties discredit heroics and expose the banality attendent upon social malignancies (*The Illegal Operation,* 1962 [cat. no. 75]; *Five Car Stud,* 1972), institutionalized brutalities *(The Birthday,* 1964; *The State Hospital,* 1966), adolescent alienation and lonely aging *(The Back Seat Dodge '38,* 1964; *The Wait,* 1964–65), time's wastage *(The Beanery,* 1965), and the insanities of a doomsday world (*The Portable War Memorial,* 1968). In these and other tableaux the viewer is disoriented by the contrast between big-concept absolutes and extreme specificity. Crucial to this tension is Kienholz's manipulation of space and time. His use of a rational stage space and correct "historical" detail sets up expectations of a safe world; dreamlike fragmentation and metamorphosis of objects then subvert that world. The impact of objects once handled by real, if anonymous, people is at odds with the distancing of art. Equally, the seductions of sentiment are jarred by sympathy with the timelessness of human pain. Thus, if Kienholz's art is an "easier experience" intellectually, it is all the more emotionally disconcerting. The sport of viewer participation is mocked by the act of public voyeurism, and storytelling accessibility deepens conflict—compassion and fear rival disgust and denial.

Kienholz's empathy for suffering speaks to a smashing of childhood promises and a sadness for an admired American value system gone awry. It suggests a secular puritanism concerned not with flawed souls but with neurosis and distorted social conditioning. The impulse to expose sham reveals an idealism consistent with the distress and moral challenges of the sixties. In a powerful mix characteristic of assemblage's history, Kienholz serves moral commentary by linking modernism's anti-aestheticism with the accessibility of nineteenth-century genre sculpture.

> But all my work has to do with living and dying, our human fear of death. —*Edward Kienholz*[34]

> ART IS LOVE IS GOD. —*Wallace Berman*

Whether its history was modernist venture or idiosyncratic usage, assemblage in the sixties appears in retrospect as something of a period style and a response to the period's social turbulence. It was during the counterculture revolutions that the need to break down rigid polarities of thought struck a chord with great numbers of people. Artists turned to assemblage as a way of returning spiritual value to the objects of the world; to combat, that is, what Robert Duncan has called the "trashing of the world-mind."[35] With the malignant proliferation of waste comes a deeply felt, if not precisely understood, withdrawal of meaning from life. Writing persuasively on the "normal" state of schizophrenia in twentieth-century culture, John Vernon has commented that, "Waste is created by the structure Western thought gives to objects, for waste is possible only when objects whose full meaning is "use" have become useless. Schizophrenics... are fascinated by waste, by their own waste deposits and the waste deposits of the object world, that is, by junk."[36]

The assemblage artist, rather than simply hoarding junk, reformulates and develops new contexts for the detritus of the world. Assemblage can make manifest the body-self split inherent in Western dualist thought and intensified by a civilization honoring materialism. When objects have only "use" value, human beings are themselves reified. They become fragmented and interchangeable objects—brothers and sisters to the horrific figures of Kienholz's tableaux. Another possibility of assemblage is the re-inspiriting of forgotten objects: in the process, the mysterious continuity of human beings and their world is affirmed—as in the meditative assemblages of Wallace Berman.

In Southern California, where social eruptions and esoteric interests seem magnified, the art of Berman and

Kienholz had an idiosyncratic look, sidestepping as it did the aesthetic issues dominating assemblage in New York. Instead, the potency of their art as revelation and sermon developed in two opposing directions reaching back to earlier American traditions. Barbara Novak has distinguished two tendencies of religious experience: "On the one hand, the traditional projection of the self into an anthropomorphic baroque ecstasy; a form of appropriating the world. On the other, a serene, almost Oriental absorption of the self into the cosmos, an annihilation of the self."[37] These tendencies, traced through nineteenth- and early twentieth-century art, again present themselves in the secular morality of Kienholz's *Roxys* and the hermetic spiritualism of Berman's 1957 Ferus exhibition. For Kienholz, the artist projects his fantasies into reality; for Berman, the artist is the meditative center through which the cosmos flows. In the sixties in Los Angeles, the baroque opera of Kienholz and the arcane doxology of Berman represent polar aspects of the city's extensive assemblage activity.

Notes

[1]*Los Angeles Art Community Group Portrait: Edward Kienholz,* interviewed by Lawrence Weschler, 1977, Oral History Program, University of California, Los Angeles, vol. 1, p. 109. Quotations from the UCLA transcript occasionally have been corrected by the artist for the purposes of this essay.

[2]William C. Seitz, *The Art of Assemblage,* The Museum of Modern Art, New York, 1961.

[3]Wallace Berman, *Semina 2,* 1957, back cover.

[4]Kienholz interview, vol. 1, p. 133. Kienholz is comparing Los Angeles with San Francisco.

[5]In the late fifties and sixties artists as distinct in character as Wallace Berman, Bruce Conner, George Herms, and Edward Kienholz spearheaded an assemblage "movement" in Los Angeles. Although Bruce Conner is a San Francisco artist, his one-man show at the Ferus Gallery in 1962 and his inclusion in major group exhibitions at the Pasadena Art Museum, the U.C. Irvine Art Gallery, and the Los Angeles County Museum of Art made him an influential force in Los Angeles. Assemblage attracted many first and second generation practitioners, and a partial list spanning the sixties would include Tony Berlant, Sabato Fiorello, Llyn Foulkes, Dennis Hopper, Sandra Jackson, Fred Mason, Richard Pettibone, John Reed, Betye Saar, Dean Stockwell, John Schroeder, Ben Talbert, Edmund Teske, and Gordon Wagner. Emerging to exhibit in the seventies were, among others, Simone Gad, Bruce Houston, Phil Orlando, and Nancy Yodelman.

[6]Quoted in "An Interview with Walter Hopps," *Wallace Berman Retrospective,* ed. Hal Glicksman, Otis Art Institute Gallery, Los Angeles, 1978, p. 9.

[7]Letter from Warren M. Dorn, Los Angeles County Supervisor, to Edward W. Carter, President of the Los Angeles County Museum of Art Board of Trustees, March 17, 1966, quoted in Gerald D. Silk, "Ed Kienholz's 'Back Seat Dodge '38,'" *Arts Magazine,* vol. 52, no. 5, January 1978, p. 117, n. 1; also see "Kienholz Scrapbooks," Los Angeles County Museum of Art Library or the Archives of American Art, San Francisco, microfilm roll 1042, 1-209.

[8]Alfred Frankenstein, "Kienholz Stirs Up a Storm," *San Francisco Chronicle,* April 3, 1966, p. 23; quoted in Silk, "Back Seat Dodge," p. 114.

[9]The offending item in the Berman exhibition was presumed to be the close-up photograph of sexual intercourse forming part of the assemblage *Factum Fidei.* In a comedy of errors, it was overlooked by the arresting officers who seized instead upon a relatively inoffensive drawing. Brief discussions of the arrest are provided in Merril Greene, "Wallace Berman: Portrait of the Artist as Underground Man," *Artforum,* vol. 16, no. 6, February 1978, pp. 56–57; Betty Turnbull, *The Last Time I Saw Ferus 1957–1966,* Newport Harbor Art Museum, Newport Beach, California, 1976, n.p.; *Berman,* p. 9. In Kienholz's exhibition at the Los Angeles County Museum of Art, the prostitute *Five Dollar Billy* of the *Roxys* tableau proved particularly objectionable; the figure lay on her back on a sewing machine treadle that could be activated by the viewer; a four-letter obscene word was carved into the assemblage. Compromise was reached when Kienholz agreed to enlarge the platform upon which *Five Dollar Billy* rests, thus slightly distancing the viewer. The sexually en-

gaged couple within *The Back Seat Dodge '38* was revealed only to groups touring with museum docents. Those under eighteen years of age were not admitted to the exhibition unless accompanied by responsible adults. For Kienholz's extensive comments on the ruckus, see Kienholz interview, vol. 2, pp. 376–99; see also "Kienholz Scrapbooks," for a compilation of newspaper and magazine coverage.

[10]Berman's mature work is comprised of three-dimensional "junk" assemblages (c. 1949–57), untitled "parchment" paintings (1956–57), *Semina* (vols. 1–9, 1955–64), cover designs for small press publications, and a body of photography. He is perhaps best known for an extensive group of collages made with an old Verifax copying machine; and for assemblages of small stones, as well as *in situ* boulders and walls, inscribed with Hebrew characters.

[11]Quoted in "Hopps," *Berman,* p. 9.

[12]As interpreted by Hesse's hero Joseph Knecht, "The Game encompasses the player at the conclusion of his meditation in the same way as the surface of a sphere encloses its center, and leaves him with the feeling of having resolved the fortuitous and chaotic world into one that is symmetrical and harmonious." Herman Hesse, *Magister Ludi,* trans. Mervyn Savill, New York, 1949, p. 10. Parallels between the Bead Game and the Cabala are drawn by Herbert Weiner in *9½ Mystics: The Kabbala Today,* New York, 1969, pp. 118–19.

[13]Kirby Doyle, Allen Ginsberg, Philip Lamatia, Michael McClure, and David Meltzer are among the poets included in *Semina* associated with the San Francisco renaissance. The French tradition was represented by Antonin Artaud, Charles Baudelaire, Jean Cocteau, Paul Eluard, and Paul Valery. Drug allusions and "stoned" thought processes are pervasive in the *Semina* series.

[14]Hesse, *Magister Ludi,* p. 390–91; *Semina,* 1955; *Semina 2,* 1957. For personal reminiscences and a discussion of Berman's literary influences, see Robert Duncan, "Wallace Berman: The Fashioning Spirit," *Berman,* pp. 19–24.

[15]Greene, "Underground Man," p. 56.

[16]Because Berman's work offers itself to open-ended interpretation, his symbolism is enriched by a reference from the "Acts of John" in the *New Testament Apocrypha:* "The twelfth number/ dances on high. Amen...I am a mirror to you/ who know me. Amen./ I am a door to you/ who knock on me. Amen./ I am the way to you/ the traveler. Amen." Quoted in Elaine H. Pagels, "To the Universe Belongs the Danger: The Jesus Round Dance in the Acts of John," *Parabola,* vol. 4, no. 2, pp. 6–9.

[17]David Meltzer's illuminating essay on the Jewish mystical tradition of the Cabala discusses the creation of the universe from the Hebrew alphabet. Meltzer writes that "One of the central sources of mystery and contemplation in the Kabbalah is the Hebrew alphabet. It is believed that God created the universe by means of the Hebrew alphabet. The twenty-two letters of the alphabet are twenty-two realms, twenty-two states of consciousness. Each container embodies an essence of existence. It is a four-dimensional alphabet. Each letter represents a literal self, a number, a symbol, and an idea. They are hard to classify because they include all the qualities they designate, and when a letter is placed together with other letters to form words, the meanings within the meanings interact and multiply in infinite combinations. See Meltzer, "Door to Heaven," *Berman,* p. 92. See also Gershom G. Scholem, *On the Kabbalah and its Symbolism,* trans. R. Manheim, New York, 1965; and Papus, *The Tarot of the Bohemians,* trans. A. P. Morton, third ed., rev., preface by Arthur E. Waite, North Hollywood, California, 1978, pp. 105–14. See also the three issues (1942–44) of the New York published Surrealist Journal *VVV* (edited by David Hare, with André Breton, Max Ernst, and—later—Marcel Duchamp as advisers), of which Berman was aware. Of particular interest for Berman research is issue no. 2–3, which reproduced a Surrealist card deck: Love, Revolution, Dream, and Knowledge replace the conventional suits, and historical and fictional figures valued by Surrealists reign as face cards.

[18]Kienholz interview, vol. 2, p. 361; Stéphane Mallarmé, "Art for All," (1862), quoted in Roland N. Stromberg, ed., *Realism, Naturalism, and Symbolism: Modes of Thought and Expression in Europe, 1848–1914,* New York, 1968, p. 200.

[19]Conversation with Charles Brittin, October 14, 1980; conversation with Rachel Rosenthal, November 26, 1980. The photograph collaged to *Veritas Panel* (open) also records a Rosenthal dance event; both photographs are turned on their sides.

[20]George Herms remembers that Berman's Ferus exhibition gave him his first sense of the art gallery as a sacred space. Conversation with the artist, October 9, 1980.

[21]Formally, Berman's use of a panel structure with collages, photographs, letters, numbers, etc., is similar to contemporary developments in New York—for instance, Allan Kaprow's *Grandma's Boy* (1957). But unlike Kaprow and Rauschenberg—e.g., the freestanding "combines" *Monogram* (1955–59) and *Odalisque* (1955–58), Berman's Ferus assemblages deemphasize painterliness and gestural expressionism. They are directed toward outside referents rather than toward self-referential aesthetic queries; and they are insistently "junky" rather than self-consciously "jokey." Surrealism lurks in the background of the entire assemblage movement, but West Coast artists tended to stress the magical and associational power of objects and to play down the object as a formal substitute for conventional media. For example, Bruce Conner connects his assemblages with theater experience, and he feels that, "Rauschenberg was a painter and these were paintings that he was doing, that rather than being a paint stroke it is a piece of cloth." *Bruce Conner,* interview with Paul Karlstrom, 1974, Archives of American Art, Washington, D.C.

[22]George Herms, "Wallace Berman Exhibition," gallery notes, Timothea Stewart Gallery, Los Angeles, July–August 1977.

[23]An extended discussion of the Verifax collages is beyond the scope of this essay; so too is an analysis of Berman's late work, primarily composed of the outdoor walls and boulders and the small mixed-media assemblages of stones inscribed with random associations of Hebrew letters. Counterpoised with the frenetic compilation of the Verifax collages, the stones return to the meditative stillness of the early *Homage to Hesse* sculpture. On a more serious level than the "stoned" puns and perceptions of the sixties, the stone as symbol and actuality becomes the quintessential image in Berman's work, as it similarly functioned for Hesse in his best-known novel, *Siddhartha.* For Berman, the

stone appears as the void made manifest—the ground for a seeding of Hebrew letters and a Cabalistic meditation on the eternally present moment.

[24]Carl Jung, quoted in Arthur Koestler, *The Roots of Coincidence,* New York, 1972, p. 108. Although Berman's processes were not influenced directly by John Cage, they suggest similar investigations. Cage's interests, which saw popular currency in the sixties, channeled distrust of the structured intellect into highly sophisticated concepts of indeterminacy. Chance operations are seen as revealing "the world of nature, where gradually or suddenly one sees that humanity and nature, not separate, are in this world together." John Cage, *Silence: Lectures and Writings,* Cambridge, Massachusetts, 1967, p. 8.

[25]By the end of the sixties, John Coplans characterized the California mode of assemblage as a "covert" activity; he commented that the style "belongs to a small, arcane group of underground artists who draw upon a common source of literary, symbolic, and visual metaphors which derive from a shared ambience." John Coplans, *Assemblage in California: Works from the Late 50's and Early 60's,* Art Gallery, University of California, Irvine, 1968, p. 5.

[26]Berman's upbringing as a street-wise youth of Los Angeles' Jewish ghettos serves as background to his enigmatic art. Urban survival brings complex strategies to quotidian encounters. Cultural heterogeneity and overpopulated spaces both enrich and threaten. Keeping one's own counsel becomes an art of self-protection, as do the permissions received from shifting personae. There is a necessary sympathy for in-group exclusiveness and the safety of jargons. Drugs, too, provide escape from the reality of poverty and boredom, but they also stimulate vivid fantasies, ease passage into separate realities, and urge acquaintance with recesses of the censored mind. Berman appears to have been temperamentally at one with the drug mystique of the sixties and with the decade's yearning for esoteric solutions to existential discontents. Compare the perceptive analysis of the matter by Merril Greene in "Underground Man," the pioneering article for Berman research. See also, Merril Greene, *Art as a Muscular Principle,* John and Norah Warbeke Gallery, Mount Holyoke College, South Hadley, Massachusetts, 1975.

[27]Kienholz interview, vol. 2, p. 345.

[28]Ibid., p. 351.

[29]Meltzer, "Door to Heaven," *Berman,* p. 99. In contrast, Meltzer described Berman as "soft-spoken, wry, inward, uneasy about committing himself to big concept words...he gave the illusion that all of his work came about accidentally, a random happening." Ibid., p. 99. Berman's storefront studio on Sawtelle Boulevard (where he co-founded "Stone Brothers Printing" with Bob Alexander) was also a center of random art activities attracting artists, poets, dancers, filmmakers.

[30]Critical writing has discussed at length Kienholz's formal progression toward his tableaux of the sixties. See especially Maurice Tuchman, *Edward Kienholz,* Los Angeles County Museum of Art, 1966.

[31]The evocative power of doll fragments had a particularly strong attraction for Los Angeles assemblage artists; it was used to advantage by George Herms and Fred Mason in the late fifties and early sixties, and it continued to be minded throughout the seventies by, for instance, Phil Orlando and Bruce Houston. The Hollywood celebrity icon in a small stage-box presentation is the special province of Sabato Fiorello.

[32]"When I decided to make a whorehouse, it was just a funny gesture or a funny idea. I wanted to make it as good as possible. So I went back in memory to going to Kellogg, Idaho, to whorehouses when I was a kid, and just being sort of appalled by the whole situation—not being able to perform because it was a really crummy, bad experience, a bunch of old women with sagging breasts that were supposed to turn you on, and like I say, it just didn't work right. So I took those feelings and the name from Las Vegas of a whorehouse that was there, a very famous one, which I'd never been in.... But later, when I decided to name my whorehouse *Roxys,* then I was really sorry that I hadn't been inside the original, I hadn't seen what the decor was like, what the ambience was like. So my *Roxys* is a combination of eighteen-year-old rememberings, blue movies, imagination, and whatever." *Los Angeles Art Community Group Portrait: Edward Kienholz,* interviewed by Lawrence Weschler, Oral History Program, University of California, Los Angeles, 1977, pp. 231–33.

[33]Kienholz, quoted in Silk, "Back Seat Dodge '38," p. 118, n. 15.

[34]Kienholz interview, vol. 2, p. 342.

[35]Duncan, "Wallace Berman," *Berman,* p. 23.

[36]John Vernon, *The Garden and the Map: Schizophrenia in Twentieth-Century Literature and Culture,* Urbana, Illinois, 1973, p. 25.

[37]Barbara Novak, *American Painting in the Nineteenth Century: Realism, Idealism, and the American Experience,* New York, 1969, p. 219.

Los Angeles Painting in the Sixties: A Tradition in Transition

The decade of the 1960s was the significant moment for painting in Los Angeles. The city had always looked promising as Stanton Macdonald-Wright, Morgan Russell, the Arensbergs, Frank Lloyd Wright, Man Ray, and a host of others observed with affection and enthusiasm. It was a place to come from, a place to visit, a place linked to older more cultivated cities. They described it as a city of great vitality holding the promise of things to come. In the sixties the era of the cultivated visitor ended, and the era of the dynamic, unabashed, plain-speaking native began. At long last, the promises started to come true.

In abstract art the groundwork had been laid as early as the thirties in the highly personal, innovative work of Oskar Fischinger and Peter Krasnow. By the early fifties, painters such as Lorser Feitelson and John McLaughlin had established a tradition of abstraction that combined modernist reductivism with idiosyncratic but rigorous interpretations of the means and purposes of abstract art.

The impact of San Francisco in the fifties was important, too, especially the Abstract Expressionism practiced by Bay Area artists as diverse in style as Richard Diebenkorn, Jay DeFeo, Sonia Gechtoff, Frank Lobdell, David Park, Hassel Smith, and others. These artists had been exposed to the tradition of Abstract Expressionism as early as 1930, when Hans Hofmann accepted his first American teaching position at Berkeley. A decade later this involvement with abstract painting was further encouraged by Clyfford Still, Mark Rothko, and Ad Reinhardt, each of whom taught at the California School of Fine Arts for a brief period of time.

By the late fifties a great number of the gifted young Los Angeles painters were adapting the loose, calligraphic forms of Abstract Expressionism to their own purposes. The early work of John Altoon, Robert Irwin, Craig Kauffman, Ed Moses, and Paul Sarkisian, although diverse in many ways, shares this basic structure. Many of these artists had studied and worked in San Francisco and most had also spent time in New York, where they came into contact with the work of the second generation of New York Abstract Expressionists. There they discovered their own restlessness mirrored in the attitudes of young New York artists who shared a growing determination to break through to a newer, fresher situation more completely their own.

When the Ferus Gallery opened in March 1957, this generation of younger California artists came into focus for a broader public. The first Ferus exhibition included some of the more prominent Bay Area expressionists: Richard Diebenkorn, Sonia Gechtoff, Hassel Smith, and Clyfford Still. Soon, however, the undeniable energy of Southern Californians such as John Altoon, Billy Al Bengston, Wallace Berman, Craig Kauffman, Ed Kienholz, and Ed Moses asserted itself and became the central force of the Ferus scene. Founders of the gallery—Walter Hopps and Ed Kienholz—and, later, director Irving Blum, projected an aura of professionalism and reached beyond the boundaries of Los Angeles to make Ferus part of a national scene. For the first time the art of Southern California commanded the attention and respect of a national audience. As Bengston observed, "that was the time when we all decided to go professional."[1] The ambitiousness and verve of the Ferus environment drew artists such as Larry Bell, Robert Irwin, Ken Price, Ed Ruscha, and others to itself within a short time.

In abstract painting the critical breakthroughs of the Ferus artists during the late fifties were subtle, based more upon nuances of sensibility than their brash public images might indicate. John Altoon's softened, tactile forms and open, light-filled fields projected a vibrant sexuality laced with irony. His imagery spoke of tangible experiences—the wisdom of the body, not the grander, more cerebral metaphysics associated with the later phases of New York Abstract Expressionism. If Abstract Expressionism had become an academy, Altoon played truant with such high spirits and obvious gifts that his irreverence could only be viewed with delight and a measure of relief. Important, too, was the lightness of his palette, the transparency of his color, the throbbing sensuality he projected upon even the most mundane and everyday objects and events. This stood in contrast to the studied seriousness of much of the painting admired during this period, such as the late work of Still, Newman, and Rothko. Altoon was one of several Southern California artists who turned the language of expressionism into a living thing of the city streets, immediate and direct, without philosophical or literary pretentions.

The work of Ed Moses and Craig Kauffman during the late fifties shares some of these stylistic qualities—the open forms, the frank eroticism, the sureness and elegance of tactile, calligraphic passages (cat. nos. 82 and 66). Moses' drawing of the late fifties exhibits a great intensity of focus and touch as individual areas are confidently delineated, then warmed and enriched by soft tonal areas and the physical interaction of overlapping forms. Moses had uncovered the possibility of working across the entire plane, shifting the placement of his imagery to suggest a space with multiple points of visual access. His floral and phallic images suggest an up-front eroticism while the casual sureness, indeed virtuosity, of his line gives evidence of a fine-tuned aesthetic sensibility.

After an almost two-year stay in New York, from 1958 to 1960, Moses returned to Los Angeles. In December 1961, at Ferus, he showed a number of large-scale drawings. These were fields of floral and leaf forms placed at regular intervals across a highly textured, subtly modulated field of soft graphite. Moses transformed the rose pattern of an ordinary piece of Mexican oilcloth into a highly structured planar field. Dealing with a basically graphic form derived from a printed source—not a real rose but a picture of a rose—he exposed its true identity by barely outlining it and flattening the form, then giving it three dimensions by pushing the graphite to near-black, then allowing the rose to flatten once more and fade into the soft gray of his modulated background. This work gave evidence of his awareness of the issues of

[1]Conversation with the artist, September 1980.

modernist painting of the early sixties. It was a self-confident, personal exploration of the issues of graphic imagery, something which was at the same time occupying the thoughts of Johns, Rauschenberg, and others in New York in more direct and obvious ways. This work also revealed Moses' basic modernist sensibility, the aestheticism which would remain the hallmark of his career, handled at this point with a warmth that was immediate and physical, full of the traces of the artist's own character.

The following year Moses pushed this format further, achieving an even more impressive level of intensity in his drawing. In a large format, some forty by sixty inches, he shifted the figure-ground balance of his imagery to place major emphasis upon the ground (cat. nos. 83–89). Covering the plane with acute gestural passages, he embedded the by now almost unreadable roses within a dense graphite structure. Light is trapped and partially reflected by the soft layer of graphite, sending a shimmer of metallic gray across the surface of the work. One is acutely conscious of the presence of the medium on the paper, recalling certain Japanese printmakers' use of mica to achieve a state of absolute physical density on the surface of their prints. Moses' drawing of this period stands as a technical tour de force, achieving a studied awareness of the medium by redefining it, using it not as a tool for delineation but as a means of establishing a material presence on the plane of the paper.

By all accounts, one of the most gifted and precocious of the Ferus artists was Craig Kauffman. Confident and accomplished beyond his years, Kauffman was only twenty-five when he took part in the Ferus opening exhibit of 1957; even more surprising, he had already had a one-man show at the prestigious Felix Landau Gallery in 1953. Kauffman's paintings of this period are high in color and his line is buoyant; his imagery playfully erotic, with vast bright fields of open space suggestive of the physical and emotional landscape of Southern California.

Another of Kauffman's strengths was his cosmopolitanism, also unusual in so young an artist. He spent time in San Francisco from 1959 to 1960, he had already been to Europe in 1956, and would go again in 1960–61. His knowledge of New York art included a grasp of the concepts involved in color-field painting. Most important of all, Kauffman had the ability to transpose this wealth of information and observation into his own key, one which seemed so appropriate to the time that it immediately established a stylistic base for a host of other California artists.

One who acknowledged the importance of Kauffman's spatial and coloristic vision was Billy Al Bengston, a perceptive iconoclast with unusual resources of his own. Bengston came to Los Angeles as a teenager and enrolled at Manual Arts High School in 1948. After a somewhat troubled but productive period as an art student he found employment as a beach attendant during the summer of 1953. There he discovered a life-style uniquely suited to his needs at the time, a life of swimming and surfing and making art which he shared with his friend Ken Price, whom he met at the beach during that summer of 1953. Bengston and Price also shared an intense involvement in ceramics. For Bengston, the opportunity to study with Peter Voulkos at the Otis Art Institute was especially significant. Bengston also pursued his own study of Japanese ceramics, which led him to the decorative and refined aesthetic of Oribe and Shino ware as well as the more widely known and much-admired Raku ware.

The rich diversity of Bengston's life, especially his serious pursuit of motorcycle racing and his knowledge of techniques involved in their maintenance and repair, made him expert in the use of sprayed enamels and lacquers and the action of such paint upon metal surfaces. Unencumbered by academic biases concerning high and low art forms, Bengston was capable of a remarkable synthesis. He went about making a painting with the cool confidence of someone constructing a well-tooled object. Bengston's centered images can and should be compared to Johns' targets and flags, which the younger Californian saw at the Venice Biennale in 1958. But with the loose parallel of a centered format the similarity ends. Bengston's work of the early sixties is all gleam and gloss and shiny hard, achieved by applying the devices of layering and spraying he had learned so thoroughly while working on the smooth surfaces of motorcycles. Choosing Masonite instead of canvas, he found a hard surface that would receive the pigment without absorbing it and altering its physical qualities.

Bengston's paintings of this time also exhibit the ambitiousness of scale that was so typical of this moment in American art. His magnified, large-scale chevrons (cat. nos. 10–13) and irises and concentric circles challenge the viewer to place them in a new lexicon of graphic imagery. Suggestive of the emblems on uniforms, of floral imagery on decorative screens, or of a host of other contexts, they are none of these. In order to serve as signifiers in the usual sense, they would require a human—that is to say, an intellectual—context, a world of related imagery in which to reveal their identity. Within Bengston's paintings such images can only discover their physical location. Even their physical situation has been so neutralized, plunged so completely into a controlled world of evenly modulated pigment, of graded light and symmetry, that the image may be said to be engaged in a solo flight within an enclosed environment. If there is anything metaphysical about these emblems, it is more likely to be revealed by their physical situation within the painting than in the meanings of the symbols themselves.

Bengston's decision to work within a symmetrical, centered format is part of a desire, very common among his generation, to evade or destroy the issue of composition, particularly Cubist-derived concepts of dynamic asymmetry. Johns' targets, Stella's symmetrical stripes and chevrons, Noland's concentric circles, and many other examples might be cited as contemporary parallels. When questioned about this, however, Bengston's motives seem to differ significantly from theirs: he speaks of eliminating or "locking in" the aspect of composition to get on with the job of making a painting, freeing himself to address the compelling issues of surface, imagery, and physical structure. For whatever reason he has adopted it, Bengston's symmetry is anything but calming and cerebral; it creates something of a confrontation between viewer and image, between the viewer and that object which is the painting. Like so many of his contemporaries in Los Angeles, Bengston sought to eradicate the possibility of seeing the painting as a window or even as a metaphor. Relentlessly, Bengston made the painting so completely a physical presence that it could not possibly be mistaken for anything else.

The power of these paintings to affect the viewer is all the more surprising in view of their cool factuality, not unlike that cool outward posture masking controlled tension which was so carefully cultivated in the social sphere of the sixties. Bengston chooses to show us the result, not the process; he offers a finished object, a state of being sufficient unto itself. His paintings are as real and unromanticized as the bare facts of contemporary life: they repel sentimentality and iconographic interpretation. Now, twenty years later, this may seem a cool and unrelieved attitude, but it is one which requires a good deal of discipline and clearness of vision, qualities that are perhaps still to be admired.

During the early sixties in Los Angeles, New York, and elsewhere, long-held assumptions concerning the basic physical structure of a painting were being torn apart and redefined. During the era of Minimalism, paintings were frankly acknowledged to be objects, a special class of objects, perhaps, but ones that existed in the real world of tangible physical space. In New York, Frank Stella's shaped canvases required the viewer to become aware of the outward contours of the painting, to see and acknowledge the shape and thickness of the stretcher bars and the visible grain of the canvas itself. Ellsworth Kelly's painted metal planes functioned in much the same way: they were vivid, assertive, based upon the primacy of shape and a merging of color and physical contour. In the work of these artists and many others of this time, the boundaries between painting and sculpture broke down, the variety of media available to the artist expanded, and the old world of canvas, easel, and brush was abandoned, if only temporarily, in favor of a brave new world of contemporary technological form.

By the early 1960s a particular aesthetic began to be identified with Los Angeles. It was lean, cool, well-crafted; it involved unusual materials such as metal, new plastics, glass, resins, and industrial pigments. The "L.A. Look" was never completely defined but found its most typical expression in certain works by Larry Bell, Billy Al Bengston, Robert Irwin, Craig Kauffman, John McCracken, and Ed Ruscha. As the careers of these artists have unfolded, we may now see more differences than similarities in their work. It is likely that these differences were there all along.

The softened, painterly forms of Craig Kauffman's paintings of the late fifties had depended upon their clear if uneven contour lines for physical definition. During the early sixties, Kauffman invested his buoyant, playfully suggestive forms with a new clarity and rigor. He began working with Plexiglas, employing crisp, flat shapes with beautifully rounded contours and intense areas of color. They had the sleek good looks of a well-made machine, animated by strong sexual overtones. As such, they are late twentieth-century counterparts to the mechano-erotic visions of Duchamp and Picabia.

Kauffman's ability to employ complex technology developed along with the deepening clarity of his imagery. By 1968, two years after the end of the Ferus era in Los Angeles, Kauffman produced a group of large, vacuum-formed Plexiglas works which seemed to place color and light into a state of pure physical suspension (cat. nos. 67–72). In these works, colored air is made to hover in space. We look through and into the form, never discovering its source of support, so diffuse and subtle is Kauffman's handling of the layers of material from surface to ground. He has exchanged the earlier erotic imagery of his art for a direct embodiment of an exquisitely controlled but powerfully sensuous form. At its best, the hard gleam of the "L.A. Look" is able to produce precisely this paradox, a cool, fine-tooled form exhibiting a refined but seductive sensuality. Departing from the somewhat more conceptualized form of New York Minimalism, exponents of the "L.A. Look" celebrated the lush physicality of their art, pushing their imagery and material to new heights of tactile, coloristic, and technical complexity.

In 1965 Ron Davis moved to Pasadena from San Francisco, where he had been studying and working. At the time, Davis was making enormous shaped canvases in separate panels positioned to form interlocking geometric configurations. His was ambitious work, even if it was somewhat more involved with the abstract formal issues of painting than that of many of his contemporaries in Los Angeles. Within little more than a year, Davis had changed the physical structure of his work and modified his imagery to allow the interplay of a radically altered form of perspective. The paintings were now made of polyester resin and fiberglass. They were large, intensely colored, strong geometric forms with translucent interior depths capable of trapping light within the layers of their material.

Davis, moreover, achieved a daring, unexpected equivalence of literal and depicted form. He had created the graphic image of a three-dimensional geometric object that appeared to exist in real space, cut free from the confining edge of the rectangle. During a decade that prided itself upon a frank admission of the literal flatness of the painted plane, Davis' powerful illusionistic forms appeared to overturn cherished norms of the period. In a 1966 *Artforum* essay, "Shape as Form: Frank Stella's New Paintings," New York critic Michael Fried had argued for "the primacy of literal over depicted shape."[2] Davis, on the other hand, had just achieved a congruence of literal and depicted shape.

In the same essay, however, Fried went on to suggest

---

[2]Michael Fried, "Shape as Form: Frank Stella's New Paintings," *Artforum*, vol. 5, no. 3, November 1966, p. 19.

that the advent of Minimalist painting had opened the door to a reconsideration of purely fictive, optical imagery. Quoting Greenberg, he found support for his own intuition: "The heightened sensitivity of the picture plane may no longer permit sculptural illusion, or *trompe l'oeil,* but it does and must permit optical illusion.... Only now it is strictly pictorial, strictly optical third dimension."[3] It is just this distinction between *trompe l'oeil* and pictorial illusionism that marks the critical boundaries in Davis' art. Davis does not show us a slice of the visible world but uses the pictorial convention of perspective to propose a reality of his own making, to convince us of the reality of a powerful illusion sharing our own space. Not only did Davis' hovering forms appear to exist in the rooms they inhabited, their acute two-point perspective expanded these rooms as if the interior perspective of the painting were connected to a space more grand and expansive than the real contours of the room itself.

In 1967 it was Fried who recognized the important step Davis had taken. Reviewing Davis' one-man show at the Tibor de Nagy Gallery in New York, Fried expressed his enthusiasm for the young Californian's work: "What incites amazement is that ambition could be realized *in this way* that, for example, after a lapse of at least a century, rigorous perspective could again become a medium of painting."[4] If Davis' particular accomplishment was unusual for his time and for Los Angeles, so were his sources which involved a reconsideration of long-standing traditions. Davis was an avid admirer of the Renaissance painter and mathematician Paolo Uccello, who opened up grand vistas in his painting through the use of the new art of perspective. Also important to Davis was the then neglected art of Patrick Henry Bruce, the early twentieth-century American whose clear, conceptualized still-life compositions have a compelling beauty prophetic of Davis' own ambitions for his work.

Davis' dodecagons of 1968 and 1969, measuring slightly more than eleven feet in width, are notable for their complex color, massive scale, and aura of completeness (cat. nos. 37–42). As Davis worked on this group of paintings, internal divisions of space shifted and clear tonal planes gave way to complex, densely painted areas of color. During Davis' progress from *Dodecagon* (63) to the later *Zodiac* (96), we see a change in his conception of this stable geometric form, seen first as an open, translucent configuration in which each segment is known, then as a heavier, nearly opaque structure in which each painted segment introduces another mood and direction, like the contradictory but interrelated phases of a complex cycle. Davis liked to observe these paintings on a large black wall in his studio, where they must have appeared as extraordinary phenomena, beautifully articulated visions cast within believable geometric forms. If there is a significant link between Davis' work of this time and that of Bell, Bengston, Kauffman, and others employing unusual media, it is perhaps in the phenomenological aspect of their work, the way it is able to convince one of the beauty and believability of a world perceived and understood by the senses.

At the same time in Southern California another remarkable painter, John McLaughlin, pursued quite a different path in order to "liberate the viewer from the tyranny of the object."[5] Although McLaughlin was born in 1898 and was much older than any artist of the Ferus generation, we are still in the process of understanding and discovering his art. McLaughlin was known in this area as early as the 1950s and had numerous shows at the Felix Landau Gallery in Los Angeles. But it was not until the late sixties and seventies that his work had its greatest impact upon the younger painters of Southern California. In one sense, McLaughlin was the oldest painter in this area; he had patiently absorbed and evaluated the traditions of European abstract art, of Malevich and Mondrian, while also penetrating the aesthetics and philosophies of the Far East. McLaughlin's art involved a well-reasoned rejection of the aesthetics of late twentieth-century formalism, a distrust of technical virtuosity as an end in itself, and a desire to achieve a state of unfettered clarity in his life and art. By freeing himself of dogma, symbolism, beautiful design, and even of his own willfulness, McLaughlin distinguished himself from his peers and remained the youngest and least time-bound of them all.

Born in Sharon, Massachusetts, McLaughlin had been a dealer in Japanese prints, a translator during World War II in Japan, Burma, and China, as well as a serious part-time painter. When he and his wife settled in Dana Point, California, in 1946, forty-eight-year-old McLaughlin made a decision to devote himself completely to his painting. His work matured during the fifties as he practiced a rigorous discipline, reducing the number of elements in his canvases, eliminating niceties of design, eventually producing paintings that were able to convince both the artist and the viewer of what McLaughlin termed "the power of withholding."[6]

Even a cursory examination of McLaughlin's work cannot fail to disclose his early influences: he admired Mondrian for taking the crucial step beyond Cubism and emulated the large, powerful, non-objective forms of Malevich. McLaughlin could not, however, accept many of the basic concepts motivating the work of these two modern masters and eventually came to regard their achievements as incomplete. For example, McLaughlin observed that, "Mondrian's greatness rests in his prodigious effort to bridge the gap between factual and the essential qualities of nature."[7] But McLaughlin ultimately rejected the art of Mondrian because, to his mind, the Dutch artist had reduced his grasp of nature to a single concept, that of dynamic equilibrium.

[3]Ibid.

[4]Michael Fried, "Ronald Davis: Surface and Illusion," *Artforum* vol. 5, no. 8, April 1967, p. 37.

[5]Archives of American Art, "John McLaughlin Papers," Smithsonian Institution, Washington, D.C., West Coast Area Center, San Francisco.

[6]Ibid. [7]Ibid.

In my mind there may be some reason to think that he failed in this because his was a "concept" and in a sense a discipline involved to some degree with morality. To him the real content in art was "the expression of pure vitality which reality reveals through the manifestation of dynamic movement." In this concept lies the paralyzing element of aggressive logic.[8]

McLaughlin applied the same kind of penetrating analysis to his study of Malevich. He particularly admired Malevich's painting *White on White*. Speaking of Malevich he offered high praise and some strong objections:

Here we witness the act of annihilation, the destruction of one void by the superimposition of another void. Malevich stated that his black square on a white ground "was by no means an empty space but the feeling of the absence of an object." While these paintings are singularly devoid of intellectualization, or of any other means that we regard as reasonable means of communication, they are in their simplicity, extraordinarily compelling because of their lack of a guiding principle. In other words, all resistance to the fullest possible participation was removed.[9]

These things he admired and we see them reflected in McLaughlin's art, but even so he voiced significant reservations about the physical qualities of Malevich's art and suggested an alternate stance, one which he was to pursue in his own work: "It is my own opinion that implementation of this profound aesthetic suffered in that the destruction of form takes on the appearance of a physical act. This is in contrast to the more effective means of destruction by implication."[10]

Some of the most difficult qualities to understand and accept in McLaughlin's mature painting are its quietude, its devotion to a peculiar form of symmetry, its plain craftsmanship, and the strange power that derives from McLaughlin's grasp of understatement (cat. nos. 77–81). He said that he wanted his forms to be neutral and that his desire for them was that they "destroy themselves by implication." Clearly, for McLaughlin, it was unworthy of an artist to strive for physical beauty in a painting; even less to be admired was the urge for self-expression. He viewed it as "presumptuous of me, or even narcissistic to present to the viewer my own feelings."[11] He was not trying to solve any problems or achieve some new style. What McLaughlin appeared to seek was a state of silence in his art, a type of focus in which the viewer would be encouraged to confront himself and contemplate his own relationship to nature.

In McLaughlin's art this is not to be accomplished by simply telling the viewer to do so, but by removing all specifics, all subjects, all theories, all forms which engage the mind and prevent it from seeing things whole. This, then, is the crucial difference between McLaughlin's approach to abstraction and that of most other abstract art of the twentieth century. His painting was not created to embody some spiritual truth but to attain that state of quietude in which the viewer might approach wisdom on his own terms. As McLaughlin observed, "Quite naturally our objective is to attain a state of palpable wisdom. The real danger here is in believing that this has been achieved."[12]

If, as it is often said, Los Angeles has experienced a talent drain of its younger painters who have moved to New York and elsewhere, it has also been extremely fortunate to welcome other painters of great stature and vitality. One such artist is Sam Francis, a native Californian who was born in San Mateo and lived in virtually every part of the world before settling in Santa Monica in 1962. Francis' grasp of color and space is truly inimitable. No other painter in our time has even attempted to achieve the wonderful openness Francis can give to a canvas on any scale. His work redeems the very notion of beauty by giving bone and sinew to his complex passages of color, lending them dignity and articulation.

Crucial changes had occurred in Sam Francis' art just prior to his move to Santa Monica. The interiors of his paintings had opened and lightened, and a new vocabulary of forms now moved with buoyant grace within a breath-filled atmosphere. Assessing Francis' achievements of the early sixties, one thinks particularly of his brilliant Blue Balls series of 1960–62, paintings filled with an unusual and potent dynamism. Images in paintings have traditionally moved across the plane, from left to right or vice-versa. The Italian Futurists traced straight linear movements in vectors indicating speed. The photographs of Muybridge, the experiences of the motion picture, and centuries of Western painting (except perhaps in the Baroque era) have reinforced our pictorial conventions for movement in space. In Francis' Blue Balls, however, we witness movement as it typically occurs in nature. One form revolves around its own axis, another slides through space on a subtly curved path, other forms hover like microscopic particles in air or tiny organisms alive in a pool of water. His forms are as awkwardly beautiful as the legitimate creations of nature, no doubt finding their authenticity in the artist's own understanding of the biological world.

In Los Angeles during 1963, Francis spent a productive period at the Tamarind Lithography Workshop. Throughout the sixties his color brightened and intensified as raw, unmixed pigments were juxtaposed and even overlapped to create brash new combinations allowing the penetration of light. By the end of the decade, Francis' work projected a heightened sense of drama bordering on severity. He pushed his vivid areas of color to the edge of his compositions, laying open a large white field that Francis has likened to the white sails of a great ship. Not only did his interior space gain in importance, but the paintings attained a state of tension and compression.

The intensity of this time can best be seen in the emphatic *Berlin Red* of 1968–70, created for the Nationalgalerie in Berlin. Powerfully articulated islands of dense

[8]Ibid. [9]Ibid. [10]Ibid. [11]Ibid.

[12]Ibid.

color stand face to face across an open field of space. Lush color turns sober and dramatic as dark malachite, blood red, bright orange, blues, and greens collide and submerge each other. Working on a vast scale, some twenty-six by forty feet, Francis achieved in *Berlin Red* an emotionally charged, deeply evocative image of human confrontation.

Berkeley of 1970 (cat. no. 52), in the collection of the University Art Museum at Berkeley, is characterized by a similar, strongly asymmetrical space with dense, rough-hewn passages of pigment. Here Francis' color is bright and transparent, dominated by clear reds and red-purples. We experience these forms as constellations in a vast field, but they press toward each other across a highly charged irregular ground. In *Looking Through* (cat. no. 53) of the same year a new structure appears, one that ties edge to edge through a framework of strong diagonals. With this and other related canvases, Francis made a major move toward a heavier, firmer structure, alive with fluid, glowing pigment.

During almost two decades as a working artist in Los Angeles, Francis has lent his sophistication, deep social conviction, and lively wit to the artistic community of this area. More than any other artist in the city, Francis is a citizen of the world; his outlook as an artist, like his painting, removes and erases boundaries, embraces many cultures and makes them his own. His achievements have given the younger members of the community something to measure themselves against, not something to imitate but a generous attitude to take note of and comprehend.

In 1966 Richard Diebenkorn moved to Santa Monica from the Bay Area. A much-admired painter of major stature who had exhibited in Southern California many times and had already played a part in the artistic life of the area, Diebenkorn set up his studio in the Ocean Park section of Santa Monica and accepted a teaching post at UCLA. During the next year, 1967, he embarked upon a new group of paintings, shifting his direction from a rich, evocative, abstract form of figuration to a new, expansive abstraction in the paintings he now entitled Ocean Park (cat. nos. 43–47).

Among the enduring qualities of Diebenkorn's Ocean Park period has been his ability to offer the viewer an intense experience of space, light, and depth within an abstract format. Long vertical and horizontal lines span his compositions from edge to edge, measuring then declaring their dimensions, teaching the eye to move quickly, to traverse long distances with assurance. The work is powerful and clean though modified by complex tonal passages and remnants of the artist's handwriting. Diebenkorn's approach to the canvas is assertive, his process is reflective. The effect of scale is not always determined by size. Drawings in the Ocean Park group are often massive and spacious, while some of the larger canvases are quite intimate and tangible. The final measurement is one of the eye and the mind, based upon perceived equivalence as well as absolute and measurable scale.

Diebenkorn's Ocean Park paintings present an experience of space and light that is similar to experiences in nature but intensified, rendered more vivid and accessible. The high horizon lines of these paintings are unbounded and far-reaching, the space beneath is deep and limitless, the edges of the paintings open rather than enclose interior space. Diagonal cuts provide a dramatic counterweight to his horizontals and verticals, seeming to move easily beyond one plane and through another. Sensations of vastness, rapid passage through planes, the strength of large wedges of color—all involve physical experiences beyond the actual dimensions of the painting, suggesting an encounter with real space that might be found in soaring, in aerial mapping, or in the special qualities of the landscape of the western United States. But in the Ocean Park paintings such space is not distant and reduced; it is luminous, immediate, near to us, and wedged into a stable structure.

Responding to a question which suggested this relationship of pictured space to perceived scale, Diebenkorn replied, "I think it is something of the same kind of thing that—who was it, Fry or Bell?—who said, 'significant form.'... I think with space the same thing can be applied. You don't really think much of that area of two-dimensional space until it is related in such a way that it becomes, their word, 'significant,' not mine."[13]

The Ocean Park paintings of Richard Diebenkorn, begun in the late sixties and continuing to the present, are a profound achievement, a powerful synthesis which reflects the maturity of a lifetime of painting. They cannot be placed securely within any decade, being the product of a painter's patient, thoughtful cultivation of a refined and vital form. Within the artistic community of Los Angeles, Diebenkorn has made multiple contributions, most significantly of course as an artist of great breadth and vision, as a man of exceptional dignity and humor, and as one who shares his experience of the working process, its pleasures and pains, with fellow artists as both teacher and friend.

The presence of artists of major stature is important to the cultural vitality of any city, as artistic achievements give character and form to historical periods, show us ourselves, and become the living record of our time. The splendid natural climate of Southern California has attracted and sustained many gifted individuals, and it is hoped that the next two hundred years will witness a flowering of the cultural climate to rival the one nature has so generously provided.

---

[13]Conversation with the artist, July 1977.

The Word Made Flesh: L.A. Pop Redefined

It is by now well known that much of what was swept up into the dizzying international movement called Pop art in the 1960s shares only the most superficial of characteristics. If one can identify a "pure Pop," surely it is the work of Warhol, Lichtenstein, and Rosenquist, in which the ubiquitous symbols of mass culture are rendered with techniques derived from mass communications. Yet artists as disparate as George Segal and Marisol, Richard Artschwager and George Brecht, R. B. Kitaj and Larry Rivers were, at one time or another, seen through the lens of Pop.

Among the artists at work in Los Angeles in the early and mid-sixties, Billy Al Bengston, Joe Goode, Ed Ruscha, and David Hockney were similarly perceived.[1] The first three were included in such exhibitions as Walter Hopps' *New Painting of Common Objects* at the Pasadena Art Museum (September 1962); *Six More,* Lawrence Alloway's addendum to *Six Painters and the Object* at the Los Angeles County Museum of Art (July 1963); and John Coplans' *Pop Art, USA* at the Oakland Museum (September 1963). Hockney, who first came to Los Angeles at the beginning of 1964, had quickly acquired the curious appellation of "the British Andy Warhol." While it is true that those artists identified with Pop shared certain interests in topical subject matter, the work of these four artists is vastly different from that of Warhol, Lichtenstein, and Rosenquist. Indeed, topicality itself—the particularity of a locale or place at a certain time—may account for the unique point of view evident in the art produced in Los Angeles. Bengston's pristine, sprayed lacquer paintings of chevrons and irises trapped in a luminous space; Goode's paintings of the sky, torn in layers or captured in the frame of an actual window; Ruscha's hard-edged manipulations of graphic iconography; and Hockney's suburban landscapes with their harsh, planar clarity—these are not literally images of mass culture rendered by techniques of mass communication, although they draw on the shared experiences of popular culture. It has been suggested that the reason for this is that Los Angeles itself is as close as one can get to a "pure Pop" environment;[2] if this is so, it is reasonable to assume that, as an expansionist aesthetic, as a way of relating art to the environment, Pop art in Los Angeles would be at variance with work produced elsewhere.

"Pop art is neither abstract nor realistic," Lawrence Alloway has written, "though it has contacts in both directions."[3] Abstract knowledge (the conceptual or ideal) is wedded to the real (material presence or the depiction of objects). A unique relationship of object to idea, of the real and the ideal, characterizes much American art from the late eighteenth century to the present. The separate traditions of the real and the ideal have, at various times, become so perfectly overlaid on one another as to produce what has been termed a "conceptual realism," a preoccupation with *things* amplified by concerns with light, space, and time that serves to make the real somehow more than real.[4] This magical union of idea and object takes its place beside the late Gothic tradition of conceptual realism embodied in the work of Jan van Eyck. In a sense, the secularization of Christianity transposed traditional symbols until, by the mid-nineteenth century, they were firmly lodged in landscape motifs. The convincing means of expressing religious experience that had been channeled into the themes of Christian art were now called into service for the revelation of divinity in nature. For instance, van Eyck's *God the Father* from the Ghent altarpiece is rendered, with the new medium of oil paint, in a shimmering splendor of color. The radiance of gems, the brittle luster of pearls, and the tactility of brocade suggest a magical scrutiny of the microcosm as a vehicle for the revelation of a divine macrocosm personified by the figure of God.[5]

The translation of the sacred into the secular in nineteenth-century landscape painting finds its apogee in Luminism, the most indigenous of American styles (fig. 1). The hard, precise light, the linear clarity of rocks, trees, and surfaces of water, the unbroken integrity of objects raised nature to a higher coefficient of reality. The raw, untouched land, sea, and sky of the American continent (the real) was perceived as the New Eden (the ideal).

In our own century the popular mythology of the earthly paradise was embodied in the landscape of Southern California. The reality of the horizontal expanse, the limitless sky, and the shimmering Pacific, all infused with an amorphous, sun-bleached light, held for the twentieth century consciousness the possibility of becoming the ideal. If nineteenth-century Americans had no cultural traditions of their own, no ideal past, then at least they had their ancient trees. And if the semi-arid desert of Los Angeles had no cultural traditions, at least there was the technologically inspired dream of the ideal future. The nineteenth-century natural Garden exists in Los Angeles as an invented Garden. Primeval forests were planted as clusters of imported palms. Virgin lakes were dug and contained as concrete swimming pools (fig. 2). Majestic waterfalls were trapped by pipes from the Owens Valley and reemerged in front yard lawn sprinklers. Nature became a vernacular invention, constructed by the language of technology. Nature and culture were so exactly superimposed as to obscure one another. The invented "real" fused with the natural "ideal" in a sun-drenched luminescence.

---

[1]Anthony Berlant, Llyn Foulkes, Phillip Hefferton, Robert O'Dowd, and Richard Pettibone, among others, have also been seen in this context.

[2]Peter Plagens, *Sunshine Muse: Contemporary Art on the West Coast,* New York, 1974, p. 139; and Nancy Marmer, *Pop Art,* New York, 1966, p. 140.

[3]Lawrence Alloway, *American Pop Art,* Whitney Museum of American Art, New York, 1974, p. 3.

[4]Barbara Novak, *American Painting of the Nineteenth Century,* New York, 1969; Novak discusses the nature of conceptualism and the object in nineteenth-century American painting and suggests provocative relationships to contemporary art.

[5]Robert Rosenblum, *Modern Painting and the Northern Romantic Tradition: Friedrich to Rothko,* New York, 1975, p. 16.

Fig. 1
Anonymous American
Meditation by the Sea,
c. 1850–60
Oil on canvas
13½ x 19½ in. (34.3 x 49.5 cm.)
Museum of Fine Arts, Boston,
M. and M. Karolik Collection

Fig. 2
David Hockney
Portrait of an Artist (Pool with Two Figures), 1971
Acrylic on canvas
84 x 120 in. (214 x 275 cm.)
© David Hockney
Courtesy Petersburg Press

The Los Angeles landscape consists of the conflicts and confusions between nature and culture. "California is two separate things," John Baldessari has said, "the reality and the state of mind." This landscape was the subject of much art of the sixties and seventies. In Los Angeles, the tradition of the visual arts is the tradition of movies and television, of billboards and advertising (fig. 3).[6] These traditional visual arts take the shape of a vernacular narrative: the word (the Hollywood sign) is superimposed on nature (the hills).

In the static art of painting, this flow of narrative visualization becomes the frozen absolute of the sign, the symbol, and the common object. Time stops, becoming timeless and contained, and the narrative is embodied in the transcendent object, in actionless existentialism. The word is made flesh, the jump from word to idea is made by way of the *thing*.[7]

An orientation to the "thing" pervades the work of Bengston, Goode, Ruscha, and Hockney. The physical work of art as both object and image is restated in Bengston's choice of subject matter, typified by the chevron. His endless layers of highly polished spray lacquer give his paintings of the early sixties (cat. nos. 10–22) an undeniable corporeality that becomes even more evident in the later "dentos" (fig. 4), painted sheets of aluminum pounded and gouged with a hammer. The central image of a chevron also hovers between the abstract quality of a symbol and the physical reality of a military badge. The material bent of Bengston's work may in part be traced to the influence of Richard Diebenkorn, with whom he studied in 1955 ("Diebenkorn showed me how I might physically approach a painting");[8] to his friendship with Ken Price and study of ceramics with Peter Voulkos at the Otis Art Institute in 1956; and to his admiration for the similarly ambiguous "physical images" of Jasper Johns.

Joe Goode also acknowledges his interest in the work of Johns.[9] Goode, whose art has been compared to that of the nineteenth-century trompe l'oeil painters John Peto and William Harnett (fig. 5), progressively incorporated common objects into his paintings until the paintings themselves became objects.[10] The early milk bottle paintings (fig. 6) included a real but hand-painted glass bottle standing before a loosely brushed, painterly canvas. On occasion, the canvas carried a painted "ghost image" of the bottle. In his 1963 series of house paintings, the image was traced from photographic reproductions in the real-estate section of newspapers and transferred to tactile fields of brushy paint. Goode's "cloud triptychs" and "unmade bed" paintings (cat. nos. 55–57) extended this object orientation to encompass the entire painting. Images of the sky were encased in mullions and set behind Plexiglas, making the ephemeral sky a concrete object seen from a concrete window. The "ghost image" reappears in these works in the form of twisted or torn drawings of unmade beds or Polaroids of the sky, distressed images that underscore their material quality. The conundrum is stated in reverse in two series of staircases constructed in 1964 and 1971. The staircases, aligned against walls or in corners in the manner of relief sculpture, are too narrow and constricted to be walked on and physically experienced. Rather, they are things that must be visually perceived and conceptually experienced.[11]

Ed Ruscha, who grew up and went to school with Goode in Oklahoma City, almost literally approaches the notion that the jump from word to idea is made via the thing, a notion first stated by the eighteenth-century New England theologian Jonathan Edwards. Ruscha's hard-edged word paintings, begun while he was a student at Chouinard in 1961–62, incorporated word environments: the logo of 20th Century-Fox and gas stations dominated by trademarks. Like Johns' use of the word as object in paintings such as *Tennyson,* Ruscha's words are divorced from contextual meaning; they are rendered either in imitation of physical substance (maple syrup, water) as in *Steel* (fig. 7) or by the use of actual physical substance (gunpowder). Henry Hopkins has noted that, given Ruscha's commercial art training and his sense of composition and design, it may at first seem peculiar that he chose to deal with figurative subject matter rather than abstract formalism: "Perhaps the reason is quite simple. Things mean something to Ruscha—things to be

[6]Kim Levin, "Narrative Landscape on the Continental Shelf: Notes on Southern California," *Arts Magazine,* vol. 51, no. 2, October 1976, pp. 94–97.

[7]Novak, *American Painting,* p. 22.

[8]James Monte, *Billy Al Bengston,* Los Angeles County Museum of Art, 1968, n.p.

[9]Goode, according to Henry Hopkins, saw and wanted to buy a Jasper Johns lithograph, *Coathanger,* which was shown at the Everett Ellin Gallery. Unable to afford the $75 purchase price, Goode made his own print of a screwdriver "in the manner of Johns." See Henry T. Hopkins, *Joe Goode: Work until Now,* Fort Worth Art Center Museum, Texas, 1972.

[10]Philip Leider, "Joe Goode and the Common Object," *Artforum,* vol. 4, no. 7, March 1966, pp. 24–27.

[11]Michele D. De Angelus, "Isolated Imagery: Joe Goode," Los Angeles Institute of Contemporary Art *Journal,* no. 20, October 1978, pp. 34–35.

Fig. 3
Edward Ruscha
Hollywood, 1968
Silkscreen
17½ x 44½ in.
(44.5 x 113.1 cm.)
Collection Douglas Cramer

Fig. 4
Billy Al Bengston
John, 1966
Polyurethane, lacquer, aluminum
34 x 31 in. (86.3 x 78.8 cm.)
Sterling Holloway Collection

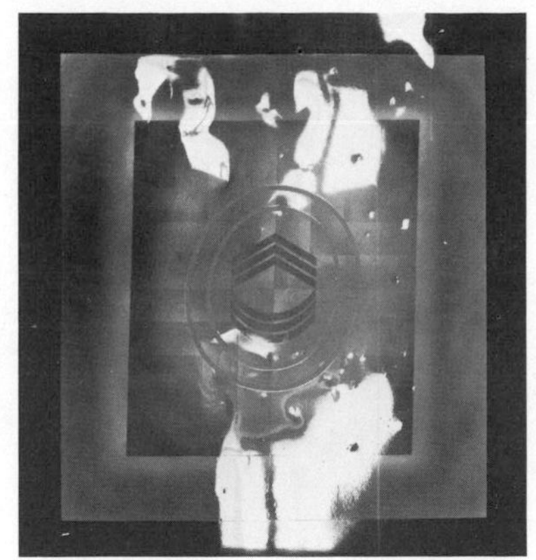

Fig. 5
William Harnett
The Old Cupboard Door, 1889
Oil on canvas
61½ x 41 in. (154.9 x 104.2 cm.)
Graves Art Gallery, Sheffield, England

Fig. 6
Joe Goode
Milk Bottle Painting (Happy Birthday), 1961–62
Oil on canvas with object
67 x 67 in. (170.2 x 170.2 cm.)
Janss Foundation, Thousand Oaks, California

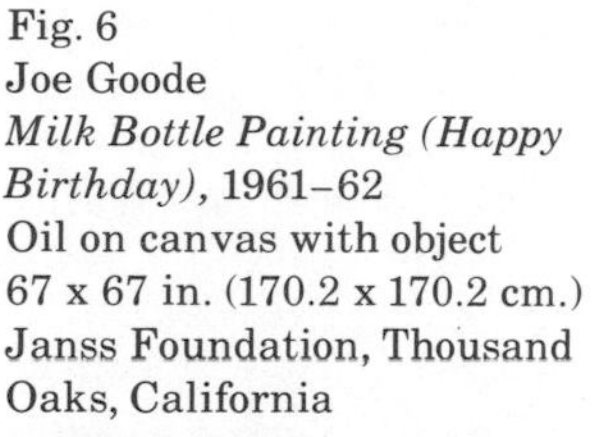

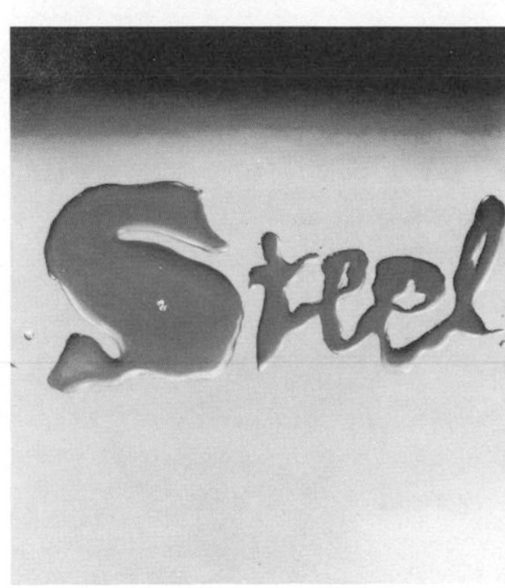

Fig. 7
Edward Ruscha
Steel, 1960s
Oil on canvas
60 x 54 in (152.4 x 137.2 cm.)
Collection Walker Art Center, Minneapolis.
Purchased with the aid of funds from The Clinton and Della Walker Accessions Fund and the National Endowment for the Arts

recorded and collected through time."[12] This interest is clearly seen in his books such as *Every Building on the Sunset Strip, Twentysix Gasoline Stations, Thirtyfour Parking Lots in Los Angeles,* and *Royal Road Test* (all 1966–67) (cat. nos. 107–110). The photographs in these books are "dumb," uncomposed snapshots, cropped to support the layout of the book rather than to manipulate the content of the image. Attention is focused on layout, typography, scale, sequence—in short, on the physical properties of the object. "They are simply a collection of 'facts,'" he has said. "One of the purposes of my books has to do with making a mass-produced object."[13] *Royal Road Test,* which records the event of hurling a typewriter from the window of a speeding car, is of particular interest. The "words" of the narrative are photographs (significantly, photographs of a typewriter) that are objectified in the book in much the same manner that the word "Steel" is written in a painted illusion of liquid in a late 1960s painting.

This interest in real things also occurs in David Hockney's choice of subject matter. "The one thing that had happened in Los Angeles," the artist has stated, "was that I had begun to paint the real things that I had seen: all the paintings before that were either ideas or things I'd seen in a book and made something from."[14] This new attraction to real things as the subject of his art developed between 1964 and 1966, and can be seen in the shift from the pure invention of forms in *California Art Collector* to the specific portraiture and landscape of *Beverly Hills Housewife* (cat. no. 58) and *Portrait of Nick Wilder.* While speculation on why Hockney's arrival in Los Angeles occasioned this shift in focus is risky, it may not be presumptuous to suggest that popular mythology about the place, disseminated through the channels of popular culture (and in Hockney's case, specifically through magazines like *Physique Pictorial*), turned out to be less fiction than fact. Los Angeles, Hockney has noted, was "just how I imagined it would be."[15]

The physical materials with which Hockney was working at the time changed as well, from oils to the clear, intense colors of acrylic paint. The hard-edged, usually unmodulated areas of color reinforce the frontal, planar organization of space in these paintings. In a nearly classicist manner, foreground, middle ground, and background are delineated in brittle planes. A similarly frontal and planar organization of space dominates the work of Bengston, Goode, and Ruscha, and combines with a clear spatial organization of depicted (or actual) objects.

---

[12]Henry T. Hopkins, *Joe Goode and Edward Ruscha,* The Fine Arts Patrons of Newport Harbor, Balboa Pavilion Gallery, California, 1968, n.p.

[13]John Coplans, "Concerning 'Various Small Fires': Edward Ruscha Discusses His Perplexing Publications," *Artforum,* vol. 3, no. 5, February 1965, pp. 24–25.

[14]Nikos Stangos, ed., *David Hockney by David Hockney,* New York, 1977, p. 104.

[15]Ibid., p. 97.

Through this hierarchy of placement, matter becomes an extension of mind.

Many of these paintings also evince the selection of a moment and its elevation to an Emersonian "concentrated eternity."[16] We see our reflections pass by in the window panes of Goode's sky paintings, but the sky is immobilized. Hockney's three paintings of the moment of a splash in a swimming pool, inspired by a photograph in a book, are frozen in time. Bengston's iris shape derives, according to James Monte, from the animation form used by Hollywood technicians to depict the moment of transformation from bat to human in the film *Dracula*.[17] The frozen moment and the palpable object, the precisionist and anonymous surface fill these paintings with a remarkable silence, a silence quite unlike the aggressive shriek of psychedelic Pop. Even Ruscha's trumpeting typography of the word "noise" in *Noise, Pencil, Broken Pencil, Cheap Western* (1966) (cat. no. 102) is reduced to the snap of a cracking pencil, and the hard, lacquered sheen of Bengston's *Buster* (1962) (cat. no. 11) is a glaze that captures, like a fly in amber, softly glowing, luminous orbs of color. A decidedly lyrical quality pervades much of this work.

Critically misperceived according to formalist canons is the high degree of surface finish that cuts right across style in Los Angeles art of the 1960s.[18] The so-called "L.A. Look," to use Peter Plagens' definition, "refers generically to cool, semi-technological, industrially pretty art made in and around Los Angeles in the sixties by Larry Bell, Craig Kauffman, Ed Ruscha, Billy Al Bengston, Kenneth Price, John McCracken, Peter Alexander, DeWain Valentine, Robert Irwin, and Joe Goode, among others."[19] This definition, however, belies the quiet lyricism of much of the work, a lyricism that could be described as an almost transcendent approach toward the perfection of the object. This obsessively perfectionist approach, however, does not mean that materials and techniques are the subject of the art. Rather, it reveals an attitude toward making art that is charged with an *idealism* concerning *the object.* As James Jackson Jarvis said of the methods of the Hudson River painters: "With singular inconsistency of mind they idealize in composition and materialize in execution."[20]

[16]Alfred Kazin and Daniel Aaron, eds., *Emerson: A Modern Anthology,* Boston, 1958, p. 122.

[17]Monte, *Bengston,* n.p. It is tempting to assume that this story is apocryphal. However, many of Bengston's paintings from 1960–65 are titled with names of movie actors: *Big Duke, Ava, Ingrid* (all 1960); *Tyrone* (1961); *Boris, Humphrey* (both 1963); *Alfalfa* (1964); *Chaney* (1965). Also, the central curved-lozenge form surrounded by glowing circles in such 1963 paintings as *Bela* and *Busby* is similar to a movie marquee and is currently in use in "Coming Attractions" film trailers.

[18]John Coplans, *West Coast 1945–69,* Pasadena Art Museum, California, 1969, n.p.

[19]Plagens, *Sunshine Muse,* p. 120.

[20]Novak, *American Painting,* p. 82.

It is interesting to note that the exploration of new painting materials, of acrylic and plastic and automobile lacquers, corresponds to similar experimentation at earlier periods of interest in conceptual realism. It is well known that van Eyck exploited the glowing color possible in glazes of the then newly rediscovered medium of oil paint (so much so that he was long credited with having "invented" the technique).[21] Perhaps less well known is the invention of a host of new chemically based paints, in addition to the traditional earth and vegetable pigments, that emerged in the 1850s and accompanied the development of a Luminist mode.[22]

Equally significant is the fact that, in the generation of the mid-nineteenth century, American painting was truly a popular art. Its diverse interests were those of its public, and its style, as E. P. Richardson has noted, "was simple, transparent, and easily grasped. The aesthetic problems that interested painters led toward heightening and deepening the common consciousness rather than breaking away from it."[23] Likewise, Pop art in the 1960s found strength in the shared experiences of the culture at large. But despite points of congruence, the work of Bengston, Goode, Ruscha, and Hockney differs substantially from that of Warhol, Lichtenstein, and Rosenquist, largely through the former's adherence to a unique relationship of object to idea, of the real and the ideal.

Conceptual realism, the Eyckian notion of a magical scrutiny of the microcosm as a vehicle for the revelation of the macrocosm, persisted in the nineteenth-century Luminist landscape. By the 1930s, that sharp-focused, planar, frontal, smooth-surfaced, anonymous, timeless, unbroken integrity of natural objects in the landscape had been transposed to the man-made objects of the industrial landscape. The machines and factories of Precisionist paintings were rendered with the clear silence of a transcendentalist vision. In the 1960s, that magical scrutiny still persisted in the sharp-focused, planar, frontal, smooth-surfaced, anonymous, timeless, unbroken integrity of the narrative landscape, the transcendentalism of the vernacular language of the sign, the symbol, and the common object. Pop art in Los Angeles is heir to the tradition of conceptual realism.

[21]Fidel Danieli has discussed Bengston's spray technique in this light: "One is reminded of the ancient Western tradition, moribund for a century, of endless gradations of oil and varnish fully exploited by the primitive Flemish." See Fidel A. Danieli, "Billy Al Bengston's 'Dentos,'" *Artforum,* vol. 5, no. 9, May 1967, pp. 24–27.

[22]E. P. Richardson, *A Short History of Painting in America: The Story of 450 Years,* New York, 1963, pp. 157–59.

[23]Ibid., p. 159.

Visually Haptic Space: The Twentieth Century Luminism of Irwin and Bell

As legend would have it, Los Angeles is a borderless urban sprawl transversed by a tangle of freeways, a city without a fulcrum, oozing toward its confining mountains and beyond, beneath smoggy or painfully light-saturated skies. It is Lotusland, where the catharsis of group encounters, Rolfing, and est come together with the pleasures of hot tubs, Malibu Beach, and the Sunset Strip. Home of Disneyland, Hollywood, and the aerospace industry, where the climate and luxuriant sensuality of the Mediterranean have been sanitized and packaged by the film industry as the American Dream, Los Angeles is the heartland of the future.

The city particularly sustains this role in the popular imagination as the edge where all that is zany, dangerous, offbeat, and experimental comes to rest after shaking loose or being forcibly extradited elsewhere. In Los Angeles, so the cultural mythology would have it, these things take root and thrive. In the American mind, Southern California is the frontier.

Within this ambience grew up an art predicated on the Southern California environment—the sea, desert, and sky. An art of light, space, and color, its aim and preoccupation, like that of Narcissus, was alleged to be transparency and reflection. Supposedly born of a union of the new aeronautical technology and eastern religious philosophies, it was purportedly midwifed by the dazzlingly clear, intense light and atmospheric haze of L.A.'s urban sprawl and freeway snarl. Since this new art showed a predilection for difficult, sophisticated techniques and for shiny space-age materials of glass, plastic, and metal, its mentors were assumed to be NASA and the automotive body shop. It was portrayed in contemporary criticism as a latter-day Impressionism, flourishing in the capital of the Me Generation, fed on hedonism and health food.

It is this art—the so-called "plastic presences" of Alexander, Kauffman, and Valentine, the illusive glass tonnage of Bell, the ephemera of Irwin, Orr, Nordman, Asher, Turrell, and others—that, more than any other art, has come to embody the myths of West Coast culture in the national and international art world.

Although "Transparency, Reflection, Light, Space"[1] have occupied many significant Southern California artists working with plastics or "situational" installations, this does not imply a coherent aesthetic movement or language. The real issues are to be found in something other than the common use of certain materials, tools, or methods of presentation.[2] Even within the seemingly homogeneous intangibles made by Robert Irwin, Michael Asher, James Turrell, Maria Nordman, and Eric Orr, the intentions, meaning, and success of the work vary significantly between artists' oeuvres.

Historically as well as tangibly, this is an elusive art. When collectively discussing these works, particularly those of Irwin and others, the historian, confined to the symbolic generalizations of the written language, strives futilely to reconstruct what is already legendary. Though made only within the last decade, most of these works are as nonexistent and as mythical as ancient Greek painting. Beyond the specifics of their time and place of creation, they are perpetuated through memory and oral myths. Shreds of the works' essences are caught in the critical writings like the skeletal remains of a caged bird. The life of this art persistently evades the photograph and the printed word.

Though different in its avowed intent and apparent illusionism, this evasive character is equally true for the multi-ton plate-glass sculptures of Larry Bell and the "situations" conjured by Robert Irwin from a handful of black string or a few yards of nylon scrim. Bell's works and those constituting the researches of Irwin have given impetus to an art of the phenomenological, grounded on the idea that the aesthetic act is best consummated on a prelinguistic level of pure sensation and perception. The progress of their work appears the most consistently influential for artists of that inclination in Los Angeles and elsewhere.

Paradoxically, this strain of California work had its origins in the decade of the sixties, at a time when the strength of art defined as discrete consumable object was at its apogee. The primacy of the object during that era was such that its physical qualities were critically read as the imperative for the formative process, art's subject and its content. Formalism reigned supreme. Perhaps not surprisingly, with this uncompromising emphasis on the formal qualities of a work of art came the necessity to expand the dimensions and formal possibilities of paintings.[3] The easel painting of Pollock, Newman, and Still had already become wall-sized canvases; with Stella, Flavin, Bladen, Artschwager, and others, painting became sculpture; sculpture was subsumed by architecture and engineering for Smithson and Heizer. Against this prevailing formalist tide, Robert Irwin and Larry Bell wrestled their way toward their mature concerns of the seventies.

During the 1960s Robert Irwin and Larry Bell numbered among the irascible, independent, sometimes physically violent group of artists for whom the Ferus Gallery and Barney's Beanery served as social nuclei. Los Angeles in that decade offered only the most anemic of art environments. Eccentric and highly personal art works emerged without benefit of—and perhaps due to the lack of—cultural density, historicity, or a substantial critical or stylistic dialectic. The dialogue between artists had little to do with art: "We didn't talk the art out. If we sat around the Beanery, we talked about who was a good

[1]Title of an exhibition and catalog presented by the UCLA Art Galleries, January 11–February 14, 1971, which included the work of Peter Alexander, Larry Bell, Robert Irwin, and Craig Kauffman. (Catalog foreword by Frederick S. Wight; artist interviews.)

[2]Among the first to make valuable distinctions about Southern California art in the sixties was Jane Livingston in "Two Generations in Los Angeles," *Art in America*, vol. 57, January–February 1969, p. 94.

[3]Lucy R. Lippard, "As Painting Is to Sculpture: A Changing Ratio," *American Sculpture of the Sixties*, ed. Maurice Tuchman, Los Angeles County Museum of Art, 1967, p. 32.

Fig. 1
Larry Bell
Little Blank Riding Hood, 1962
Oil on canvas
65 x 65 in. (165.1 x 165.1 cm.)
Sterling Holloway Collection

fuck and where we were going to get the six dollars so we could buy gas for a car to go to, you know, the Valley and get drunk. It was a whole different thing."[4] Art magazines were a more visually informative resource than art museums or galleries. In the face of an indifferent if not hostile milieu, the necessity to develop and project a tough, distinctive, coherent persona was common to all in the Ferus group. Bell and Irwin were not exceptions.

In a city with few artistic institutions and role models, the company of one's peers was of extreme importance in shaping professional direction and ambition. The rules were few but rigorous, tinged with a kind of moral imperative that has characterized West Coast artmaking in talents as diverse as Clyfford Still and Bruce Nauman. Irving Blum describes the Ferus group as "very, very isolated to begin, and at the same time very critical of each other.... You have to remember that they were the only audience they had.... They kind of relied on each other, and they were extremely positive, one to the next; they were critical, yet supportive at the same time."[5]

Irwin cites Billy Al Bengston, Ed Moses, Craig Kauffman, and later Ken Price as contributing significantly to his artistic sophistication. As he recalls, "those two or three people had, in a sense, more to do with my education than any school that I went to or any activity that I had."[6] For Bell, too, certain individuals of the Ferus group were primary influences, instrumental in shaping and reinforcing his personal ambitions.

Local academicism and a mannered but tenacious Abstract Expressionism held sway in Los Angeles art of the late 1950s when Robert Irwin, teaching at the Chouinard Art Institute from 1957 to 1958, encountered Larry Bell as a student. Irwin's enormous pedagogical influence begins in these years. His obvious talent and commitment were impressive to his students at Chouinard; his emerging belief in the power and integrity of artistic inquiry was already in evidence. Irwin's relationship with Bell has been ongoing, subtle, and pervasive. Recognizing Bell's "extraordinary possibility," Irwin devoted considerable amounts of time and attention to him.[7] At a certain point, he encouraged the younger artist to leave school to work as a professional on his own, and Irwin was later instrumental in bringing him into the Ferus Gallery in the early sixties.

Earlier, in 1957, when associated with the Felix Landau Gallery, Irwin had exhibited competently painted beach scenes and landscapes remembered by dealer Irving Blum as being of notably "curious organization."[8] Surprisingly, Irwin recalls that at that time he had little or no awareness of the work of Pollock or the achievements of the New York School.[9] Two years later, in 1959, Irwin had switched over to the Ferus Gallery with a one-man show of large gestural abstract paintings. Like Bell's works of that year, these heavily impastoed canvases are remarkable only for a rich and intimate intensity.

In the early 1960s Los Angeles art began to attract national attention, and a sluggish but bona fide art market began to simmer. The art of Irwin and Bell swung into its stride during these same years. The objects made by both men in the opening years of the decade employed the current formalist vernacular of flatness, monochromism, taciturn and pristine hard-edged geometric forms, and were consequently counted as part of the reductivist impulse called Minimalism. But in the works of these years—Irwin's line- and dot paintings, and Bell's monochrome canvases and the mirrored and glazed boxes—both artists began to divert the prevailing vernacular so as to break the normal identity of the formalist object as cool, impassive, and self-contained. Their works, with increasing aggression, acknowledged their environment as an operative part of the artwork.

Only in the line paintings was Irwin composing his pictures in a deductivist mode in order to eliminate the Abstract Expressionist baggage acquired in the late 1950s Ferus milieu. Thereafter, his was an additive process, an intuitive progression toward a felt goal. In the earliest line paintings, dating from 1961–62, a web of lines congregate at the center of the canvas. In the later line paintings of 1962–65 (cat. nos. 62–65), Irwin carefully adjusted the placement of several straight horizontal lines within and in relation to the confining limits of a single-colored canvas. The lines were placed in such a way, however, that the eye could not read them simultaneously, nor could it pursue the movement of a relational composition. The lines were no longer the point of focus. Irwin recognizes these works as his first attempt "not to paint a painting."[10] It is interesting to note that, despite the pared-down look of these paintings, Irwin felt it critical to lay in each line "not crudely, but by hand,"[11] rather than with a rule, as though already conscious that his direction was toward an art of such refinement that small distinctions could effect enormous visual resonance.

Larry Bell's work of 1961–62 was also moving toward an emphasis on the extra-formal, straining at the confining perimeters of the concrete object. In his first one-man show at the Ferus Gallery in March–April 1962, Bell showed shaped canvases of a lozenge configuration achieved by truncating two of the opposing corners of

---

[4]Interview with Edward Kienholz conducted by Lawrence Weschler between June 1, 1975, and March 31, 1977, part of the series *Los Angeles Art Community: Group Portrait,* produced under the auspices of the UCLA Oral History Program, transcript no. 300/152, Department of Special Collections, UCLA Research Library, p. 208.

[5]Interview with Irving Blum conducted by Joanna Phillips and Lawrence Weschler between December 27, 1976, and January 3, 1979, *Los Angeles Art Community: Group Portrait,* UCLA Oral History Program, transcript as yet unnumbered, Department of Special Collections, UCLA Research Library, p. 55.

[6]Interview with Robert Irwin conducted by Frederick S. Wight between July 1, 1975, and March 31, 1977, *Los Angeles Art Community: Group Portrait,* UCLA Oral History Program, transcript no. 300/152, Department of Special Collections, UCLA Research Library, p. 13.

[7]Blum interview, p. 133.

[8]Ibid., p. 117. [9]Irwin interview, p. 12. [10]Ibid., p. 26. [11]Ibid., p. 21.

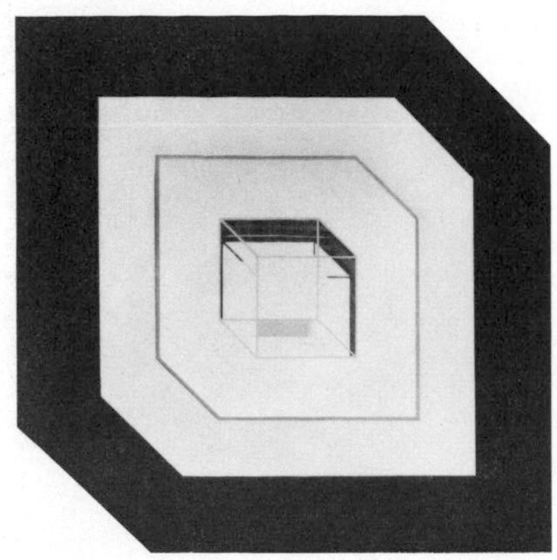

Fig. 2
Larry Bell
Untitled, c. 1964
Mixed media painting
36½ x 36½ x 3 in. (92.7 x 92.7 x 7.6 cm.)
Los Angeles County Museum of Art
Gift of Dr. and Mrs. Sanders Goodman
M.67.24

a rectangle. Each was painted in a single warm hue, leaving areas of blond raw canvas. Exercises in a kind of geometric shadow play, such as *Little Blank Riding Hood* of 1962 (fig. 1), are rife with the tension of their spatial ambiguities. The exterior shape of such canvases is at first glance echoed and compounded by the noncommittal geometry of its interior figure. Almost immediately, however, the internal configuration torques into depth, twisting the forms into a three-dimensional illusion and complicating the paintings' apparently simplistic composition.

Critically, the flatness and deadpan geometry of these pictures admitted them to the then-august company of hard-edged, "post-painterly" abstraction. Vasarély was invoked to explain their disloyal flirtation with an illusion of optically forged depth. The paintings themselves, however, subtly denied these allegiances.

In the works that followed in 1962–64, Bell expanded the two-dimensional illusion of a geometric form into actual space: his canvases became thick panels with the addition of clear and opaque, black and white glass and mirrors; his axonometrically projected solids now presented in relief grew into shallow boxes and then cubes (cat. nos. 2 and 3). Ellipses, squares, or projected solids of clear or mirrored glass broke open the centers of a cube's six sides or the mid-parts of such panels as *Conrad Hawk,* 1962, *Ghost Box,* 1964 or *Untitled,* c. 1964 (fig. 2), to expose an infinitely shifting and recessive space. Such works are but distant kin to Minimalist abstraction and its "all-over" compositional directives. Breaking the grip of formalism with a magician's sleight-of-hand (its power only hinted at in the earlier pieces), these works conjure fantastical worlds; their space, existing only in the vision of the viewer, is a mélange of the real and the illusory.[12] Their mirrored checkerboard patterns or diagonally twisting ellipses confound and undermine the space perceived as does a circus hall of mirrors.

With a perceptible quieting, the cubes of 1966–69 became simultaneously larger and more evanescent (cat. nos. 7–8). Up to two feet square on a side, the glass panels were held in place by a colored metal framework which, being narrower, was less obstrusive than the shiny structural elements of the earlier cubes. Like planar soap bubbles, the glass sheets were of unnameable, iridescent hues, modulating imperceptibly in color, tone, and density as the viewer navigated around them. In their incessant and diffuse transitions, these more closely resemble halations of the breath than still and solid objects. The viewer extrapolates, from their atmospheric clouds and shifting, breathy color, a whole world of spatial relationships. The qualities of the space in Bell's cubes, though visually perceived, are kinesthetically sensed. They are significant not only in their transposition of the realm of painterly concerns to three dimensions, but in their impulse toward a new sculptural arena, that of visually haptic space, in which the artwork is the phenomenological event.

Perhaps more conscious of and verbally better able to formulate this as his direction than could Bell, Robert Irwin arrived at a similarly inclusive stance toward artmaking in his dot paintings of 1964–66.[13] These works firmly establish Irwin's direction toward an art that was without mark, image, or boundary. The dot paintings, consisting of large, square canvases stretched over slightly bowed, hardwood frames, were carefully painted with spaced red and green dots. The interaction of color and the convex curve of each painting effects the illusion of a centered cloud of colorless energy which hangs, dancing formlessly, in front of the painting's surface. Paradoxical objects, these are works whose total effect is more than the sum of their material parts.

In his disc paintings of 1966–69, Irwin further erased the distinction between optic and haptic that had traditionally segregated painting and sculpture.[14] These works embody an effort to abolish a way of perceiving art that had to do with hierarchies of vision and experience. To do this, Irwin did away with the delimiting rectangular edge, tacit signifier of the exclusive aesthetic terrain. In these aluminum and acrylic "paintings," subtly sprayed convex discs were lit with low-intensity spots to dematerialize their edges. Free-floating apparitions without visible support, the discs fuse with their background and the surrounding ambience. The viewer contemplates an indefinite, misty, glowing composite of light and shadow and abstract presence, more appropriately called a concentration or coalescence of pure energy than a form or an image.

Much was made in the art journals at this time of a California obsession with materials and techniques. The meticulous craftsmanship and concentrated attention

[12]Curiously similar in their intent to create self-defined worlds within intimate, box-like objects were a series of rarely seen small paintings done by Robert Irwin much earlier, about 1959. Thickly encrusted tactile works, perhaps no more than a foot square, these paintings were framed, at Irwin's instructions, in handsome, deep, walnut boxes. They were intended to be held and scrutinized close up, or to be set on a table, or to be hung. Each constitutes a dark, roily world of paint.

[13]Though both artists came to this position in their respective oeuvres about mid-decade, Irwin's ideas have been the more widely known and discussed due to his enormous verbal abilities to formulate and disseminate them through teaching and extensive travel and lecturing. Bell, however, though less overtly verbal and intellectualizing, has acknowledged the applicability of many of Irwin's dicta in regard to his own work: "I was so in awe of his ability to talk, when I just found myself not able to talk at all, about things in my mind. I didn't have to, if he was talking. He said all kinds of stuff I felt so I didn't have to say it; I could repeat what he said, if I could remember it." (Interview with Larry Bell by the author, conducted under the auspices of the California Oral History Project of the Archives of American Art, Smithsonian Institution, between May 25 and June 2, 1980, p. 78.

Irwin, Bell's senior and former teacher, has been enormously influential on the younger man. Never mentioned and yet to be explored is the possibility that the influence may also have flowed in the other direction, with an observant teacher learning from a gifted and innovative student.

[14]John Coplans, "The New Sculpture and Technology," *American Sculpture of the Sixties,* p. 23.

Fig. 3
Larry Bell
The Iceberg and Its Shadow, 1975
Iconel and silicon dioxide on plate glass
Varying heights x 60 x ⅜ in. (152.4 x 10 cm.)
Permanent Collection, Massachusetts Institute of Technology. Gift of Albert and Vera List Family Collection

to detail of Irwin and Bell earmarked their work as part of this allegedly localized preoccupation called "finish fetish." Irwin, for example, was known to have spent a year fabricating the hardwood stretchers for his dot paintings, strutting the curve like an airplane wing and then laying on a thin veneer of wood. Bell's working process, after he acquired his own vacuum-coating equipment in 1966, was an expensive and painstaking procedure, demanding rigorous attention to detail.[15] The glass sheets as well as the machine had to be meticulously cleaned and maintained to achieve the remarkable consistency of his immaculate surfaces. The onanistic taint of the finely wrought consumer object, intuited from West Coast car culture and Beverly Hills values, was adhered like a decal to their artworks.

The severe insistence by these artists on artistic integrity was mistaken for an obsessive involvement with surfaces and perfection. They believed that uncompromising attention to detail would result in an indescribable but perceptible wholeness unattainable otherwise. "Any gesture or any act that you're involved in should read all the way,"[16] counseled Irwin; he explained his impetus in the dot paintings as proceeding from "the feeling that somehow if all those things were consistent... everything was consistent... that the sum total would be greater, even though it would not be definable in some causal, connected way."[17] In an art involving slight distinctions and close viewer scrutiny, "Being a craftsman is directly in relation to what you want to accomplish."[18]

The attention to presentation that characterizes the work of Bell, Irwin, and others such as Price and Bengston, who came to maturity in L.A. in the sixties, arises out of similar concerns. Ken Price's explanation could apply equally to all their work:

> People call it perfectionism, but it's not really, it's kind of... you want to have the thing resolved to a level where it actually really functions like it's supposed to. You can't tell me an Albers is still okay with a great big Crayola mark over on the side.... But people think of things that way. You know, it's like, "let's pretend we don't see this over here," when in fact, there it is. You know what I mean?[19]

By the early 1970s, both Irwin and Bell were working on a much-expanded scale on works that melded the traditionally distinct optic and haptic modes. To encompass and more totally affect the viewer, room-sized pieces were designed and installed to relate specifically to a particular space. These works incorporated into their appearance and their subject much that the viewer had formerly been conditioned to consider as extraneous: the action of light on an object, the effect of viewer movement in relation to a space or objects, the space around objects, and the transitions between them. These artists were making works whose physical materials were catalysts for a dialectical, perceptual process. Their sculptures functioned as stimuli to perception, as "instruments for seeing."[20]

Acquiring a much larger, expensive vacuum-coating machine in 1969, Bell was able to apply thin quartz and metallic film to glass sheets of unprecedented dimensions, a possibility he had first considered one year earlier:

> I had this feeling always that... the answer to what to do next was always in the last work you did, but you had to look at it very carefully to find it. And then I realized that in the last cubes that I was doing I was making the coatings fade off at the corners. So what I decided was to get rid of the cube format and just work with the corners, just right-angle relationships. Basically it was just a series of right angles. And so then I decided if I did that, then I could make them bigger. Because if I just used the corner, I could stand it on the floor, and it could be big and encompass your peripheral vision.[21]

Noticing that the junctures of the cube's glass sheets tended to collect the cloudy coalescense of tone, Bell enlarged the sheets so that they became room-sized pieces which actually enclose the viewer. However massive or numerous, the rectangular or triangular glass plates stand effortlessly in angled configurations, belying both their weight and fragility. Designed for close viewer scrutiny and interaction, they are scaled to human height and arm's breadth. They therefore maintain a kind of intimacy and conversational relationship, however extensively they proliferate, as in *The Iceberg and Its Shadow* of 1975 (fig. 3), which is made up of fifty-six ⅜-inch-thick plates.

Constantly renewed by light changes and different angles of vision, their transitory hues and illusive surfaces undermine a sense of objectness. The surfaces, made mysterious by their thin, vacuum-applied coatings, subsume the viewer and his surroundings in spaces of indeterminate depth and kaleidoscopic color. Forms surface from these depths unexpectedly, and their reflection and refraction play on and subvert our spatial expectations learned from mirrors and store windows. Disorienting and surprising the viewer, these works initiate a perceptual and kinesthetic dialogue.

Here, Bell is sculpting translucency, shadow, reflection, and refraction. Glass and the metallic inconel[22] and quartz that coat it in these works are but the sculptor's tools, not medium or subject. His true medium is light;

---

[15]For a detailed description of Bell's technique, see Fidel A. Danieli, "Bell's Progress," *Artforum,* vol. 5, no. 10, June 1967, pp. 68–71.

[16]Irwin interview, p. 46.

[17]Ibid., p. 47.

[18]*Transparency, Reflection, Light, Space,* p. 69.

[19]Interview with Kenneth Price by the author, conducted under the auspices of the California Oral History Project of the Archives of American Art, Smithsonian Institution between May 30 and June 2, 1980, p. 18.

[20]Michael Kirby, *The Art of Time: Essays on the Avant Garde,* New York, 1969, p. 20.

[21]Bell interview, p. 36.

[22]An alloy consisting of a specific combination of nickel, chrome, manganese, cobalt, and iron.

Fig. 4
Robert Irwin
Untitled, 1971
Fluorescent light and scrim
Size variable
Walker Art Center, Minneapolis, Minnesota
Gift of the artist

the sculptures give it shape and substance. The thin films, unlike pigment, are without inherent color. They are in themselves, structures that shape and fracture light and form, as do the configurations of the glass sheets. What appears as mutable color is in fact an "interference layer." As Bell has explained, "the coatings interfere with the light, with the wave length of light that is equivalent to the thickness of the coating."[23] Essentially clear, like quartz, they function as does a prism to bend and refract the light as one moves about them, causing light in its different wave lengths to create changing colors. They are like gasoline on water, an analogy frequently invoked by Bell to explain these mysterious colorations: "The phenomena [sic] is the same. The different thicknesses of gasoline determine the colors that you see."[24]

Robert Irwin, prior to the execution of the disc paintings, also realized that his medium was indeed light, not aluminum or acrylic: "I had been working with a lot of light systems prior to doing these paintings, using every kind of rented light I could get my hands on, laser beams, collimated light systems, and everything else. I'd never exhibited any of those things. But I did a lot of things with just pure light."[25]

Like an apprentice learning the tools of a trade, Irwin experimented with various lighting situations trying to discern the language and vocabulary of his medium. The goal that emerged was to separate the "light from its source... the phenomena of light from the light bulb," to achieve a situation that was "rich in terms of the phenomena, the energy... the light itself, the colors and the ambience without definable source."[26]

Even less materially substantial than the discs were Irwin's acrylic columns of 1969–70. Immaculately machined, with a clarity .06 percent better than that of glass,[27] the columns were situated vertically below a skylight or in relation to a natural light source. There they would dematerialize as concrete object, acting instead like an invisible optical instrument to transmit and focus light and color. Transient volumes, they appeared as light flashes or as briefly glimpsed black or white edges of light.

In striving toward an unfettered artmaking process, Irwin arrived at the position that working regularly in a studio—the same studio, of a given size and shape and in the same place—could only serve to circumscribe his choices. It would, of necessity, elicit and reinforce certain limited and similar solutions. Giving up his studio left Irwin, an eminently tactile person who has avowed his pleasure in the perceptual manipulation of material, bereft of a tactile, and with only a mental way of thinking.[28]

An answer to this dilemma was presented in the person of Dr. Ed Wortz, whom Irwin met through the auspices of the Art and Technology program of the Los Angeles County Museum of Art. Wortz, a perceptual psychologist of wide-ranging intellect, headed an open research facility at the Garrett aerospace corporation. In Wortz Irwin found a companion and mentor for his researches into philosophic and artistic attitudes and questions of perception. Together, as similarly perceiving, sensate beings, they set up and explored a series of perceptual situations, sharing their ideas and impressions.

By 1970 Irwin was using the information and processes garnered through this collaboration in creating "situations" or "installations," "responses" to specific places such as a service stairwell at UCLA in 1971 or to a room in The Museum of Modern Art in New York, his first scrim installation done one year earlier. Subtly, often imperceptibly, Irwin doctored each space to heighten the viewer's perception of the nature of that space, calling attention to some integral but formerly unnoticed character or aspect. Evocative volumetric spaces, as perceptibly real as they were physically intangible, were called into being and defined by nylon scrim at the Walker Art Center in Minneapolis in 1971 (fig. 4), or by a few yards of dark string at the Fort Worth Art Museum in 1975–76, or by a roll of black tape at the Museum of Contemporary Art in Chicago in 1975.

As vehicles for perceptual experience, these works, like those by Larry Bell, have three aspects: (a) *the tangible identity* of the physical materials constituting the piece. Whether string or scrim, light or glass sheets, these are the physical triggering devices for (b) *the intangible product*—the perceptible illusion, which is this art's subject. Constituted of illusory visual or haptic phenomena, these perceptible illusions are often qualifiable, for example, in Bell's work as reflections or refracted images, or in Irwin's installations as "halations," "imageless presence," "volumetric moistness." The point of this work, its goal and content, is (c) *the psychological, perceptual experience* that is initiated in the viewer. This temporal synesthetic complex is constituted of states of being or modes of consciousness, variously experienced and described by viewer/participants as "displacement," "disorientation," meditative or alpha states, and other terms.

The preponderance of critical writing about works such as these has relied heavily on descriptions of their first two aspects. It is no doubt irksome to deal collectively and verbally with what is so clearly individual and experiential. In an age in which the art world still relies heavily on the imprimatur of art publications, an art that eludes literal description and defies photographic isolation is given limited currency.[29]

Impressionism has been the historical antecedent most usually cited for a Southern California art of light and space.[30] Rather more analogous to this work in both

[23]Bell interview, p. 104. [24]Ibid., p. 108.

[25]Irwin interview, pp. 70–71.

[26]Ibid., p. 71. [27]Ibid., 109. [28]Ibid., pp. 117–18.

[29]For a discussion of the ideology that effects this rejection, see Germano Celant, "Bonds between Art and Architecture," *Andre Buren Irwin Nordman: Space as Support,* trans. Camilla Sbrissa, ed. Mark Rosenthal, University Art Museum, University of California, Berkeley, 1979, p. 12.

[30]For one such comparison, see Melinda Wortz's essay in *California Perceptions: Light and Space, Selections from the Wortz Collection,* The Art Gallery, California State University, Fullerton, 1979, p. 10.

subject and content is an American nineteenth-century manifestation called Luminism. With Impressionism, the immediacy of perception offered a pseudoscientific way of seeing, an analytic technique by which objects and vistas could be translated into a shimmering, atmospheric dissolve of light *cum* paint. Luminism was a lyric rather than an analytic approach to painting:[31] "If we can say that Impressionism is the *objective* response to the *visual* sensation of light, then perhaps we can say that luminism is the *poetic* response to the *felt* sensation."[32] In Luminist painting, as with this contemporary work, the art object is an instrument or catalyst that initiates a transcendent experience in the viewer. The works themselves are but points of entry for the viewer, channels of access to the perceptual and spiritual engagement that is the work's content. For the Luminists, as with Irwin and Bell, light was the vehicle chosen to effect this transubstantiation.

Not only an attitude toward light, Luminism was a way of seeing that proceeded from the artists' ideas of the world and their relation to it,[33] ideas surprisingly like those of many current artists: "The American nineteenth century in particular... tended to define in terms of process rather than product, to emphasize the view and the vision, a way of seeing, rather than to judge the thing seen as a work independent... of the perception of the viewer."[34]

The role of these nineteenth-century American artists was that of an anonymous "clarifying lens"[35] which unobtrusively facilitated a perceptual communion. As tenets of a secular priesthood of sorts, their aesthetic philosophies were thick with didactic moral overtones regarding the culturally renovating role of art. These are remarkably close in tenor to Robert Irwin's philosophical conversations. Irwin's realization that "if light is a medium, then in a sense the universe is a medium"[36] is also strikingly consonant with the Emersonian ideas of the Luminists.

In both nineteenth-century Luminist paintings and works by Irwin and Bell, light, the most impalpable of substances, is medium and subject. Luminist paintings paradoxically combine idealized, illusionistic compositions depicting landscape vistas with meticulously rendered details of flora and fauna. Their linear clarity of form is nevertheless combined with a tonal handling that impregnates the whole with a charged and radiant light. This emanant light, though all-pervasive, is without visible source. The immaculate, vitrescent surfaces of these pictures reveal no trace of the artist's hand through brush stroke, allowing the viewer's direct engagement with the work.

Equally light-filled and illusionistic, the work of Bell and Irwin is formally similar in their effect. Pristine surfaces are meticulously crafted and highly finished. In the viewer's perception these works evoke formless ambient light and atmosphere, and become the agents of a perceptual (some would say spiritual) drama. Whether one comes nose up against the nylon scrim of an Irwin installation or the sleek *trompe l'oeil* surfaces of a Luminist work, the revelation of means in no way diminishes the intimacy and mystery of their effect.

Integral to nineteenth-century Luminist art was the assumption that spiritual awareness could be initiated and heightened by the contemplation of the American landscape, and of natural light as an attribute of divinity. In the nineteenth century there was an "American faith that the land itself was a sufficient source to nourish both American forms and American feelings, whether intellectual, sensuous, spiritual or aesthetic in character."[37] Underlying the Luminist work was a cultural myth that identified the American land as the New Eden. Without the ruins of decayed and corrupt civilizations, it was a tabula rasa, mankind's second chance.

The work of Irwin and others, such as James Turrell or Maria Nordman, has also been enriched by the artists' immersion in the landscape experience of the American West. Their works evoke an energy through the manipulation of impalpable light which, though experientially real, is without concrete identity. Such works recreate a charged "presence" that Irwin, for one, has observed in particular locations of the Southwestern desert:

> It's a place where you go along for a while, and there seems to be nothing happening... it's all just flat desert, you know, no particular events, no mountains or trees or what have you. And then all of a sudden it just takes on this sort of—I mean it's hard to explain, but it takes on almost a magical quality. It just suddenly stands up and almost hums, it becomes so beautiful... incredibly, the presence is so strong. Then in twenty minutes it will simply stop. And I began to try and wonder why—what those events were really about—because they were so close to my interest, the quality of the phenomena.[38]

This formally intangible art, concerned with the transcendent perceptual event, has been portrayed as arising from the specifics of California light and landscapes. However much it may be a distillation of "cross-sections of sky, chunks of smog, panes of atmosphere, and radiant space,"[39] it is as much a product of the *idea* of the place as of its reality.

If California does appeal to the popular imagination

---

[31]Barbara Novak, *American Painting of the Nineteenth Century,* New York, 1969, p. 85.

[32]Ibid., p. 91.

[33]Ibid., p. 95.

[34]Roger B. Stein, *The View and the Vision: Landscape Painting in Nineteenth-Century America,* The Henry Gallery, University of Washington, Seattle, 1968, p. 5.

[35]Novak, *American Painting,* p. 97.

[36]*Transparency, Reflection, Light, Space,* p. 98.

[37]Stein, *The View and the Vision,* p. 8.

[38]Irwin interview, pp. 139–40.

[39]Kim Levin, "Narrative Landscape on the Continental Shelf: Notes on Southern California," *Arts Magazine,* vol. 51, no. 2, October 1976, p. 94.

as the playground of material spiritualism described at the beginning of this essay, one must recognize that it has also represented to the American mind the New Eden, embodied in an urbanized frontier. To the thousands of people who journeyed from the East, the South, or the Midwest, California was the land of orange groves and opportunity, swathed in a continuously temperate environment. A fantastic albeit man-made paradise, California embodied a new spiritual and economic beginning where everyone had an equal chance to strike oil or be discovered at Schwabs. Here, everyone is without a past; there is only the ever-present golden now and the hoped-for tomorrow.

This future-oriented optimism permeates the writings and expressions of many of these artists. The underlying hope implicit in these works is that they will purify and renew human perception, resensitizing the viewer to the aesthetic experiences that lie, not only within the confines of the museum or gallery, but in the world beyond. The perfectibility of man through aesthetic experience and fresh perception has been one of Robert Irwin's messages in his peripatetic lecturing. Perhaps the most articulate artist in phrasing this ambition, Irwin claims a culturally transforming role for his art: if perception is a paradigm of culture, then the art experience is a tool for cultural change. If art, he reasons, can modify attitudes of consciousness, then the configuration of our culture's boundaries will change as do the limits of perception.[40] Perhaps, then, this work is most significant in its attempts not merely at a transformation of the object, but in its conversion of art's content.[41]

Despite such hopeful ambitions, however, the "situations" of Irwin, Nordman, Turrell, and Asher and the polished sculptures of Bell, Valentine, Kauffman, and Alexander are isolated in their impact on contemporary life and culture. These streamlined environments and artworks of nylon, plastic, and glass, pristine and mysteriously light-transfused, exist like period room settings, although of limited tenure, within the museum context; they stand as testaments to a 1930s vision of the twentieth century. The "space-age" technology used in their fabrication is more *moderne* than modern, as the artists themselves are quick to acknowledge. (Bell's vacuum-coating process, Orr's ionizers, and Irwin's light systems have been available and industrially or commercially used for the last forty years.) Their materials—glass, chrome, and stainless steel—are no more modern than the Bakelite plastic or Monel metal used by American industrial designers in the 1930s in their self-conscious effort to create a technological utopia. Impelled by the bleak economics of the Depression era, those designers envisioned a coherent, machine-made environment in which life would be clean, efficient, and harmonious. Embodied in interiors, commercial packaging, automobiles, motion pictures, and so forth, this conception fast permeated the American consciousness at a time when the common people looked to the future for the solution to their problems.[42]

The streamlined, expressionistic style of that time, its technology and concomitant vision of a bright, seamless, sanitary, better world, is not so far removed from the California art of the 1960s discussed above. Like movie-made images of futuristic environments, these contemporary machined forms and ambient mists remind us of a 1930s belief in industrial design and modern technology, of an optimistic futurism that has gone unrealized with the decay and pollution of a petroleum-based civilization.

[40]*Transparency, Reflection, Light, Space,* pp. 71–99.

[41]Celant, "Bonds between Art and Architecture," p. 18.

[42]For an excellent study of the role and impact of industrial design in America, on which these remarks were based, see Jeffrey L. Meikle, *Twentieth Century Limited: Industrial Design in America, 1925–1939,* Philadelphia, 1979.

Coated glass (engraved)
14 x 14 x 14 in. (35.6 x 35.6 x 35.6 cm.)
Lent by the artist

Polymer and lacquer on Masonite
62½ x 48½ in. (158.8 x 123.2 cm.)
Artist Studio, Venice, California, and Mr. and Mrs. Jack Quinn

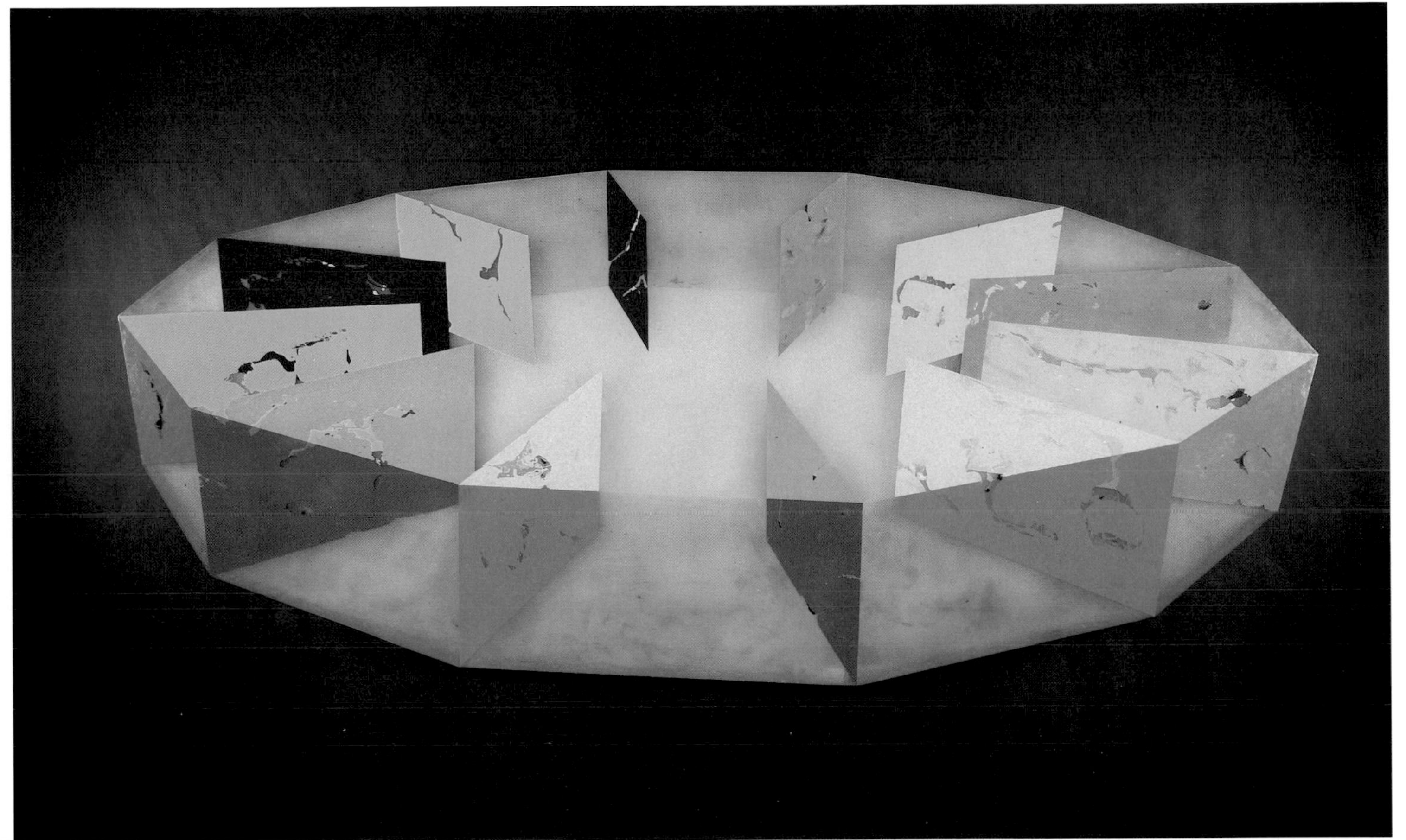

Polyester resin and fiberglass
60½ x 136 in. (153.7 x 345.4 cm.)
Los Angeles County Museum of Art
Museum Purchase, Contemporary Art Council Funds
M.69.8

Oil on canvas
93 x 80 in. (236.2 x 203.2 cm.)
Mr. and Mrs. Philip Gersh

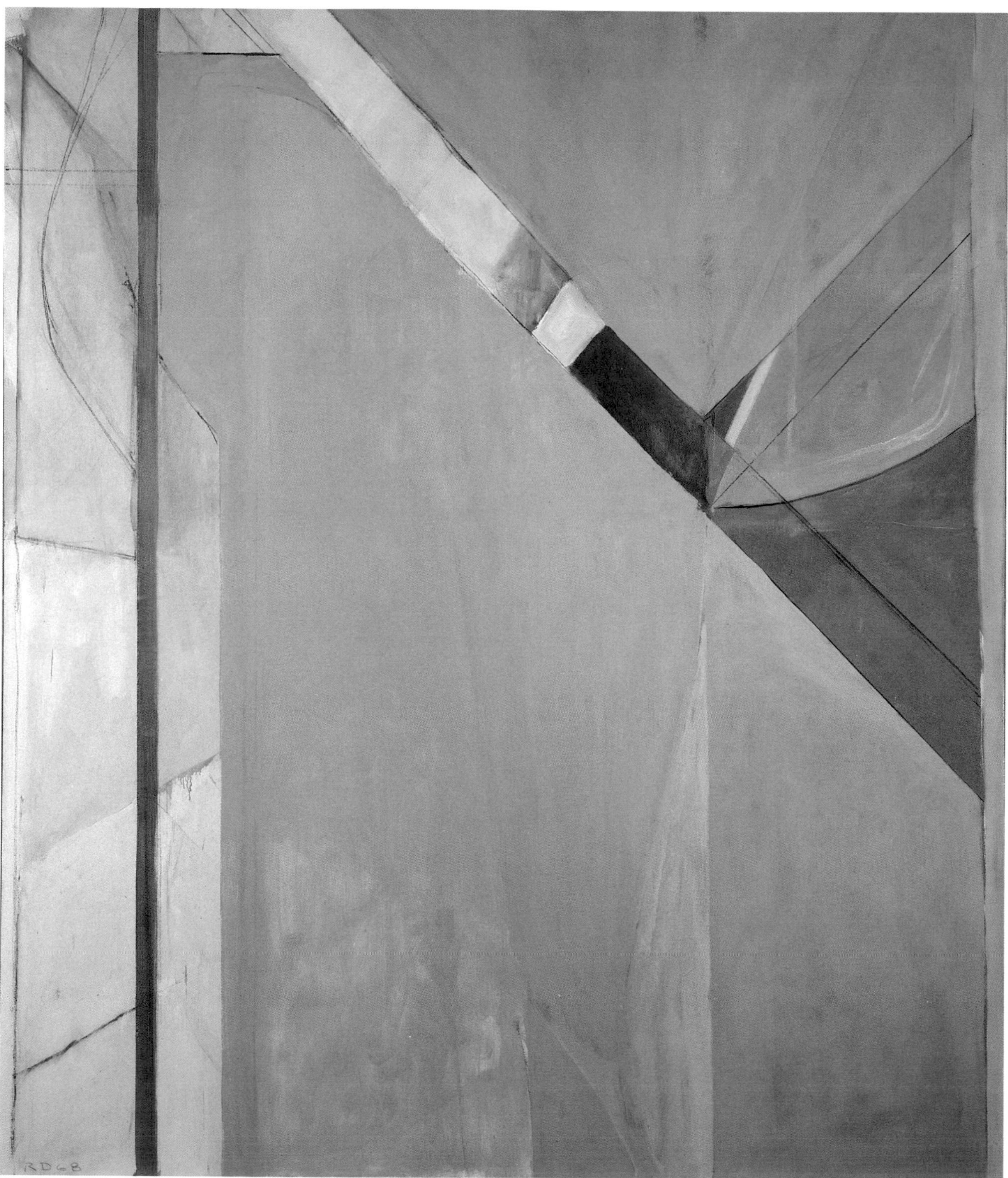

Acrylic on canvas
168 x 108 in. (426.7 x 274.3 cm.)
University Art Museum, University of California, Berkeley
Purchased with the aid of funds from the Janss Foundation
and the National Endowment for the Arts

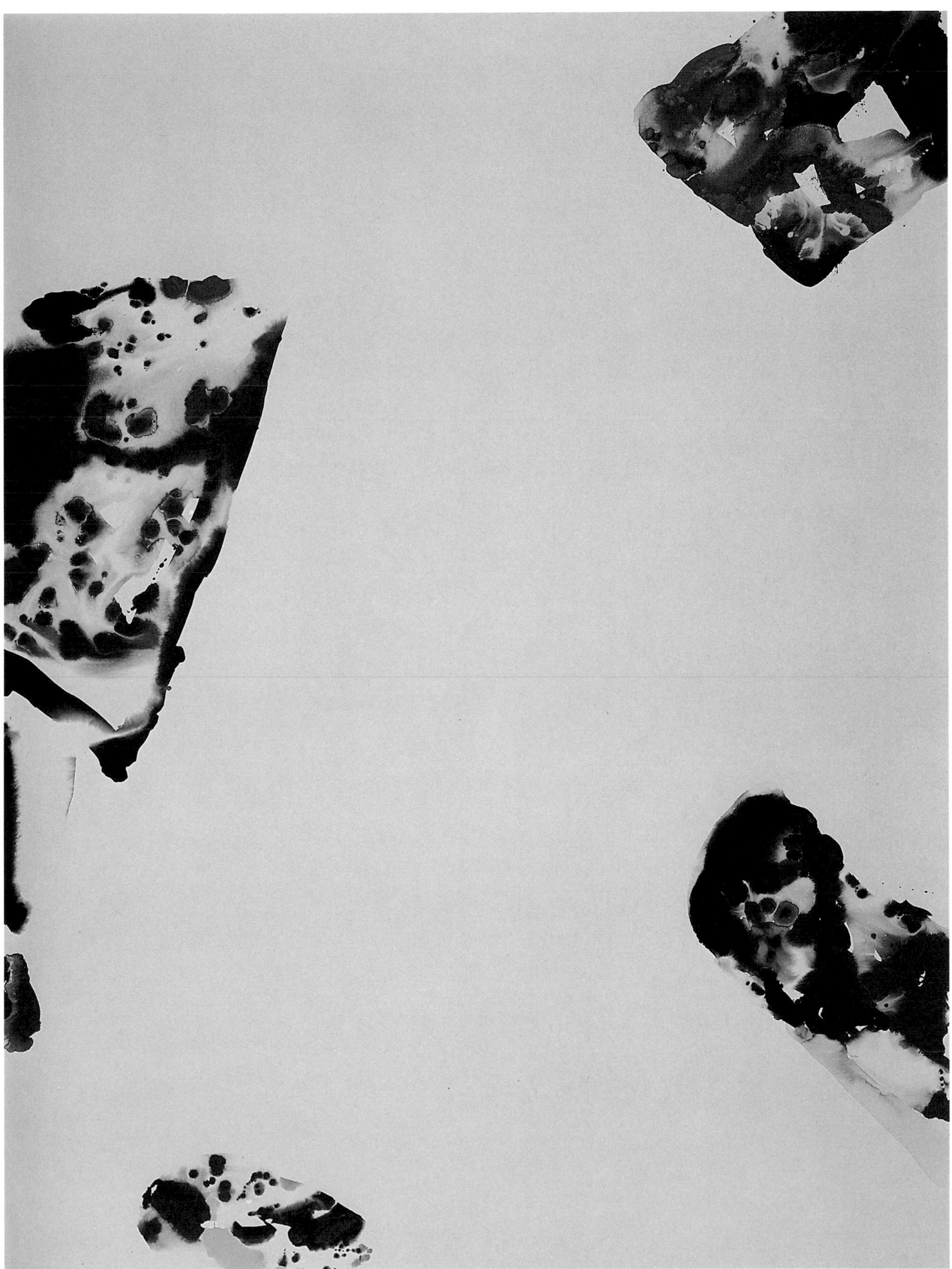

Oil on canvas with Plexiglas
3 panels, each 60 x 60 in. (152.4 x 152.4 cm.)
Lent anonymously

Acrylic on canvas (diptych)
72 x 144 in. (182.9 x 365.8 cm.)
Private collection, Los Angeles

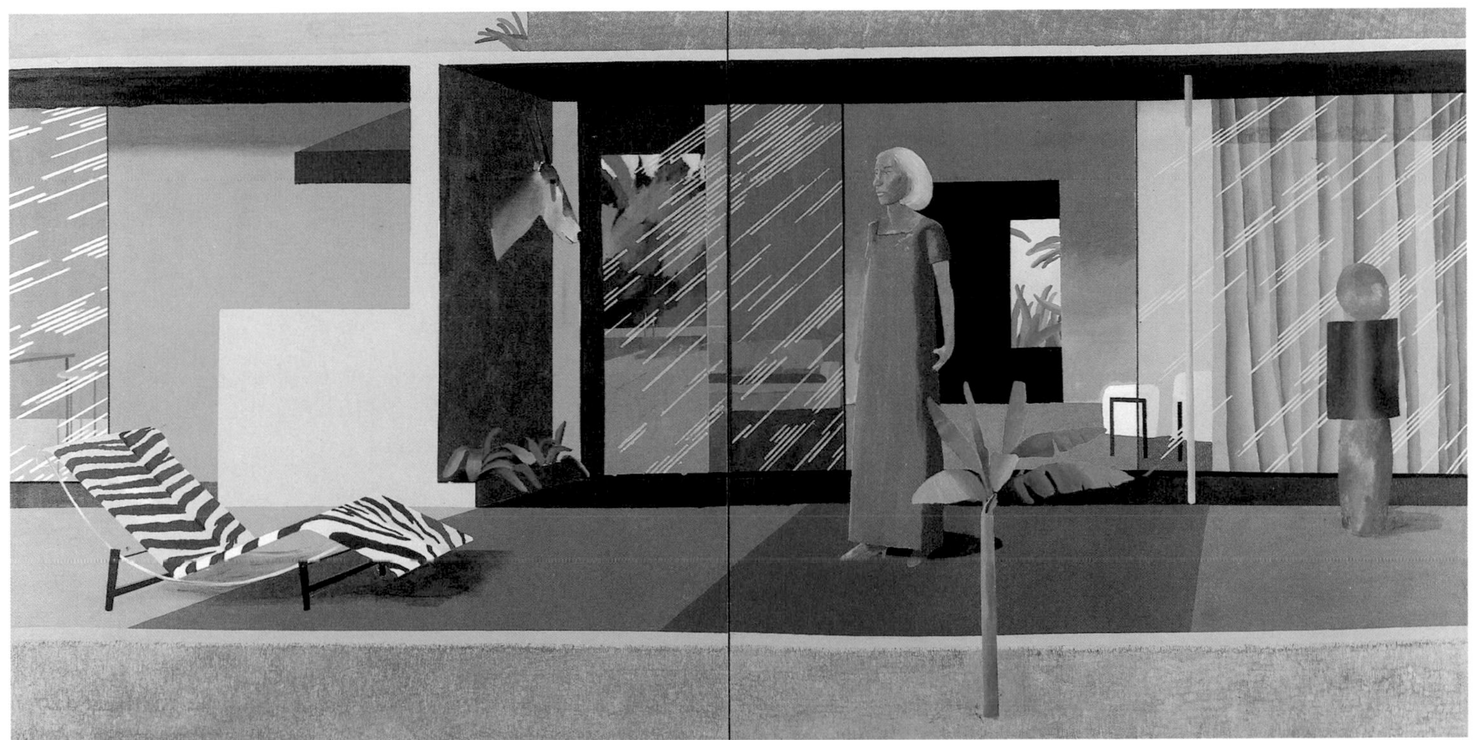

Oil on canvas
82½ x 84½ in. (209.5 x 214.6 cm.)
Collection of the La Jolla Museum of Contemporary Art, California

Sprayed acrylic lacquer on vacuum-formed Plexiglas
50 x 72 x 15 in. (127 x 182.9 x 38.1 cm.)
Los Angeles County Museum of Art
Gift of the Kleiner Foundation
M.73.38.10

Materials include paints, fiberglass, and flock, 1938 Dodge, chicken wire, beer bottles, artificial grass, cast plaster figure
66 x 240 x 144 in. (168 x 610 x 356 cm.)
Lyn Kienholz

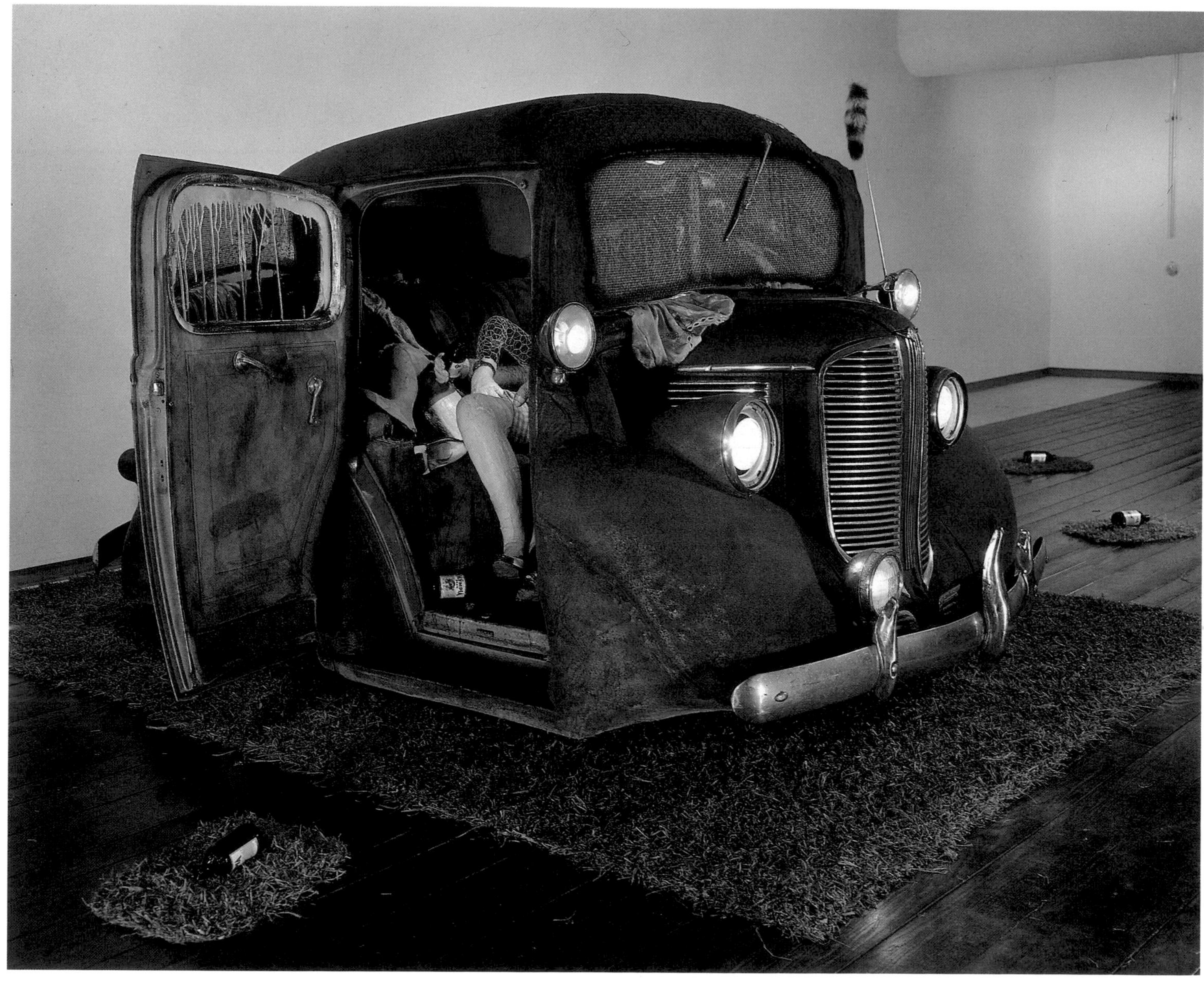

Oil on canvas
42 x 60 in. (106.7 x 152.4 cm.)
Mr. and Mrs. Morris S. Pynoos

Silver paint and graphite on paper
60 x 40 in. (152.4 x 101.6 cm.)
Lent by the artist

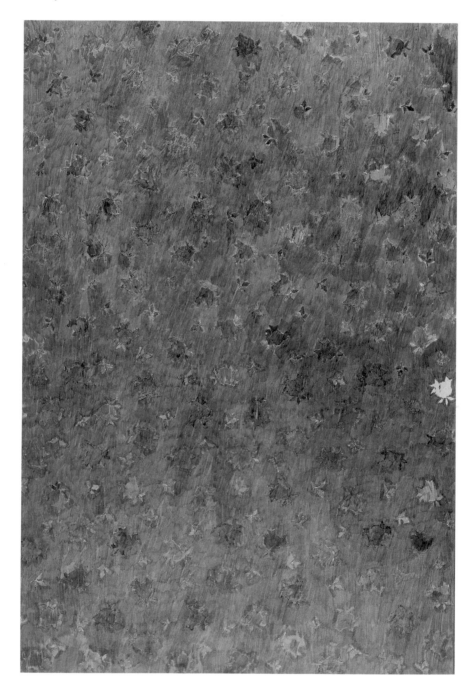

Pale purple neon tubing
63 x 33 in. (160 x 83.8 cm.)
1981 reconstruction by Los Angeles County Museum of Art
Courtesy Giuseppe Panza di Biumo, Milan, Italy
and the artist

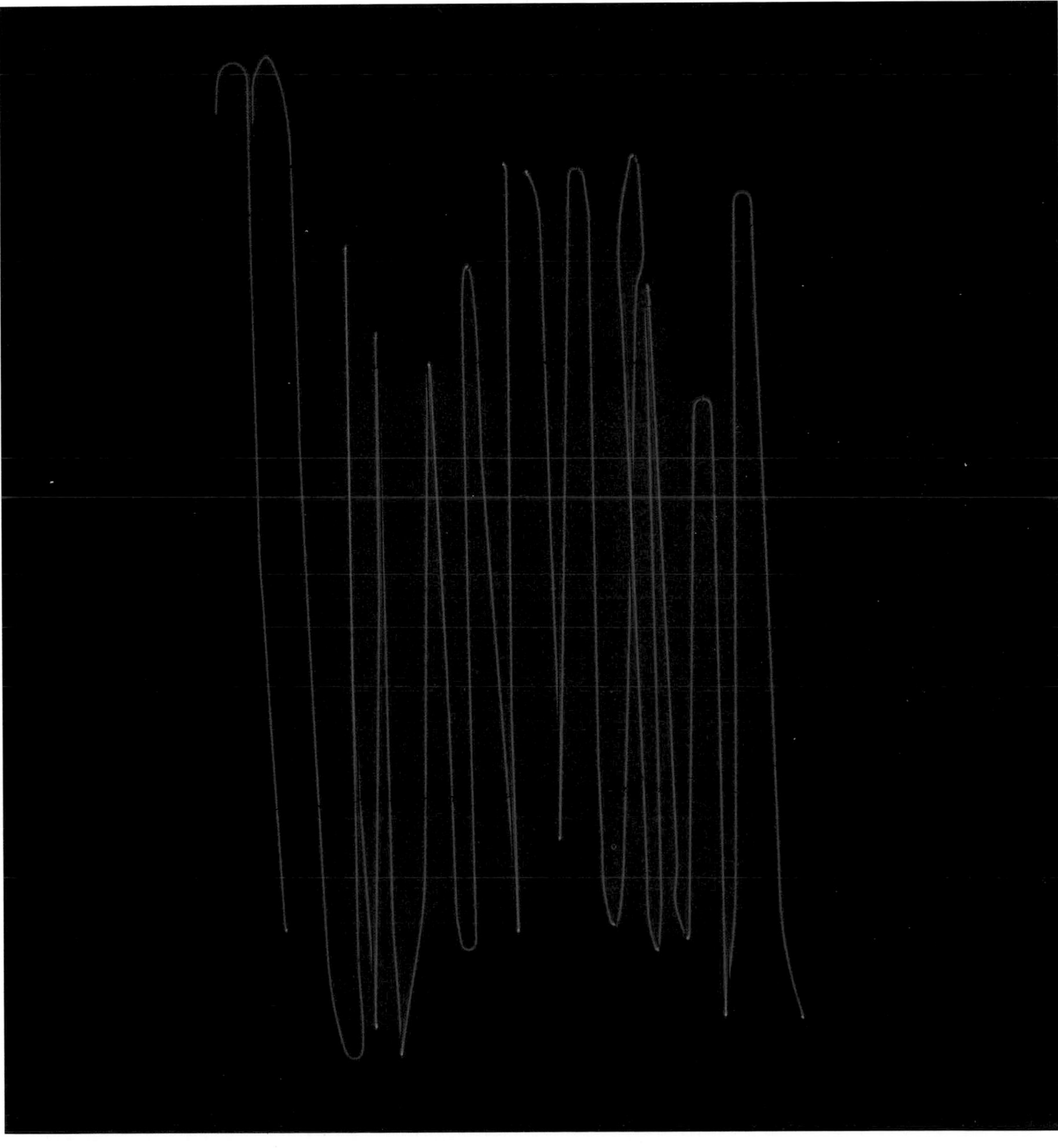

Fired and painted clay
6 x 5½ x 5½ in. (15.2 x 14 x 14 cm.)
h. with stand: 70 in. (177.8 cm.)
Betty and Monte Factor Family Collection

Oil on canvas
72 x 67 in. (182.9 x 170.2 cm.)
Los Angeles County Museum of Art
Anonymous gift through the Contemporary Art Council
M.63.14

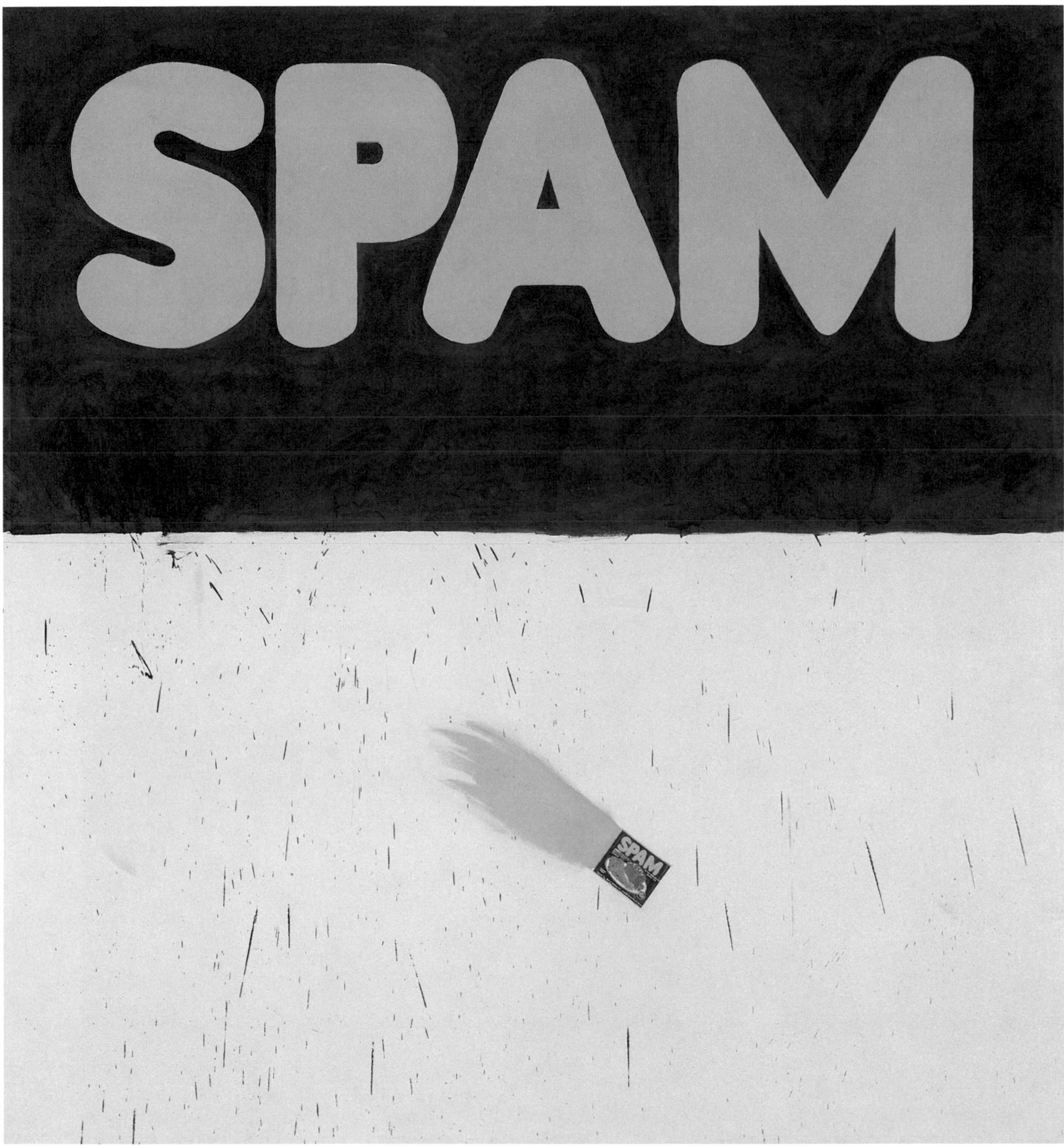

Stoneware
h: 64 in. (162.5 cm.)
Mr. and Mrs. Stanley K. Sheinbaum

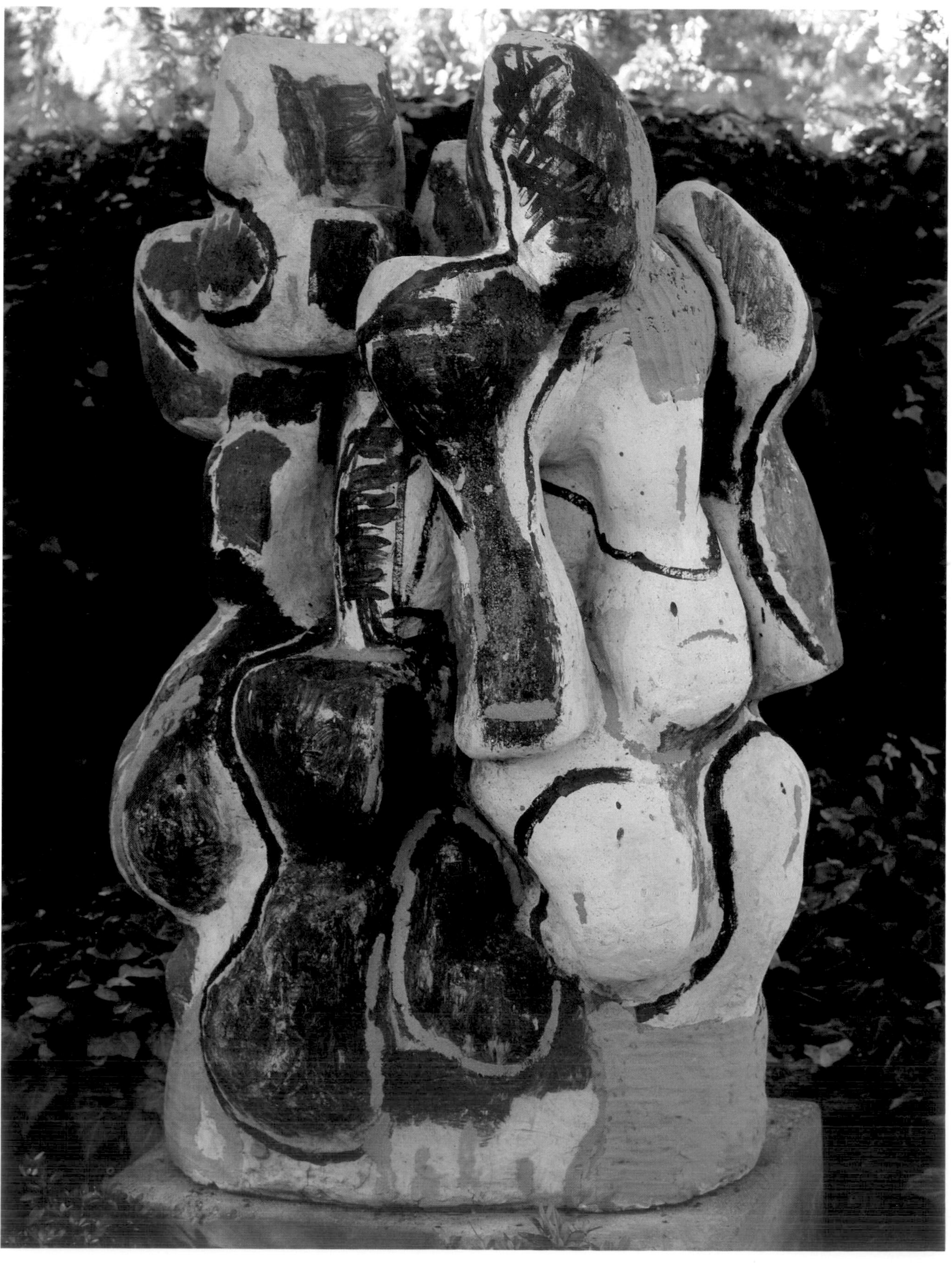

Catalog

Larry Bell

1. *Untitled,* 1958
Oil on paper mounted on canvas
43 x 43 in. (109.2 x 109.2 cm.)
Hal Glicksman

2. *Larry Bell's House, Part II*
1962–63
Glass construction
25 x 25 x 25 in. (63.5 x 63.5 x 63.5 cm.)
Lent by the artist

3. *Bette and the Giant Jewfish,* 1963
Glass and mirror
16 x 16 x 16 in. (40.6 x 40.6 x 40.6 cm.)
Betty Asher

4. *Untitled,* 1964–65
Coated glass
15 x 15 x 15 in. (38.1 x 38.1 x 38.1 cm.)
Lent by the artist

5. *Untitled,* 1964–65
Coated glass
12 x 12 x 12 in. (30.5 x 30.5 x 30.5 cm.)
Lent by the artist

6. *Untitled,* 1964–65
Coated glass (engraved)
14 x 14 x 14 in. (35.6 x 35.6 x 35.6 cm.)
Lent by the artist

7. *Untitled,* 1966
Coated glass
20 x 20 x 20 in. (50.8 x 50.8 x 50.8 cm.)
Lent by the artist

8. *Untitled,* 1968–69
Coated glass
36 x 36 x 36 in. (91.4 x 91.4 x 91.4 cm.)
Dr. and Mrs. Charles Hendrickson

2

4

Billy Al Bengston

9. *Grace,* 1960
Oil on canvas
49¾ x 42¼ in.
(126.4 x 107.3 cm.)
Betty Asher

10. *Red Ryder,* 1961
Lacquer and polymer on Masonite
48 x 48 in.
(121.9 x 121.9 cm.)
Artist Studio, Venice, California

11. *Buster,* 1962
Oil and sprayed lacquer on Masonite
60 x 60 in.
(152.4 x 152.4 cm.)
Collection of the La Jolla Museum of Contemporary Art, California

12. *Boris,* 1963
Polymer and lacquer on Masonite
62½ x 48½ in. (158.8 x 123.2 cm.)
Artist Studio, Venice, California, and Mr. and Mrs. Jack Quinn

13. *Busby,* 1963
Oil, polymer, and lacquer on Masonite
80 x 60 in.
(203.2 x 152.4 cm.)
Artist Studio, Venice, California

14. *Untitled,* 1961
Lacquer on Masonite
4 in. diameter octagon
(10.2 cm.)
Artist Studio, Venice, California

15. *Untitled,* 1961
Oil and lacquer on Masonite
5 x 5 in. (12.7 x 12.7 cm.)
Artist Studio, Venice, California

16. *Untitled,* 1961
Oil and lacquer on Masonite
5 x 5 in. (12.7 x 12.7 cm.)
Artist Studio, Venice, California

17. *Untitled,* 1961
Acrylic and lacquer on Masonite
5 in. diameter octagon
(12.7 cm.)
Artist Studio, Venice, California

18. *Untitled,* 1962
Acrylic and lacquer on Masonite
4 x 4 in. (10.2 x 10.2 cm.)
Artist Studio, Venice, California

19. *Untitled,* 1962
Oil and lacquer on Masonite
4½ x 4½ in.
(11.4 x 11.4 cm.)
Artist Studio, Venice, California

20. *Untitled,* 1962
Lacquer on Masonite
5 x 5 in. (12.7 x 12.7 cm.)
Artist Studio, Venice, California

21. *Untitled,* 1963
Acrylic and lacquer on Masonite
4 x 4 in. (10.2 x 10.2 cm.)
Artist Studio, Venice, California

22. *Untitled,* 1963
Lacquer on Masonite
5 x 5 in. (12.7 x 12.7 cm.)
Artist Studio, Venice, California

11

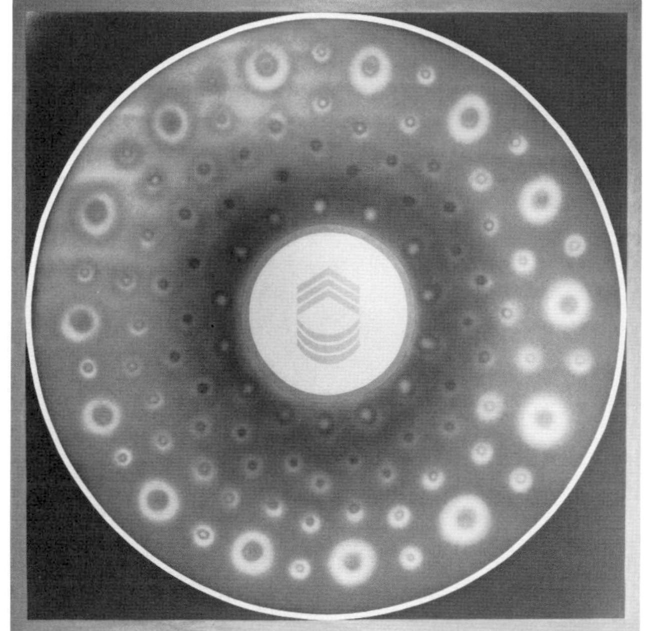

10

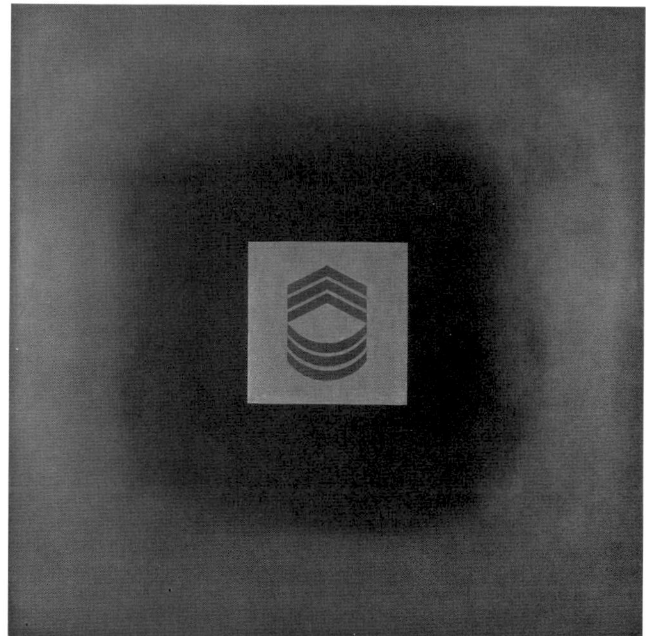

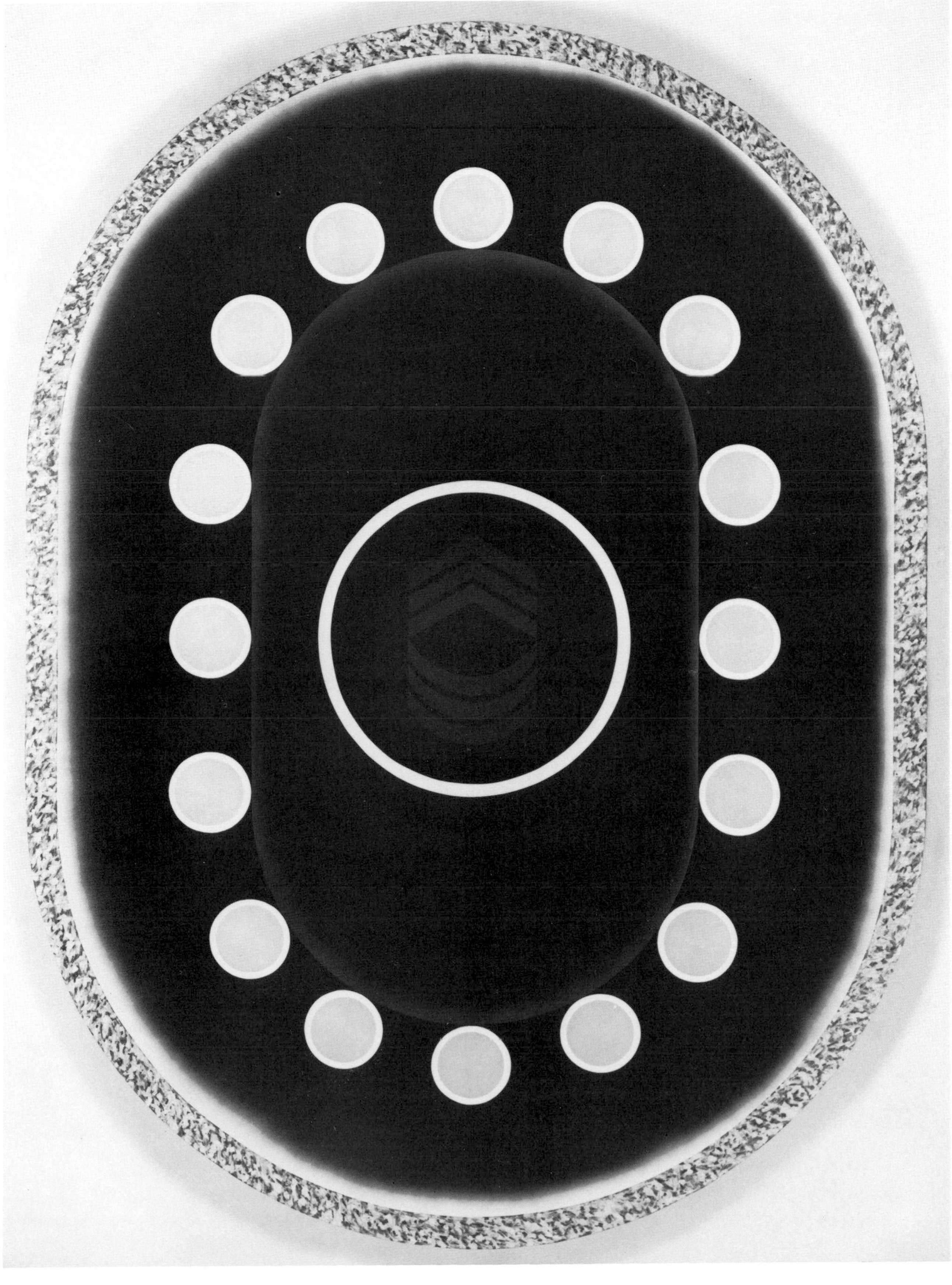

Wallace Berman

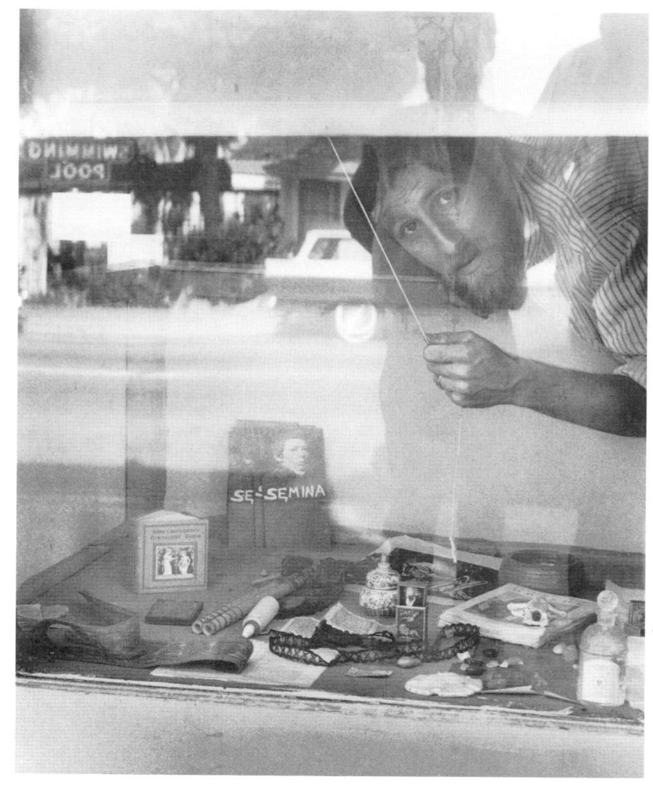

23. *Semina 1,* 1955
Printed papers and photographs
7¾ x 4 in. (19.7 x 10.2 cm.)
Hal Glicksman

24. *Semina 2,* 1957
Printed papers
8½ x 5½ in. (21.6 x 14 cm.)
Hal Glicksman

25. *Semina 3,* 1958
Printed papers
11 x 9 in. (27.9 x 22.9 cm.)
Hal Glicksman

26. *Semina 4,* 1959
Printed papers
9¼ x 7¾ in. (23.5 x 19.7 cm.)
Hal Glicksman

27. *Semina 5,* 1959
Printed papers
7⅜ x 4⅞ in. (18.8 x 12.4 cm.)
Hal Glicksman

28. *Semina 6,* 1960
Printed papers
8½ x 6 in. (21.6 x 15.2 cm.)
Hal Glicksman

29. *Semina 7,* 1961
Printed papers
7¾ x 5½ in. (19.7 x 14 cm.)
Hal Glicksman

30. *Semina 8,* 1963
Printed papers and photographs
7 x 5½ in. (17.7 x 14 cm.)
Hal Glicksman

31. *Semina 9,* 1964
Printed papers and photograph
5½ x 3⅛ in. (14 x 8 cm.)
Hal Glicksman

32. *Untitled,* 1956–57
Woodstain and ink on parchment on canvas
19½ x 19½ in. (49.5 x 49.5 cm.)
Mrs. Kathleen Bleiweiss

33. *Untitled,* 1956–57
Woodstain and ink on parchment on canvas
19½ x 19½ in. (49.5 x 49.5 cm.)
Dean Stockwell

34. *Untitled,* 1956–57
Woodstain and ink on parchment on canvas
19½ x 19½ in. (49.5 x 49.5 cm.)
Lynn Factor, Brentwood, California

35. *Untitled,* 1956–57
Woodstain and ink on parchment on canvas
19½ x 19½ in. (49.5 x 49.5 cm.)
Hal Glicksman

36. *Untitled,* 1956–57
Woodstain and ink on parchment on canvas
19½ x 19½ in. (49.5 x 49.5 cm.)
Walter Hopps, Washington, D.C.

Berman's arrest at Ferus Gallery, 1957

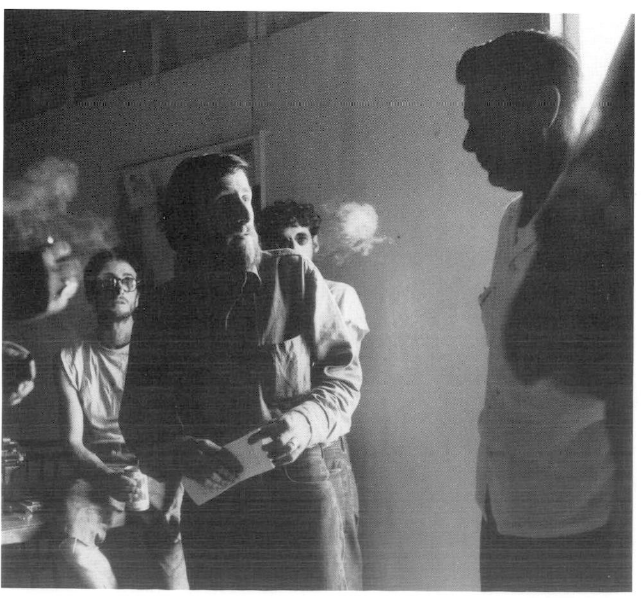

23–31

SEMINA
SEMINA 5
SEMINA 7
Fred Mason
240 N. Grand
Pasadena
SEMINA 9 '64
SEMINA
PEYOTE

36

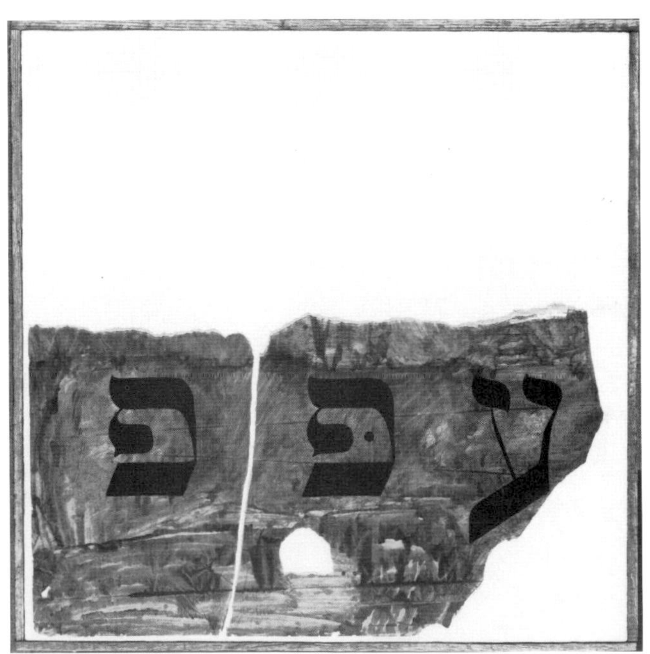

Ronald Davis

37. *Dodecagon,* 1968
Polyester resin and fiberglass
60½ x 136 in. (153.7 x 345.4 cm.)
Lent by the artist

38. *Backup,* 1968
Polyester resin and fiberglass
60½ x 136 in. (153.7 x 345.4 cm.)
Lent by the artist

39. *Roto,* 1968
Polyester resin and fiberglass
60½ x 136 in. (153.7 x 345.4 cm.)
Los Angeles County Museum of Art
Museum Purchase, Contemporary Art Council Funds
M.69.8

40. *Zodiac,* 1969
Polyester resin and fiberglass
60½ x 136 in. (153.7 x 345.4 cm.)
Lent by the artist

41. *Black Tear,* 1969
Polyester resin and fiberglass
60½ x 136 in. (153.7 x 345.4 cm.)
Robert Rowan

42. *Dual Level,* 1969
Polyester resin and fiberglass
60½ x 136 in. (153.7 x 345.4 cm.)
Lent by the artist

38

37

Richard Diebenkorn

43. *Ocean Park #7,* 1968
Oil on canvas
93 x 80 in. (236.2 x 203.2 cm.)
Mr. and Mrs. Gilbert H. Kinney

44. *Ocean Park #9,* 1968
Oil on canvas
82 x 78 in. (208.3 x 198.1 cm.)
The Times Mirror Company, Los Angeles

45. *Ocean Park #14,* 1968
Oil on canvas
93 x 80 in. (236.2 x 203.2 cm.)
Mr. and Mrs. Philip Gersh

46. *Ocean Park #16,* 1968
Oil on canvas
92⅝ x 76 in. (235.3 x 193 cm.)
Milwaukee Art Center Collection, Wisconsin
Gift of Jane Bradley Pettit

47. *Ocean Park #27,* 1970
Oil on canvas
100½ x 81⅝ in. (255.2 x 207.3 cm.)
The Brooklyn Museum, New York. Gift of the Roebling Society, Mr. and Mrs. Charles H. Blatt, and Mr. and Mrs. William K. Jacobs, Jr.

43

47

Sam Francis

48. *Untitled,* 1968
Acrylic on paper
41 x 27 in. (104.2 x 68.6 cm.)
Lent by the artist

49. *Untitled,* 1968
Acrylic on paper
41 x 27 in. (104.2 x 68.6 cm.)
Lent by the artist

50. *Untitled,* 1968
Acrylic on paper
27 x 41 in. (68.6 x 104.2 cm.)
Lent by the artist

51. *Untitled,* 1968–69
Acrylic on paper
48 x 63 in. (121.9 x 160 cm.)
Lent by the artist

52. *Berkeley,* 1970
Acrylic on canvas
168 x 108 in. (426.7 x 274.3 cm.)
University Art Museum, University of California, Berkeley. Purchased with the aid of funds from the Janss Foundation and the National Endowment for the Arts

53. *Looking Through,* 1970
Acrylic on canvas
96 x 120 in. (243.8 x 304.8 cm.)
Lent by the artist

54. *Untitled,* 1970
Acrylic on canvas
108 x 80 in. (274.3 x 203.2 cm.)
Lent by the artist

Joe Goode

55. *Unmade Bed Triptych,* 1968
Oil on canvas with Plexiglas
3 panels, each 60 x 60 in. (152.4 x 152.4 cm.)
Lent anonymously

56. *Unmade Bed,* 1968
Oil on canvas with Plexiglas
60 x 60 in. (152.4 x 152.4 cm.)
Lent anonymously

57. *Unmade Bed,* 1968
Oil on canvas with Plexiglas
60 x 60 in. (152.4 x 152.4 cm.)
Laura-Lee and Bob Woods

David Hockney

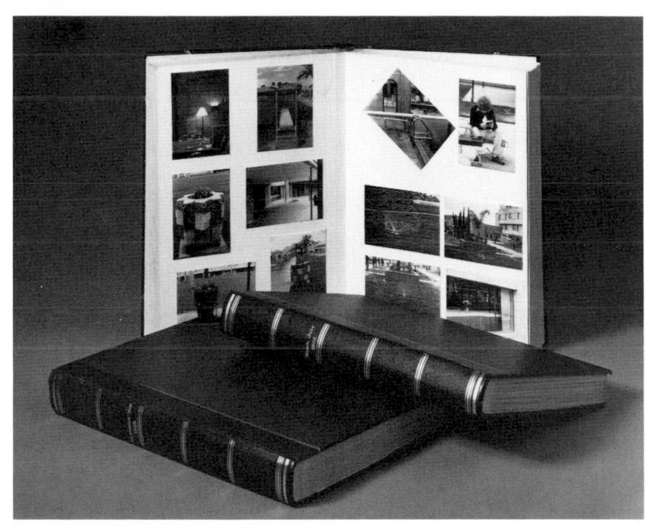

58. *Beverly Hills Housewife,* 1966
Acrylic on canvas (diptych)
72 x 144 in. (182.9 x 365.8 cm.)
Private collection, Los Angeles

59. *A Lawn Being Sprinkled,* 1967
Acrylic on canvas
60 x 60 in. (152.4 x 152.4 cm.)
Collection of Frances and Norman Lear

60. *Christopher Isherwood and Don Bachardy,* 1968
Acrylic on canvas
83½ x 119½ in. (212.1 x 303.5 cm.)
Sir John Foster

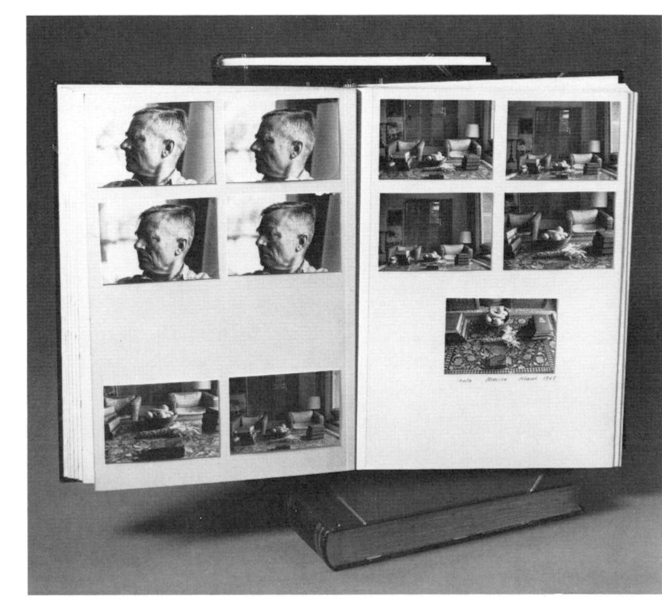

Robert Irwin

61. *Untitled,* c. 1959
Oil on canvas
65 x 66 in. (165.1 x 167.6 cm.)
Lent by the artist

62. *Untitled,* 1962
Oil on canvas
82½ x 84½ in. (209.5 x 214.6 cm.)
Collection of the La Jolla Museum of Contemporary Art, California

63. *Untitled,* 1963–64
Oil on canvas
82½ x 84½ in. (209.5 x 214.6 cm.)
Milly and Arnold Glimcher, New York

64. *Untitled,* 1963–65
Oil on canvas
82½ x 84½ in. (209.5 x 214.6 cm.)
Whitney Museum of American Art, New York
Gift of Fredric Mueller, 1977. 77.108

65. *Untitled,* 1963–65
Oil on canvas
82½ x 84½ in. (209.5 x 214.6 cm.)
Edward and Melinda Wortz

Craig Kauffman

66. *Still Life with Electric Fan and Respirator,* 1958
Oil on canvas
48 x 60 in. (121.9 x 152.4 cm.)
Artist Studio, Venice, California

67. *Untitled Wall Relief,* 1967
Sprayed acrylic lacquer on vacuum-formed Plexiglas
50 x 72 x 15 in. (127 x 182.9 x 38.1 cm.)
Los Angeles County Museum of Art
Gift of the Kleiner Foundation
M.73.38.10

68. *Untitled,* 1968
Sprayed acrylic lacquer on vacuum-formed Plexiglas
44 x 89 x 17 in. (111.8 x 226.1 x 43.2 cm.)
Asher/Faure Gallery, Los Angeles

69. *Untitled,* 1968
Sprayed acrylic lacquer on vacuum-formed Plexiglas
34⅜ x 56¼ x 8¼ in. (87.3 x 142.9 x 21 cm.)
Asher/Faure Gallery, Los Angeles

70. *Untitled,* 1968
Sprayed acrylic lacquer on vacuum-formed Plexiglas
19 x 55½ x 10 in. (48.3 x 141 x 25.4 cm.)
Judge Kurtz Kauffman

71. *Untitled,* 1968
Sprayed acrylic lacquer on vacuum-formed Plexiglas
24 x 52 x 17 in. (61 x 132.1 x 43.2 cm.)
Vivian Kauffman

72. *Untitled,* 1968
Sprayed acrylic lacquer on vacuum-formed Plexiglas
42 x 92 x 15 in. (106.7 x 233.7 x 38.1 cm.)
Edward and Melinda Wortz

70

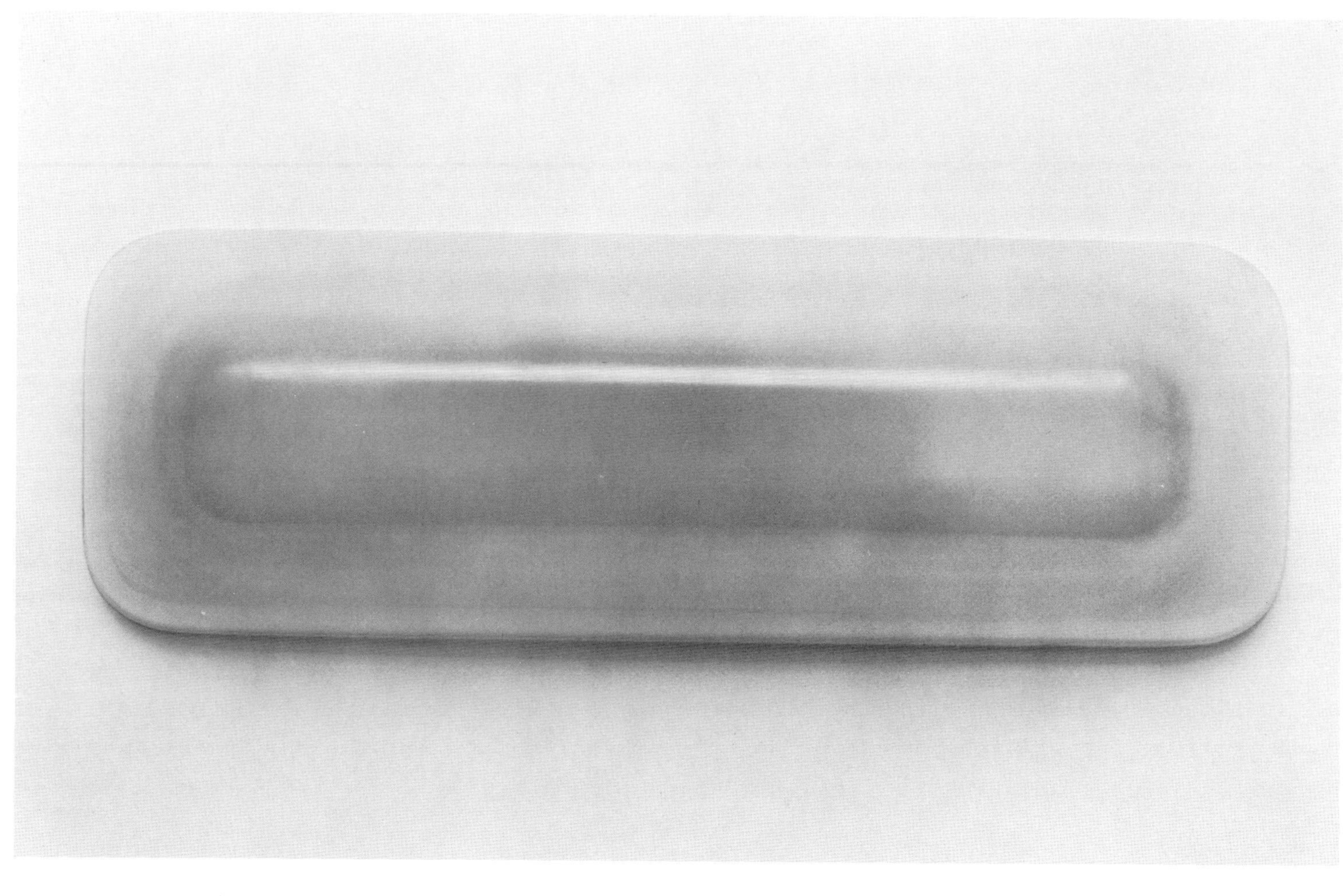

69

68

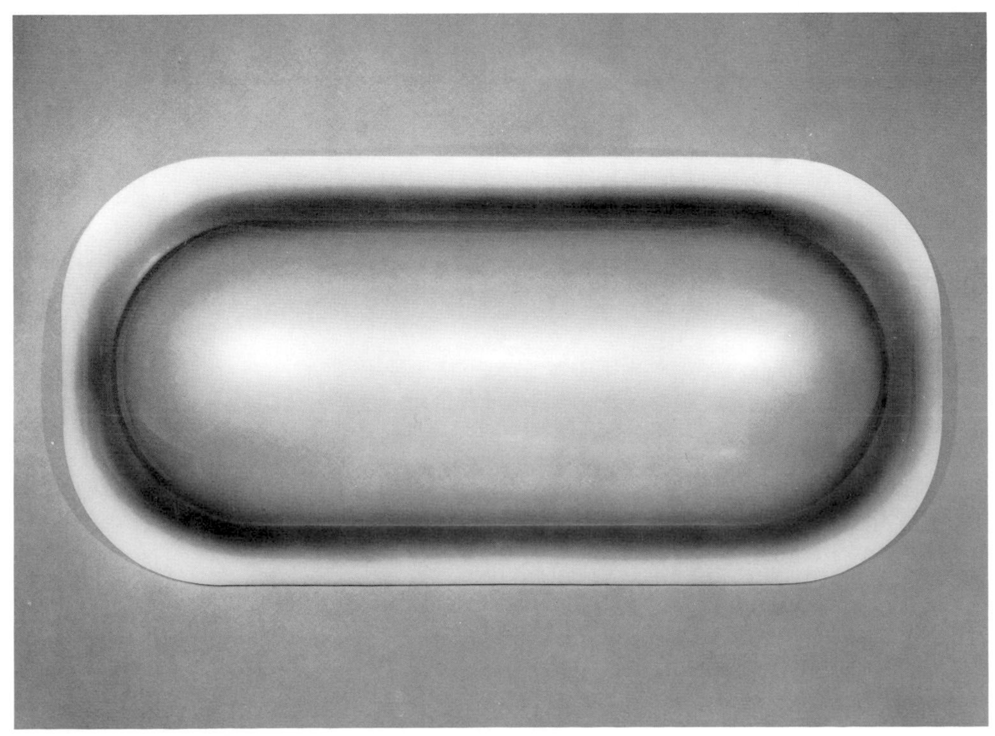

Edward Kienholz

73. *Untitled,* 1958
Mixed media
49¼ x 30⅛ in. (125.1 x 76.8 cm.)
Lyn Kienholz

74. *Hope for '36,* 1959
Mixed media
37½ x 18½ in. (95.3 x 47 cm.)
Lyn Kienholz

75. *The Illegal Operation,* 1962
Materials include fiberglassed shopping cart, furniture, concrete, medical implements
59 x 48 x 54 in. (149.9 x 121.9 x 137.2 cm.)
Betty and Monte Factor Family Collection

76. *The Back Seat Dodge '38,* 1964
Materials include paints, fiberglass and flock, 1938 Dodge, chicken wire, beer bottles, artificial grass, cast plaster figure
66 x 240 x 144 in. (168 x 610 x 356 cm.)
Lyn Kienholz

John McLaughlin

77. *#20,* 1960
Oil on canvas
48 x 36 in. (121.9 x 91.4 cm.)
Private collection,
New York

78. *#34,* 1960
Oil on canvas
36 x 48 in. (91.4 x
121.9 cm.)
Private collection,
New York

79. *Untitled,* 1961
Oil on canvas
48 x 60 in. (121.9 x
152.4 cm.)
Robert Rowan

80. *#9,* 1962
Oil on canvas
42 x 60 in. (106.7 x
152.4 cm.)
Mr. and Mrs. Morris S.
Pynoos

81. *#5,* 1963
Oil on canvas
48 x 60 in. (121.9 x
152.4 cm.)
Lent anonymously

78

79

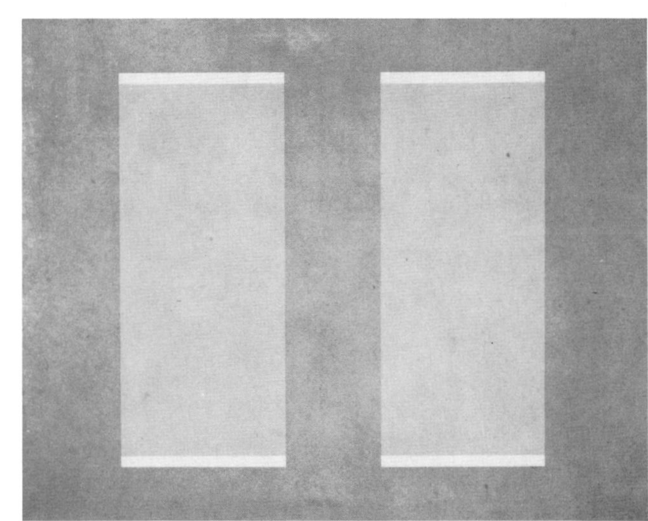

Edward Moses

82. *Rafe Bone,* 1958
Oil on canvas
72 x 64 in. (182.9 x 162.5 cm.)
Hanna Renneker

83. *Rose #1,* 1961
Graphite on paper
60 x 40 in. (152.4 x 101.6 cm.)
Lent by the artist

84. *Rose #2,* 1963
Graphite on paper
60 x 40 in. (152.4 x 101.6 cm.)
Mr. and Mrs. Henry Shapiro, Chicago

85. *Rose #3,* 1963
Graphite on paper
60 x 40 in. (152.4 x 101.6 cm.)
Laura-Lee and Bob Woods

86. *Rose #4,* 1963
Silver paint and graphite on paper
60 x 40 in. (152.4 x 101.6 cm.)
Lent by the artist

87. *Rose #5,* 1963
Graphite on paper
60 x 40 in. (152.4 x 101.6 cm.)
Lent by the artist

88. *Rose #6,* 1963
Graphite on paper
60 x 40 in. (152.4 x 101.6 cm.)
Mr. and Mrs. Richard Jerome O'Neill

89. *Rose Screen,* 1963
Graphite on paper
4 panels, each 59⅞ x 21½ in. (152.1 x 54.6 cm.)
Mr. and Mrs. Richard Jerome O'Neill

83

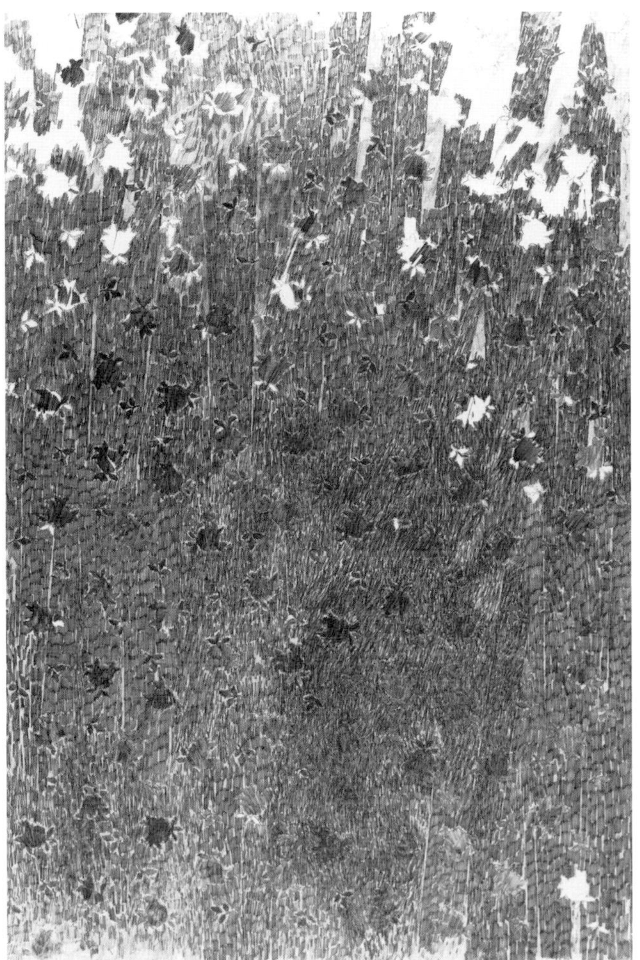

85

89

Bruce Nauman

90. *My Last Name Extended Vertically 14 Times,* 1967
Graphite and pastel on papcr
81¾ x 34 in. (207.7 x 86.4 cm.)
Gilman Paper Company Collection

91. *My Last Name Exaggerated 14 Times Vertically,* 1967
Pale purple neon tubing
63 x 33 in. (160 x 83.8 cm.)
1981 reconstruction by Los Angeles County Museum of Art
Courtesy of Giuseppe Panza di Biumo, Milan, Italy, and the artist

92. *Video Corridor: Live and Taped,* 1969
Two walls separated by 20 in. (50.8 cm.), two TV monitors, one TV camera, one play-back machine
1981 reconstruction by Los Angeles County Museum of Art
Courtesy of Giuseppe Panza di Biumo, Milan, Italy, and the artist

92

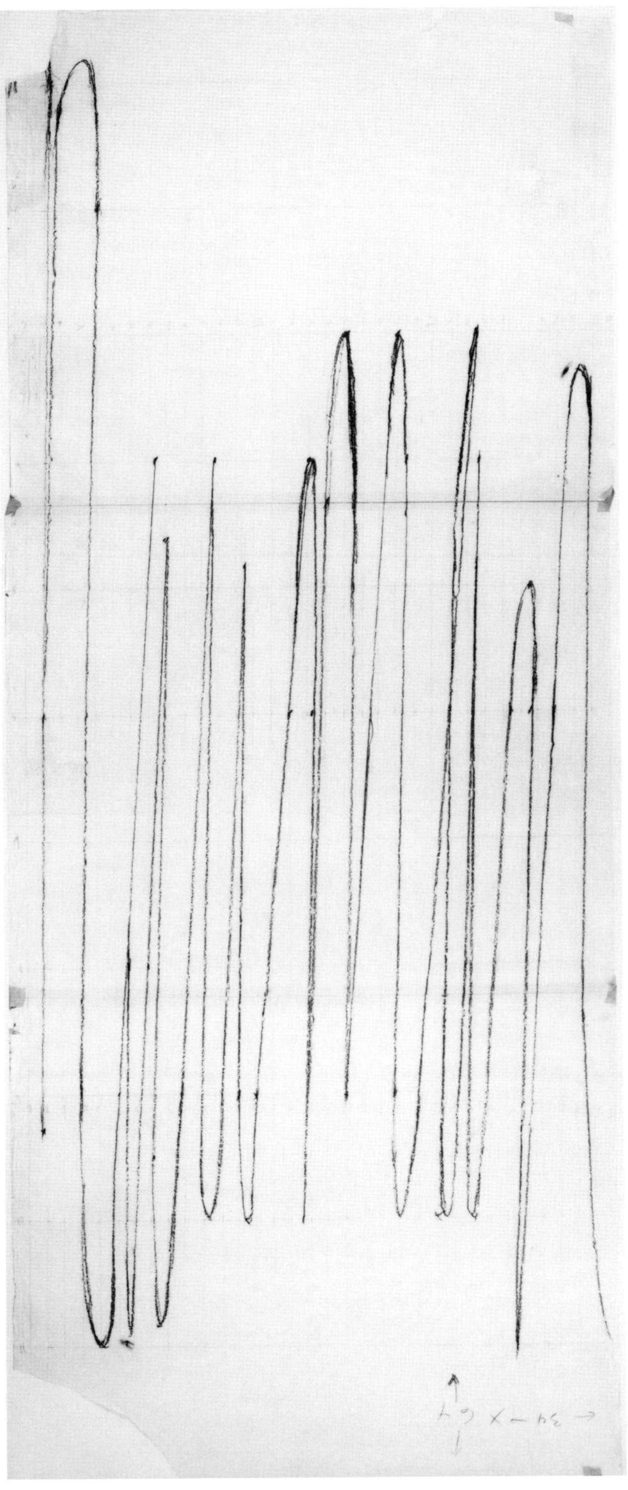

Kenneth Price

93. *Untitled,* 1959
Earthenware
h: 21 in. (53.3 cm.); w. at base: 20 in. (50.8 cm.)
Artist studio, Venice, California

94. *M. Green,* 1961
Fired and painted clay
10 x 13 x 11½ in. (25.4 x 33 x 29.2 cm.)
with pedestal: 59½ x 26 x 12 in. (151.2 x 66 x 30.5 cm.)
Betty Asher

95. *Blue Egg,* 1962
Fired and painted clay
7 x 5 x 5 in. (17.8 x 12.7 x 12.7 cm.)
Dr. and Mrs. Merle S. Glick

96. *B. T. Blue,* 1963
Fired and painted clay
10 x 6½ in. (25.4 x 16.5 cm.)
Becky and Peter Smith

97. *S. L. Green,* 1963
Fired and painted clay
9⅝ x 10½ x 10½ in. (24.4 x 26.7 x 26.7 cm.)
Whitney Museum of American Art, New York
Gift of the Howard and Jean Lipman Foundation, Inc., 1966. 66.35

98. *Pink Egg,* 1964
Fired and painted clay
6 x 5½ x 5½ in. (15.2 x 14 x 14 cm.)
h. with stand: 70 in. (177.8 cm.)
Betty and Monte Factor Family Collection

98

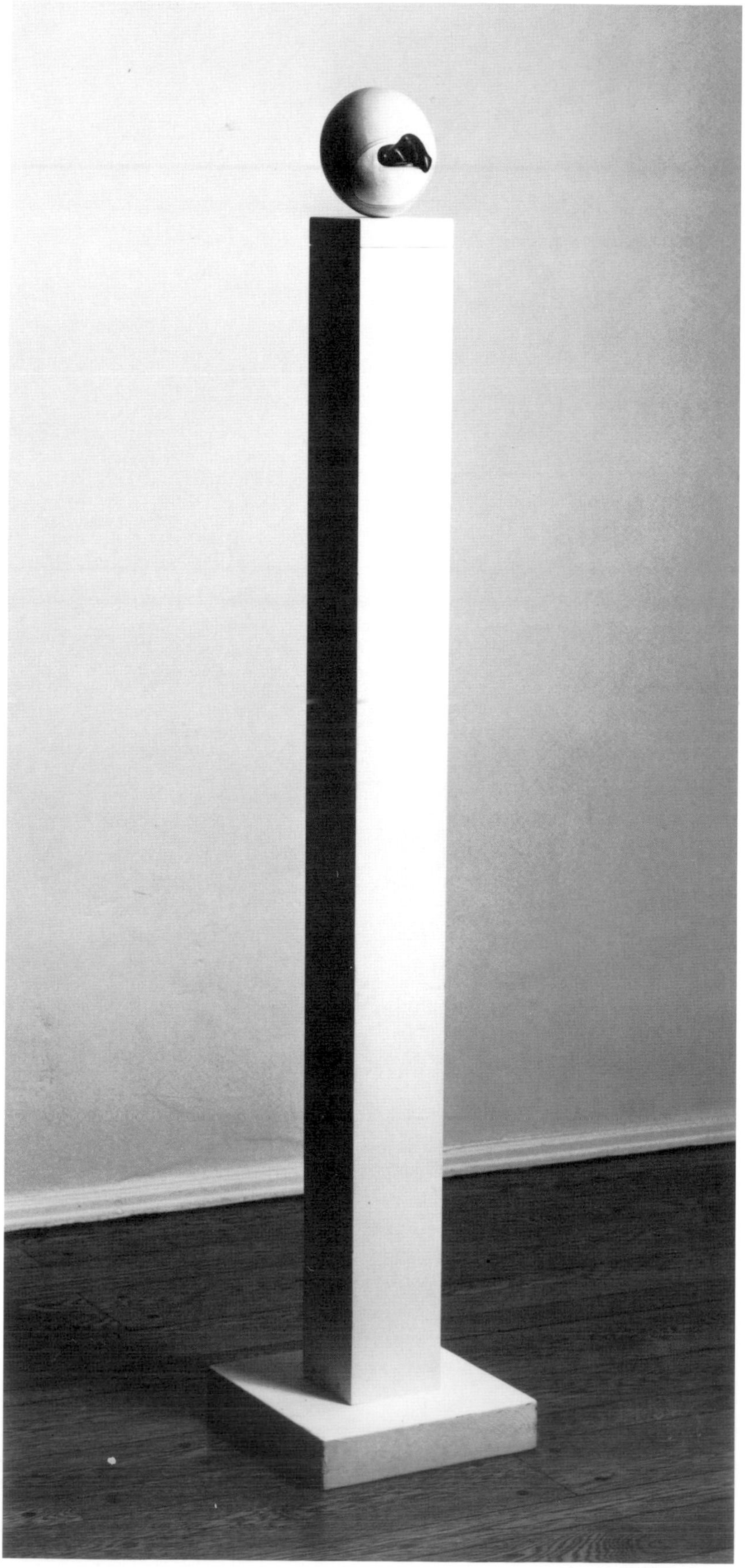

94

Edward Ruscha

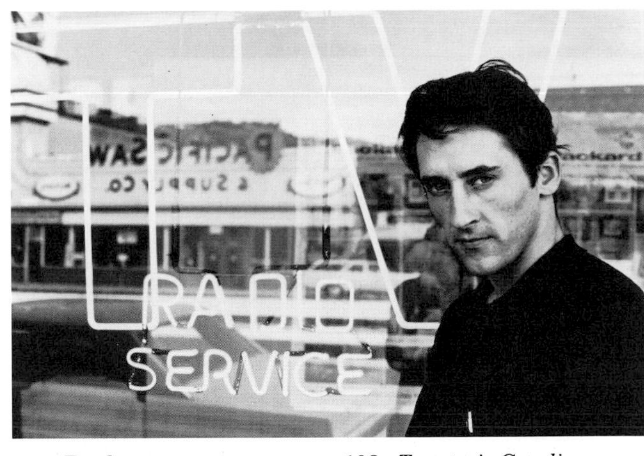

99. *Boss,* 1961
Oil on canvas
71 x 66 in. (180.3 x 167.6 cm.)
Dr. Leopold S. Tuchman

100. *Actual Size,* 1962
Oil on canvas
72 x 67 in. (182.9 x 170.2 cm.)
Los Angeles County Museum of Art
Anonymous gift through the Contemporary Art Council
M.63.14

101. *Annie,* 1962
Oil on canvas
71 x 66½ in. (180.3 x 168.9 cm.)
Betty Asher

102. *Noise, Pencil, Broken Pencil, Cheap Western,* 1963
Oil on canvas
71 x 67 in. (180.3 x 170.2 cm.)
Sydney and Frances Lewis Collection

103. *Standard Station Amarillo, Texas,* 1963
Oil on canvas
65 x 124 in. (165.1 x 315 cm.)
Dartmouth College Museum and Galleries, Hanover, New Hampshire
Gift of James J. Meeker, Dartmouth College Class of 1958

104. *Won't,* 1964
Oil on canvas
72 x 67 in. (182.9 x 170.2 cm.)
Lent anonymously

Books

105. *Various Small Fires and Milk,* 1964
Self-published in Los Angeles
First edition (1964): 400 signed
Second edition (1970): 3,000 unsigned, unnumbered,
48 pp.; softcover, sewn binding, glassine dust jacket
16 photographs
7 x 5½ in. (17.8 x 14 cm.)
Los Angeles County Museum of Art

106. *Some Los Angeles Apartments,* 1965
Self-published in Los Angeles
First edition (1965): 700
Second edition (1970): 3,000 unsigned, unnumbered,
44 pp.; softcover, sewn binding, glassine dust jacket
36 photographs
7 x 5½ in. (17.8 x 14 cm.)
Los Angeles County Museum of Art

107. *Every Building on the Sunset Strip,* 1966
Self-published in Los Angeles
First edition (1966): 1,000
Second edition (1970): 5,000 unsigned, unnumbered,
one continuous 38 ft. 4⅝ in. (11.70 m.) accordion-folded sheet, two strips of photographs (top and bottom), softcover, Mylar slipcase
7 x 9½ in. (17.8 x 24 cm.)
Los Angeles County Museum of Art

108. *Twentysix Gasoline Stations,* 1962
Self-published in Los Angeles
First edition (1962): 400 unsigned, numbered
Second edition (1967): 500 unsigned, unnumbered
Third edition (1969): 3,000 unsigned, unnumbered,
48 pp.; offset, softcover, perfect binding, glassine dust jacket
26 photographs
7 x 5½ in. (17.8 x 14 cm.)
Los Angeles County Museum of Art

109. *Royal Road Test,* 1967
(by Edward Ruscha, Mason Williams, and Patrick Blackwell)
Self-published in Los Angeles
First edition (1967): 1,000
Second edition (1969): 1,000
Third edition (1971): 2,000 unsigned, unnumbered
Fourth edition (1980): 1,500 unsigned, unnumbered,
56 pp.; softcover, spiral binding
35 photographs
9½ x 6¼ in. (24.1 x 15.9 cm.)
Los Angeles County Museum of Art

110. *Thirtyfour Parking Lots in Los Angeles,* 1967
Self-published in Los Angeles
First edition (1967): 2,413 unsigned, unnumbered
Second edition (1974): 2,000 unsigned, unnumbered,
48 pp.; softcover, perfect binding
31 photographs by Art Alanis
10 x 8 in. (25.4 x 20.3 cm.)
Los Angeles County Museum of Art

111. *Nine Swimming Pools and a Broken Glass,* 1968
Self-published in Los Angeles
First edition (1968): 2,400
Second edition (1976): 2,000 unsigned, unnumbered
64 pp.; softcover, sewn binding, glassine dust jacket
7⅛ x 5½ in. (18 x 14 cm.)
Los Angeles County Museum of Art

112. *Stains,* 1969
Self-published in Hollywood, California; Heavy Industry Publications
Edition of 70 signed, numbered (1–70)
78 loose sheets interleaved with tissue, contained in black leather box lined with white silk
11¾ x 10⅞ in. (30 x 27.6 cm.)
Lent by the artist

113. *Business Cards,* 1968
8¾ x 5⅝ in. (22.2 x 14.3 cm.)
Self-published in Hollywood, California, with Billy Al Bengston
Courtesy of Heavy Industry Publications

Annie

Peter Voulkos

114. *5,000 Feet,* 1958
Fired clay
Including base: 45½ x 21¹³⁄₁₆ x 13 in. (115.6 x 55.9 x 33 cm.)
Los Angeles County Museum of Art
Purchase Award, Annual Exhibition of Los Angeles and Vicinity
M.59.16

115. *Rondena,* 1958
Stoneware
h: 64 in. (162.5 cm.)
Mr. and Mrs. Stanley K. Sheinbaum

116. *Camelback Mountain,* 1959
Fired clay
45½ x 19½ x 20¼ in. (115.6 x 49.5 x 51.4 cm.)
Museum of Fine Arts, Boston. Gift of Mr. and Mrs. Stephen D. Paine, 1978.690

117. *Little Big Horn,* 1959
Stoneware
59¾ x 40 x 33 in. (151.7 x 101.6 x 83.8 cm.)
Collection of The Oakland Museum, California
Gift of the Art Guild of the Oakland Museum Association

118. *Sitting Bull,* 1959
Fired clay
69 x 37 x 37 in. (175.3 x 94 x 94 cm.)
Collection of the Santa Barbara Museum of Art, California. Bequest of Hans G. M. De Schulthess

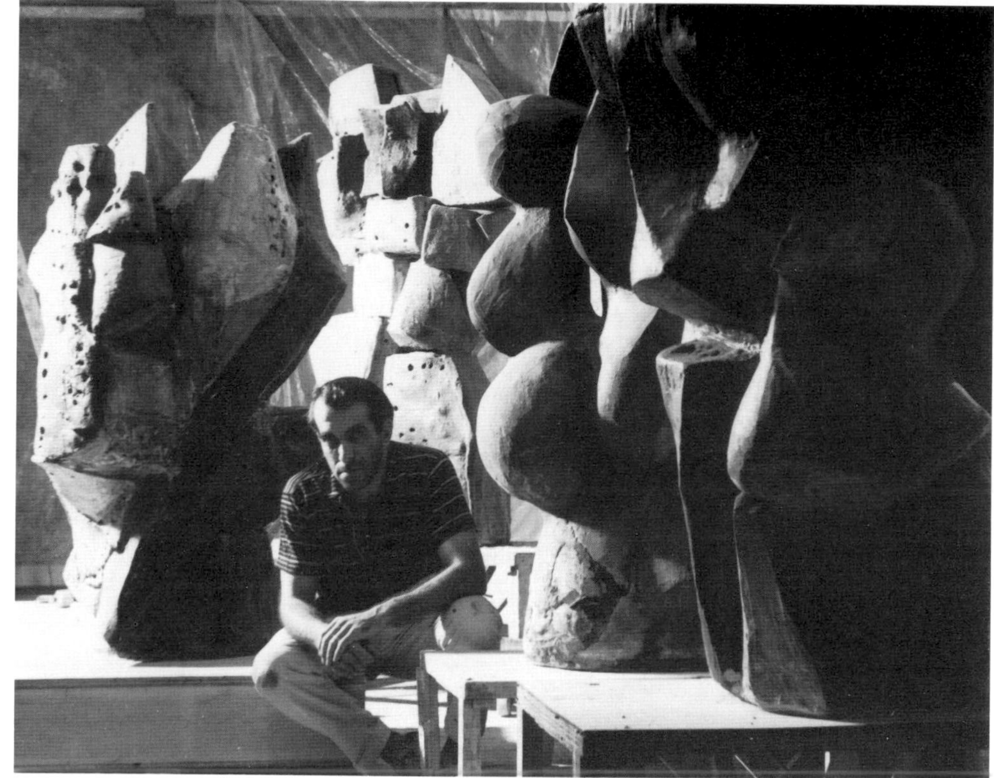

117

118

114

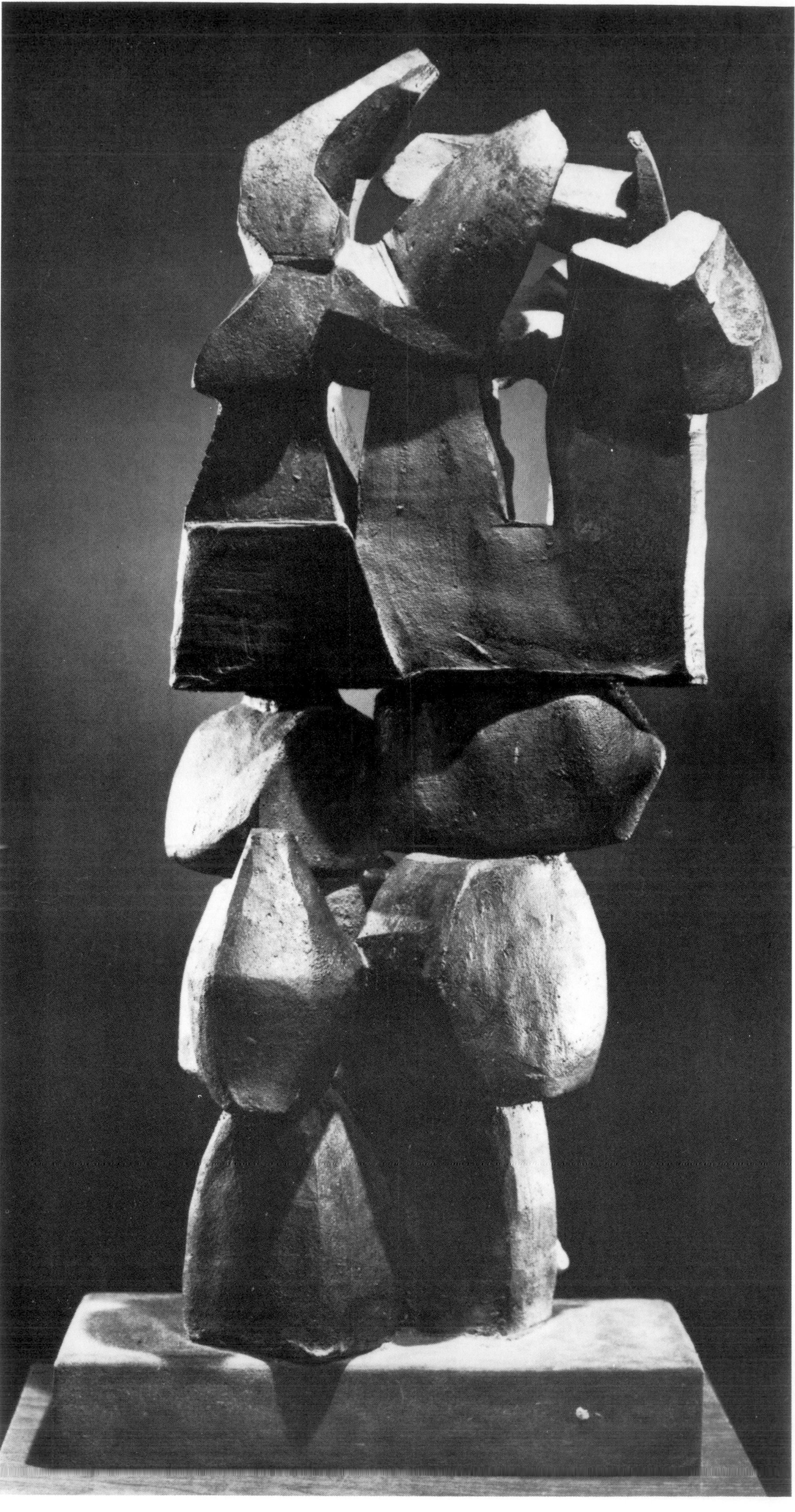

Exhibition Histories and Bibliographies

Larry Bell

Born in Chicago, 1939; resident of Los Angeles, 1945–73; lives in Taos, New Mexico. Attended Chouinard Art Institute, Los Angeles, 1957–59.

Selected One-Man Exhibitions

Ferus Gallery, Los Angeles, 1962, 1963, 1965.

Pace Gallery, New York, 1965, 1967, 1970, 1971, 1972, 1973.

Galerie Ileana Sonnabend, Paris, 1967.

Stedelijk Museum, Amsterdam, 1967.

Riko Mizuno Gallery, Los Angeles, 1969, 1971.

Ace Gallery, Los Angeles, 1970, 1971.

Galerie Rudolf Zwirner, Cologne, West Germany, 1970.

Helman Gallery, St. Louis, Missouri, 1971.

Wilmaro Gallery, Denver, Colorado, 1972.

Felicity Samuel Gallery, London, 1972.

Pasadena Art Museum, California, 1972.

Bonython Gallery, Sydney, Australia, 1973.

The Oakland Museum, California, 1973.

Marlborough Galleria d'Arte, Rome, 1974.

Fort Worth Art Museum, Texas, 1975.

Tally Richards Gallery of Contemporary Art, Taos, New Mexico, 1975, 1978, 1979, 1980.

The Santa Barbara Museum of Art, California, 1976.

Art Museum of South Texas, Corpus Christi, 1976.

Hayden Gallery, Massachusetts Institute of Technology, Cambridge, 1977.

University of Massachusetts, Amherst, 1977.

Texas Gallery, Houston, 1978.

Erica Williams/Anne Johnson Gallery, Seattle, Washington, 1978.

University of New Mexico, Albuquerque, 1978.

Roswell Museum and Art Center, New Mexico, 1978.

Multiples Gallery, New York, 1979.

Sebastian-Moore Gallery, Denver, Colorado, 1979, 1980.

Hill's Gallery of Contemporary Art, Santa Fe, New Mexico, 1979, 1980.

Hansen Fuller Gallery, San Francisco, 1979.

Janus Gallery, Venice, California, 1979.

Marian Goodman Gallery, New York, 1979, 1981.

The Hudson River Museum, Yonkers, New York, 1981.

Selected Group Exhibitions

War Babies, Huysman Gallery, Los Angeles, 1961.

California Hard-Edge Painting, The Fine Arts Patrons of Newport Harbor, Balboa Pavilion Gallery, California, 1964.

Boxes, Dwan Gallery, Los Angeles, 1964.

5 at Pace, Pace Gallery, New York, 1965.

Shape and Structure, Tibor de Nagy Gallery, New York, 1965.

The Responsive Eye, The Museum of Modern Art, New York, 1965.

VIII Bienal de São Paulo, Brazil, 1965.

Five Los Angeles Sculptors and Sculptors' Drawings, University of California, Irvine, 1966.

Primary Structures, The Jewish Museum, New York, 1966.

Ten from Los Angeles, Seattle Art Museum, Washington, 1966.

Los Angeles Now, Robert Fraser Gallery, London, 1966.

American Sculpture of the Sixties, Los Angeles County Museum of Art, 1967.

A New Aesthetic, Washington Gallery of Modern Art, Washington, D.C., 1967.

Los Angeles 6, Vancouver Art Gallery, British Columbia, 1968.

6 Artists: 6 Exhibitions, Walker Art Center, Minneapolis, Minnesota, 1968.

Documenta 4, Kassel, West Germany, 1968.

Serial Imagery, Pasadena Art Museum, California, 1968.

14 Sculptors: The Industrial Edge, Walker Art Center, Minneapolis, Minnesota, 1969.

Kompas 4: West Coast USA, Stedelijk van Abbemuseum, Eindhoven, The Netherlands, 1969.

Spaces, The Museum of Modern Art, New York, 1969.

Three from Los Angeles: Irwin, Bell, Kauffman, Dunkleman Gallery, Montreal, 1969.

Larry Bell, Robert Irwin, Doug Wheeler, The Tate Gallery, London, 1970.

American Art since 1960, Princeton University, New Jersey, 1970.

Transparency, Reflection, Light, Space: Four Artists, The UCLA Art Galleries, University of California, Los Angeles, 1971.

Works for New Spaces, Walker Art Center, Minneapolis, Minnesota, 1971.

11 Los Angeles Artists, Hayward Gallery, London, 1971 (traveled to Musées Royaux des Beaux-Arts, Brussels; Akademie der Künste, Berlin, West Germany).

USA West Coast, Kunstverein, Hamburg, West Germany, 1972 (traveled to Kunstverein, Hannover; Kölnischer Kunstverein, Cologne; Württembergisher Kunstverein, Stuttgart).

Art in Space, The Detroit Institute of Arts, 1973.

Illuminations and Reflections, Whitney Museum of American Art, New York, 1974.

The Condition of Sculpture, Hayward Gallery, London, 1975.

Sculpture: American Directions, 1945–1975, National Collection of Fine Arts, Smithsonian Institution, Washington, D.C., 1975.

The Last Time I Saw Ferus, 1957–1966, Newport Harbor Art Museum, Newport Beach, California, 1976.

200 Years of American Sculpture, Whitney Museum of American Art, New York, 1976.

Venice Biennale, Italy, 1976.

Painting and Sculpture in California: The Modern Era, San Francisco Museum of Modern Art, 1976 (traveled to National Collection of Fine Arts, Smithsonian Institution, Washington, D.C.).

Seasons of the Fountain, Larry Bell and Eric Orr, Multiples Gallery, New York, 1978.

Reflections of Realism, Albuquerque Museum, New Mexico, 1979.

California Perceptions: Light and Space, California State University, Fullerton, 1979.

Beyond Object, Aspen Center for the Visual Arts, Colorado, 1980.

Here and Now: 35 Artists in New Mexico, Albuquerque Museum, New Mexico, 1980.

Selected Bibliography

Jules Langsner, "America's Second Art City," *Art in America,* vol. 51, no. 2, March–April 1963, pp. 127–31.

John Coplans, "Three Los Angeles Artists," *Artforum,* vol. 1, no. 10, April 1963, pp. 29–31.

John Coplans, "Formal Art," *Artforum,* vol. 2, no. 12, summer 1964, pp. 42–46.

Philip Leider, "The Cool School," *Artforum,* vol. 2, no. 12, summer 1964, pp. 47–52.

Philip Leider, "Saint Andy," *Artforum,* vol. 3, no. 5, February 1965, pp. 26–28 (with statement by Bell on Warhol).

Dore Ashton, "New Sculpture Fresh in Old Techniques," *Studio International,* vol. 169, no. 866, June 1965, p. 263.

John Coplans, "Larry Bell," *Artforum,* vol. 3, no. 9, June 1965, pp. 27–29.

Donald Judd, "Specific Objects," *Arts Yearbook,* vol. 8, 1965, pp. 74–82.

Walter Hopps, *Exhibition of the United States of America: VIII Bienal de São Paulo,* Brazil, 1965.

Mel Bochner, "In the Galleries: Larry Bell," *Arts Magazine,* vol. 40, no. 3, January 1966, pp. 54–55.

John Coplans, "Los Angeles: Object Lesson," *Art News,* vol. 64, no. 9, January 1966, p. 40.

Barbara Rose, "Los Angeles, The Second City," *Art in America,* vol. 54, no. 1, January–February 1966, pp. 110–15.

Lucy R. Lippard, "New York Letter: Recent Sculpture Escape," *Art International,* vol. 10, no. 2, February 1966, pp. 52–53.

Robert Smithson, "Entropy and New Monuments," *Artforum,* vol. 4, no. 10, June 1966, pp. 26–31.

Peter Plagens, "Present-Day Styles and Ready-Made Criticism," *Artforum,* vol. 5, no. 4, December 1966, pp. 36–39.

John Coplans, *Ten from Los Angeles,* Seattle Art Museum, Washington, 1966.

Fidel Danieli, "Bell's Progress," *Artforum,* vol. 5, no. 10, summer 1967, pp. 68–71.

Robert Morris, "Notes on Sculpture, Part 3, Notes and Nonsequiturs," *Artforum,* vol. 5, no. 10, summer 1967, pp. 24–29.

Barbara Rose, *A New Aesthetic,* Washington Gallery of Modern Art, Washington, D.C., 1967 (with statement by Bell).

Barbara Rose, *American Art since 1900,* New York, 1967.

Raphael Sorin and Annette Michelson, *Larry Bell,* Galerie Ileana Sonnabend, Paris, 1967.

Michael Kirby, "Sculpture as Visual Instrument," *Art International,* vol. 12, no. 8, October 1968, pp. 35–37.

John Coplans, *Serial Imagery,* Pasadena Art Museum, California, 1968.

John Coplans, *Los Angeles 6,* Vancouver Art Gallery, British Columbia, 1968 (with Bell interview).

Barbara Rose, Christopher Finch, and Martin Friedman, *14 Sculptors: The Industrial Edge,* Walker Art Center, Minneapolis, Minnesota, 1969.

Michael Compton, "Controlled Environment," *Art and Artists,* vol. 5, no. 2, May 1970, p. 45.

Phyllis Tuchman, "American Art in Germany: The History of a Phenomenon," *Artforum,* vol. 9, no. 3, November 1970, pp. 58–69.

Michael Compton and Norman Reid, *Larry Bell, Robert Irwin, Doug Wheeler,* The Tate Gallery, London, 1970.

Maurice Tuchman, *A Report on the Art and Technology Program of the Los Angeles County Museum of Art,* Los Angeles, 1971.

Frederick S. Wight, *Transparency, Reflection, Light, Space: Four Artists,* The UCLA Art Galleries, University of California, Los Angeles, 1971.

Alistair Mackintosh, "Larry Bell," *Art and Artists,* vol. 6, no. 70, January 1972, pp. 39–41.

Peter Plagens, "Larry Bell Reassesses," *Artforum,* vol. 11, no. 2, October 1972, pp. 71–73.

Barbara Haskell, *Larry Bell,* Pasadena Art Museum, California, 1972.

Helmut Heissenbüttel and Helene Winer, *USA West Coast,* Kunstverein, Hamburg, West Germany, 1972.

Germain Viatte, "Rêver la Défense," *L'Oeil,* October 1974, p. 6.

Norman Laliberte and Alex Mogelon, *Art in Boxes,* New York, 1974.

Peter Plagens, *Sunshine Muse: Contemporary Art on the West Coast,* New York, 1974.

H. H. Arnason, *History of Modern Art,* New York, 1975.

Barbara Rose, ed., *Readings in American Art, 1900–1975,* New York, 1975.

William Tucker, *The Condition of Sculpture,* Hayward Gallery, London, 1975.

Janet Kutner, "Larry Bell's Iceberg," *Arts Magazine,* vol. 50, no. 5, January 1976, pp. 62–66.

Gerrit Henry, "Larry Bell and Eric Orr," *Art News,* vol. 77, no. 4, April 1978, pp. 152–63.

Jan Butterfield, "Larry Bell: Transparent Motif" (interview), *Art in America,* vol. 66, no. 5, September–October 1978, pp. 95–99.

"Larry Bell," interview by Michele D. De Angelus, Archives of American Art, Smithsonian Institution, Washington, D.C., May 1980.

Robert Creeley, Richard Koshalek, Melinda Wortz, and Larry Bell, *Larry Bell: New Work,* The Hudson River Museum, New York, 1981.

Billy Al Bengston

Born in Dodge City, Kansas, 1934; moved to Los Angeles, 1949; lives in Santa Monica, California.
Attended Los Angeles City College, 1952; California College of Arts and Crafts, Oakland, 1955; Otis Art Institute, Los Angeles, 1956.

Selected One-Man Exhibitions

Ferus Gallery, Los Angeles, 1958, 1960, 1961, 1962, 1963.

Martha Jackson Gallery, New York, 1962.

Los Angeles County Museum of Art, 1968 (retrospective).

San Francisco Museum of Art, 1968.

Pasadena Art Museum, California, 1969.

Utah Museum of Fine Arts, Salt Lake City, 1969.

The Santa Barbara Museum of Art, California, 1970.

Riko Mizuno Gallery, Los Angeles, 1970.

Galerie Neuendorf, Hamburg, West Germany, 1970, 1972.

Margo Leavin Gallery, Los Angeles, 1971.

La Jolla Museum of Art, California, 1971.

Galerie Neuendorf, Cologne, West Germany, 1971.

Felicity Samuel Gallery, London, 1972.

Nicholas Wilder Gallery, Los Angeles, 1973, 1974.

Contemporary Arts Museum, Houston, Texas, 1973.

Pollock Gallery, Southern Methodist University, Dallas, Texas, 1973.

Texas Gallery, Houston, 1973, 1974, 1976, 1977, 1978, 1979.

John Berggruen Gallery, San Francisco, 1974, 1978.

Jared Sable Gallery, Toronto, 1974.

Tortue Gallery, Santa Monica, California, 1975.

Portland Center for the Visual Arts, Oregon, 1976.

University of Montana, Missoula, 1977.

James Corcoran Gallery, Los Angeles, 1977, 1978, 1980.

Security Pacific Bank, Los Angeles, 1978.

University of Houston, Texas, 1978.

Conejo Valley Art Museum, Thousand Oaks, California, 1979.

Acquavella Contemporary Art Gallery, New York, 1979, 1981.

Malibu Art and Design, California, 1980.

Honolulu Academy of Arts, Hawaii, 1980.

Selected Group Exhibitions

Fifty California Artists, Whitney Museum of American Art, New York, 1962.

66th American Exhibition of Painting and Sculpture, The Art Institute of Chicago, 1963; *70th American Exhibition,* 1972.

Six More, Los Angeles County Museum of Art, 1963.

Pop Art USA, Oakland Art Museum, California, 1963.

Pop Art and the American Tradition, Milwaukee Art Center, Wisconsin, 1965.

VIII Bienal de São Paulo, Brazil, 1965.

Ten from Los Angeles, Seattle Art Museum, Washington, 1966.

1967 Annual Exhibition of Contemporary American Painting, Whitney Museum of American Art, New York; *1979 Annual Exhibition.*

Transparency/Reflection, California State College, Fullerton, 1968.

Late Fifties at the Ferus, Los Angeles County Museum of Art, 1968.

New Media: New Methods, The Museum of Modern Art, New York, 1969.

Graphics: Six West Coast Artists, Galleria Milano, Italy, 1969.

Three Modern Masters: Billy Al Bengston, Edward Ruscha, Frank Lloyd Wright, Gallery Reese Palley, San Francisco, 1969.

Superlimited: Books, Boxes, and Things, The Jewish Museum, New York, 1969.

Kompas 4: West Coast USA, Stedelijk van Abbemuseum, Eindhoven, The Netherlands, 1969.

West Coast 1945–1969, Pasadena Art Museum, California, 1969 (traveled to City Art Museum of St. Louis, Missouri; Art Gallery of Ontario, Toronto; Fort Worth Art Center Museum, Texas).

The Highway, Institute of Contemporary Art of the University of Pennsylvania, Philadelphia, 1970.

Three California Friends: Billy Al Bengston, Joe Goode, Ed Ruscha, Contemporary Arts Foundation, Oklahoma City, Oklahoma, 1970.

Looking West 1970, Joslyn Art Museum, Omaha, Nebraska.

A Decade of California Color, Pace Gallery, New York, 1970.

USA West Coast, Kunstverein, Hamburg, West Germany, 1972 (traveled to Kunstverein, Hannover; Kölnischer Kunstverein, Cologne; Württembergisher Kunstverein, Stuttgart).

The State of California Painting, Govett-Brewster Art Gallery, New Plymouth, New Zealand, 1972.

Contemporary American Art: Los Angeles, Fort Worth Art Center Museum, Texas, 1972.

Four Artists: Ruscha, Bengston, Alexander, Moses, Akron Art Institute, Ohio, 1972.

Working in California, Albright-Knox Art Gallery, Buffalo, New York, 1972.

33rd Biennial Exhibition of Contemporary American Painting, Corcoran Gallery of Art, Washington, D.C., 1973.

American Pop Art, Whitney Museum of American Art, New York, 1974.

4 from the East/4 from the West, Art Galleries, University of California, Santa Barbara, 1975.

Collage and Assemblage, Los Angeles Institute of Contemporary Art, 1975.

The Last Time I Saw Ferus, 1957–1966, Newport Harbor Art Museum, Newport Beach, California, 1976.

Painting and Sculpture in California: The Modern Era, San Francisco Museum of Modern Art, 1976 (traveled to National Collection of Fine Arts, Smithsonian Institution, Washington, D.C.).

Billy Al Bengston and Alan Shields, Art Gallery, Georgia State University, Atlanta, 1979.

Selected Bibliography

Lawrence Alloway, *Six More,* Los Angeles County Museum of Art, 1963.

John Coplans, *Pop Art USA,* Oakland Art Museum, California, 1963.

John Coplans, "Billy Al Bengston," *Artforum,* vol. 3, no. 9, June 1965, pp. 36–38.

Lucy R. Lippard, *Pop Art,* New York, 1966.

Fidel Danieli, "Billy Al Bengston's 'Dentos,'" *Artforum,* vol. 5, no. 9, May 1967, pp. 24–27.

James Monte, "Bengston in Los Angeles," *Artforum,* vol. 8, no. 3, November 1968, pp. 36–40.

Kurt von Meier, *Transparency/Reflection,* California State College, Fullerton, 1968.

James Monte, *Billy Al Bengston,* Los Angeles County Museum of Art, 1968.

Jean Leering, *Kompas 4: West Coast USA,* Stedelijk van Abbemuseum, Eindhoven, The Netherlands, 1969.

Carol Lynsley, *Three Modern Masters: Billy Al Bengston, Edward Ruscha, Frank Lloyd Wright,* Gallery Reese Palley, San Francisco, 1969.

Billy Al Bengston, "Los Angeles Artists' Studios," *Art in America,* vol. 58, no. 6, November–December 1970, pp. 100–109.

Helmut Heissenbüttel and Helene Winer, *USA West Coast,* Kunstverein, Hamburg, West Germany, 1972.

Al Radloff, *Four Artists: Ruscha, Bengston, Alexander, Moses,* Akron Art Institute, Ohio, 1972.

Michael Walls, *The State of California Painting,* Govett-Brewster Art Gallery, New Plymouth, New Zealand, 1972.

William A. Robinson, Perry Walker, and Henry T. Hopkins, "Bengston, Grieger, Goode: 3 Interviews," *Art in America,* vol. 61, no. 2, March–April, 1973, pp. 48–53.

Lawrence Alloway, *American Pop Art,* Whitney Museum of American Art, New York, 1974.

Peter Plagens, *Sunshine Muse: Contemporary Art on the West Coast,* New York, 1974.

Peter Plagens, "Billy Al Bengston's New Paintings," *Artforum,* vol. 13, no. 7, March 1975, pp. 34–35.

Fredericka Hunter, *Billy Al Bengston: Paintings of the Seventies,* Security Pacific Bank, Los Angeles, 1978.

Ruth Bass, "Billy Al Bengston," *Art News,* vol. 78, no. 9, November 1979, p. 196.

Jeff Perrone, "The Decorative Impulse," *Artforum,* vol. 18, no. 3, November 1979, pp. 80–81.

Susie Kalil, "Billy Al Bengston: Sensuality and Structure," *Artweek,* vol. 10, no. 43, December 1979, p. 3.

"Billy Al Bengston," interview by Susan C. Larsen, Archives of American Art, Smithsonian Institution, Washington, D.C., September 1980.

Wallace Berman

Born on Staten Island, New York, 1926; died in Topanga, California, 1976.
Attended Chouinard Art Institute, Los Angeles, 1944; Jepson Art School, Los Angeles, 1944.

Selected One-Man Exhibitions

Ferus Gallery, Los Angeles, 1957.

Studio Exhibition (Beverly Glen), Los Angeles, 1965.

Topanga Community House, Topanga, California, 1967 (one-day exhibition).

Los Angeles County Museum of Art, 1968 (traveled to The Jewish Museum, New York).

The Mermaid Tavern, Topanga, California, 1973 (one-day exhibition).

Gemini G.E.L., Los Angeles, 1974.

Timothea Stewart Gallery, Los Angeles, 1977.

Whitney Museum of American Art, New York, 1978.

Otis Art Institute, Los Angeles, 1978 (retrospective; traveled to Fort Worth Art Museum, Texas; University Art Museum, Berkeley, California; Seattle Art Museum, Washington).

L.A. Louver, Venice, California, 1979.

Selected Group Exhibitions

Los Angeles Now, Robert Fraser Gallery, London, 1966.

Assemblage in California, University of California, Irvine, 1968.

West Coast 1945–1969, Pasadena Art Museum, California, 1969 (traveled to City Art Museum of St. Louis, Missouri; Art Gallery of Ontario, Toronto; Fort Worth Art Center Museum, Texas).

Pop Art Redefined, Hayward Gallery, London, 1969.

Poets of the Cities/New York and San Francisco, 1950–1965, Dallas Museum of Fine Arts, Texas, 1974.

Collage and Assemblage, Los Angeles Institute of Contemporary Art, 1975.

Environment and the New Art 1960–1975, University of California, Davis, 1975.

Art as a Muscular Principle, John and Norah Warbeke Gallery, Mount Holyoke College, South Hadley, Massachusetts, 1975.

The Last Time I Saw Ferus, 1957–1966, Newport Harbor Art Museum, Newport Beach, California, 1976.

Painting and Sculpture in California: The Modern Era, San Francisco Museum of Modern Art, 1976 (traveled to National Collection of Fine Arts, Smithsonian Institution, Washington, D.C.).

Selected Bibliography

John Coplans, "Art Is Love Is God," *Artforum,* vol. 2, no. 9, March 1964, pp. 26–27.

John Coplans, "Circle of Styles on the West Coast," *Art in America,* vol. 52, no. 3, June 1964, p. 36.

John Coplans, "Los Angeles: Object Lesson," *Art News,* vol. 64, no. 9, January 1966, p. 67.

Gail R. Scott and Jack Hirschman, *Wallace Berman,* Los Angeles County Museum of Art, 1968.

James Monte, "Wallace Berman and Collage Verité," *Wallace Berman: Verifax Collages,* The Jewish Museum, New York, 1968.

Jane Livingston, "Two Generations in L.A.," *Art in America,* vol. 57, no. 1, January 1969, p. 92.

Merril Greene, "Wallace Berman," *Art as a Muscular Principle,* John and Norah Warbeke Gallery, Mount Holyoke College, South Hadley, Massachusetts, 1975.

Melinda Wortz, "Los Angeles," *Art News,* vol. 76, no. 9, November 1977, pp. 202, 204.

George Herms, *Wallace Berman,* Timothea Stewart Gallery, Los Angeles, 1977.

Merril Greene, "Wallace Berman: Portrait of the Artist as Underground Man," *Artforum,* vol. 16, no. 6, February 1978, pp. 53–61.

Hal Glicksman, Robert Duncan, David Meltzer, and Walter Hopps (interview), *Wallace Berman Retrospective,* Otis Art Institute, Los Angeles, 1978.

Ronald Davis

Born in Santa Monica, California, 1937; lives in Malibu, California.
Attended San Francisco Art Institute, 1960–64.

Selected One-Man Exhibitions

Nicholas Wilder Gallery, Los Angeles, 1965, 1967, 1969, 1973, 1977, 1979.

Tibor de Nagy Gallery, New York, 1966.

Leo Castelli Gallery, New York, 1968, 1969, 1971, 1974, 1975.

Kasmin Gallery, London, 1968, 1971.

Norman Mackenzie Art Gallery, University of Saskatchewan, Regina, Canada, 1969.

Joseph Helman Gallery, St. Louis, Missouri, 1971, 1972.

Pasadena Art Museum, California, 1971.

David Mirvish Gallery, Toronto, 1971, 1975.

Galleria dell'Ariete, Milan, Italy, 1972.

John Berggruen Gallery, San Francisco, 1973, 1975, 1978, 1980.

Gemini G.E.L., Los Angeles, 1974, 1981.

Western Galleries, Cheyenne, Wyoming, 1974.

Boise State University, Idaho, 1975.

The Greenberg Gallery, St. Louis, Missouri, 1975, 1979.

Aspen Gallery of Art, Colorado, 1976.

Seder/Creigh Gallery, Coronado, California, 1976.

The Oakland Museum, California, 1976.

University of Nevada, Reno, 1977.

Seaver College, Pepperdine University, Malibu, California, 1979.

Blum-Helman Gallery, New York, 1979.

San Diego State University, California, 1980.

Middendorf/Lane Gallery, Washington, D.C., 1980.

Selected Group Exhibitions

Hard-Edge, Rolf Nelson Gallery, Los Angeles, 1964.

New Modes in California Painting and Sculpture, La Jolla Museum of Art, California, 1966.

Some Continuing Directions, The Fine Arts Patrons of Newport Harbor, Balboa Pavilion Gallery, California, 1966.

A New Aesthetic, Washington Gallery of Modern Art, Washington, D.C., 1967.

1967 Annual Exhibition of Contemporary Painting, Whitney Museum of American Art, New York; *1969 Annual Exhibition.*

Plastics: Painting and Sculpture from Los Angeles, California State College, Los Angeles, 1968.

Los Angeles 6, Vancouver Art Museum, British Columbia, 1968.

Documenta 4, Kassel, West Germany, 1968.

31st Biennial Exhibition of Contemporary American Painting, Corcoran Gallery of Art, Washington, D.C., 1969; *34th Biennial,* 1975.

Plastics: New Art, Institute of Contemporary Art of the University of Pennsylvania, Philadelphia, 1969.

West Coast 1945–1969, Pasadena Art Museum, California, 1969 (traveled to City Art Museum of St. Louis, Missouri; Art Gallery of Ontario, Toronto; Fort Worth Art Center Museum, Texas).

Permutation: Light and Color, Museum of Contemporary Art, Chicago, 1970.

69th American Exhibition of Painting and Sculpture, The Art Institute of Chicago, 1970; *71st American Exhibition,* 1974.

Color, The UCLA Art Galleries, University of California, Los Angeles, 1970.

Six Painters, Albright-Knox Art Gallery, Buffalo, New York, 1971.

USA West Coast, Kunstverein, Hamburg, West Germany, 1972 (traveled to Kunstverein, Hannover; Kölnischer Kunstverein, Cologne; Württembergisher Kunstverein, Stuttgart).

Painting: New Options, Walker Art Center, Minneapolis, Minnesota, 1972.

Masters of the Sixties, The Edmonton Art Gallery, Alberta, Canada, 1972.

Venice Biennale, Italy, 1972.

The State of California Painting, Govett-Brewster Art Gallery, New Plymouth, New Zealand, 1972.

Art in Space: Some Turning Points, The Detroit Institute of Arts, 1973.

11 Artistes Américains, Musée d'Art Contemporain, Montreal, 1973.

15 Abstract Artists, The Santa Barbara Museum of Art, California, 1974.

Zeichnungen 3, USA, Städtisches Museum, Leverkusen, West Germany, 1975.

Current Concerns, Part I, Los Angeles Institute of Contemporary Art, 1975.

Color, The Museum of Modern Art, New York, 1975 (traveled to Museo de Arte Moderno, Bogotá, Columbia).

Ron Davis/Tom Holland: Works from the Collection of Mr. and Mrs. Robert A. Rowan, Los Angeles Municipal Art Gallery, Barnsdall Park, 1975.

Painting and Sculpture in California: The Modern Era, San Francisco Museum of Modern Art, 1976 (traveled to National Collection of Fine Arts, Smithsonian Institution, Washington, D.C.).

American Abstract Art since 1945, The Solomon R. Guggenheim Museum, New York, 1977.

California: 3 by 8 Twice, Honolulu Academy of Arts, Hawaii, 1978.

American Painting of the 1970s, Albright-Knox Art Gallery, Buffalo, New York, 1980.

Selected Bibliography

Knute Stiles, "Thing, Act, Place," *Artforum,* vol. 3, no. 4, January 1965, pp. 37–40.

John Coplans, "The New Abstraction on the West Coast U.S.A.," *Studio International,* vol. 169, no. 865, May 1965, pp. 192–99.

Donald Factor, "Ron Davis: Nicholas Wilder Gallery Exhibition," *Artforum,* vol. 4, no. 4, December 1965, p. 15.

Barbara Rose, "Los Angeles: The Second City," *Art in America,* vol. 54, no. 1, January–February 1966, pp. 110–13.

Lucy R. Lippard, "Perverse Perspectives," *Art International,* vol. 6, no. 3, March 1967, pp. 28–33.

Michael Fried, "Ronald Davis: Surface and Illusion," *Artforum,* vol. 5, no. 8, April 1967, pp. 37–41.

Barbara Rose, *A New Aesthetic,* Washington Gallery of Modern Art, Washington, D.C., 1967.

Jane Livingston, "Ron Davis," *Artforum,* vol. 6, no. 5, January 1968, pp. 60–61.

Kurt von Meier, "Painting to Sculpture: One Tradition in a Radical Approach to the History of Twentieth-Century Art," *Art International,* vol. 12, no. 3, March 1968, pp. 37–39.

Annette Michelson, "Ron Davis: Leo Castelli Gallery Exhibition," *Artforum,* vol. 6, no. 10, summer 1968, pp. 56–57.

Robert Hughes, "Ron Davis at Kasmin," *Studio International,* vol. 176, no. 906, December 1968, pp. 264–65.

John Coplans and Barbara Rose, *Los Angeles 6,* Vancouver Art Gallery, British Columbia, 1968.

Rosalind Krauss, "Leo Castelli Exhibition," *Artforum,* vol. 8, no. 4, December 1969, pp. 69–70.

Terry Fenton, *Ron Davis: Eight Paintings,* Norman Mackenzie Art Gallery, Univeristy of Saskatchewan, Regina, Canada, 1969.

Walter Darby Bannard, "Notes on American Painting of the Sixties," *Artforum,* vol. 8, no. 5, January 1970, pp. 40–45.

Charles Kessler, *Color,* The UCLA Art Galleries, University of California, Los Angeles, 1970.

John Elderfield, "New Paintings by Ron Davis," *Artforum,* vol. 9, no. 7, March 1971, pp. 32–34.

Elizabeth C. Baker, "Los Angeles, 1971," *Art News,* vol. 70, no. 5, September 1971, pp. 27–39.

Helene Winer, "How L.A. Looks Today," *Studio International,* vol. 183, no. 937, October 1971, pp. 127–31.

James N. Wood, *Six Painters,* Albright-Knox Art Gallery, Buffalo, New York, 1971.

Helmut Heissenbüttel and Helene Winer, *USA West Coast,* Kunstverein, Hamburg, West Germany, 1972.

Barbara Rose, *Ron Davis,* Galleria dell'Ariete, Milan, Italy, 1972.

Kenworth Moffett, "Kenneth Noland's New Paintings and the Issue of the Shaped Canvas," *Art International,* vol. 20, nos. 4–5, April/May 1976, pp. 8–15.

Gordon Hazlitt, with statement by Ron Davis, "An Incredibly Beautiful Quandary," *Art News,* vol. 75, no. 5, May 1976, pp. 36–38.

Fred Martin, "Ron Davis: Cycle of Work," *Artweek,* vol. 7, no. 26, July 1976, p. 1.

Charles Kessler, "Ronald Davis, Paintings, 1962–1976," *Journal,* Los Angeles Institute of Contemporary Art, no. 12, October–November 1976, pp. 20–23.

Thomas Albright, "Ron Davis, Then and Now," *Art News,* vol. 75, no. 9, November 1976, pp. 100–102.

Nancy Marmer, "Ron Davis: Beyond Flatness," *Artforum,* vol. 15, no. 3, November 1976, pp. 34–37.

Charles Kessler, *Ronald Davis Paintings, 1962–1976,* The Oakland Museum, California, 1976.

Richard Diebenkorn

Born in Portland, Oregon, 1922; moved to Los Angeles, 1966; lives in Santa Monica, California.

B.A., Stanford University, 1949; M.A., University of New Mexico, Albuquerque, 1952.

Selected One-Man Exhibitions

California Palace of the Legion of Honor, San Francisco, 1948, 1960.

Paul Kantor Gallery, Los Angeles, 1952, 1954, 1965.

San Francisco Museum of Art, 1954, 1972.

Allan Frumkin Gallery, Chicago, 1954.

Poindexter Gallery, New York, 1956, 1958, 1961, 1963, 1965, 1966, 1968, 1969, 1971.

Oakland Art Museum, California, 1956.

Pasadena Art Museum, California, 1960.

The Phillips Collection, Washington, D.C., 1961.

National Institute of Arts and Letters, New York, 1962, 1967.

M. H. de Young Memorial Museum, San Francisco, 1963.

Stanford University Museum and Art Gallery, Palo Alto, California, 1964, 1967.

Waddington Galleries, London, 1964, 1967.

Washington Gallery of Modern Art, Washington, D.C., 1964.

Nelson Gallery-Atkins Museum, Kansas City, Missouri, 1968.

Peale House, Pennsylvania Academy of Fine Arts, Philadelphia, 1968.

Richmond Art Center, California, 1968.

Los Angeles County Museum of Art, 1969.

Irving Blum Gallery, Los Angeles, 1971.

Marlborough Gallery, New York, 1971, 1975.

Smith Andersen Gallery, Palo Alto, California, 1971.

Gerard John Hayes Gallery, Los Angeles, 1972.

Marlborough Fine Art, London, 1973.

Marlborough Galerie A.G., Zurich, Switzerland, 1973.

Mary Porter Sesnon Gallery, University of California, Santa Cruz, 1974.

John Berggruen Gallery, San Francisco, 1975.

James Corcoran Gallery, Los Angeles, 1975.

The Frederick S. Wight Art Gallery, University of California, Los Angeles, 1976.

Albright-Knox Art Gallery, Buffalo, New York, 1976 (retrospective; traveled to Cincinnati Art Museum, Ohio; Corcoran Gallery of Art, Washington, D.C.; Whitney Museum of American Art, New York; Los Angeles County Museum of Art; The Oakland Museum, California).

M. Knoedler and Company, New York, 1977, 1978, 1979, 1980.

Selected Group Exhibitions

Younger American Painters, The Solomon R. Guggenheim Museum, New York, 1954.

Three Young Americans: Glasco, McCullough, Diebenkorn, Allen Memorial Art Museum, Oberlin College, Ohio, 1955.

24th Biennial Exhibition of Contemporary American Painting, Corcoran Gallery of Art, Washington, D.C., 1955; *26th Biennial,* 1959; *27th Biennial,* 1961; *28th Biennial,* 1963; *33rd Biennial,* 1973; *34th Biennial,* 1975; *37th Biennial,* 1981.

III Bienal de São Paulo, Brazil, 1955; *VI Bienal,* 1961.

1955 Annual Exhibition of Contemporary American Painting, Whitney Museum of American Art, New York; *1958 Annual Exhibition; 1963 Annual Exhibition; 1965 Annual Exhibition; 1967 Annual Exhibition; 1969 Annual Exhibition; 1972 Annual Exhibition; 1981 Biennial Exhibition.*

62nd American Exhibition of Painting and Sculpture, The Art Institute of Chicago, 1959; *70th American Exhibition,* 1972.

New Imagery in American Painting, Indiana University Art Museum, Bloomington, 1959.

New Images of Man, The Museum of Modern Art, New York, 1959.

Aspects of Representation in Contemporary Art, Nelson Gallery-Atkins Museum, Kansas City, Missouri, 1959.

American Art, 1910–1960: Selections from the Collection of Mr. and Mrs. Roy R. Neuberger, M. Knoedler and Company, New York, 1960.

Elmer Bischoff, Richard Diebenkorn, David Park, Staempfli Gallery, New York, 1960.

The Figure in Contemporary American Painting, American Federation of Arts, New York, 1961.

The Artist's Environment: West Coast, Amon Carter Museum of Western Art, Fort Worth, Texas, 1962 (traveled to The UCLA Art Galleries, University of California, Los Angeles).

Six Americans, Arkansas Arts Center, Little Rock, 1964.

American Drawings, The Solomon R. Guggenheim Museum, New York, 1964.

Seven California Painters, Staempfli Gallery, New York, 1964.

Painting and Sculpture of a Decade, The Tate Gallery, London, 1964.

Two American Painters, Abstract and Figurative: Sam Francis, Richard Diebenkorn, Scottish National Gallery of Modern Art, Edinburgh, 1965.

Selections from the Work of California Artists, Witte Memorial Museum, San Antonio, Texas, 1965.

Art of the United States 1670–1960, Whitney Museum of American Art, New York, 1966.

Late Fifties at the Ferus, Los Angeles County Museum of Art, 1968.

Painting as Painting, University Art Museum, Austin, Texas, 1968.

Venice Biennale, Italy, 1968; *Venice Biennale,* 1978.

West Coast 1945–1969, Pasadena Art Museum, California, 1969 (traveled to City Art Museum of St. Louis, Missouri; Art Gallery of Ontario, Toronto; Fort Worth Art Center Museum, Texas).

Kompas 4: West Coast USA, Stedelijk van Abbemuseum, Eindhoven, The Netherlands, 1969.

L'Art Vivant aux États-Unis, Fondation Maeght, St. Paul de Vence, France, 1970.

Looking West 1970, Joslyn Art Museum, Omaha, Nebraska, 1970.

Made in California, Grunwald Center for the Graphic Arts, University of California, Los Angeles, 1971.

11 Los Angeles Artists, Hayward Gallery, London, 1971 (traveled to Musées Royaux des Beaux-Arts, Brussels; Akademie der Künste, Berlin, West Germany).

Two Directions in American Painting, Purdue University, Lafayette, Indiana, 1971.

A Decade in the West, Stanford University Museum and Art Gallery, Palo Alto, California, 1971.

Abstract Painting in the '70s: A Selection, Museum of Fine Arts, Boston, 1972.

15 Abstract Artists, The Santa Barbara Museum of Art, California, 1974.

Twelve American Painters, Virginia Museum of Fine Arts, Richmond, 1974.

The Martha Jackson Collection at the Albright-Knox Art Gallery, Buffalo, New York, 1975.

California Landscape: A Metaview, The Oakland Museum, California, 1975.

Painting and Sculpture in California: The Modern Era, San Francisco Museum of Modern Art, 1976 (traveled to National Collection of Fine Arts, Smithsonian Institution, Washington, D.C.).

Three Generations of American Painting: Motherwell, Diebenkorn, Edlich, Gruenebaum Gallery, New York, 1976.

American Paintings of the 1970s, Albright-Knox Art Gallery, Buffalo, New York, 1978.

Selected Bibliography

Peter Selz, *New Images of Man,* The Museum of Modern Art, New York, 1959.

Thomas W. Leavitt, *Richard Diebenkorn,* Pasadena Art Museum, California, 1960.

Howard Ross Smith, *Recent Paintings by Richard Diebenkorn,* California Palace of the Legion of Honor, San Francisco, 1960.

Gifford Phillips, *Richard Diebenkorn,* The Phillips Collection, Washington, D.C., 1961.

Lawrence Alloway, *Seven California Painters,* Staempfli Gallery, New York, 1964.

Gerald Nordland, *Richard Diebenkorn,* Washington Gallery of Modern Art, Washington, D.C., 1964.

Lorenz Eitner, *Drawings by Richard Diebenkorn,* Palo Alto, California, 1965.

Norman A. Geske, *The Figurative Tradition in Recent American Art,* Venice Biennale, Italy, 1968.

Donald Goodall, *Painting as Painting,* University Art Museum, Austin, Texas, 1968.

Gail Scott, *New Paintings of Richard Diebenkorn,* Los Angeles County Museum of Art, 1969.

Gerald Nordland, *The Ocean Park Series: Recent Work,* Marlborough Gallery, New York, 1971.

Maurice Tuchman and Jane Livingston, *11 Los Angeles Artists,* Hayward Gallery, London, 1971.

Kenworth Moffett, *Abstract Painting in the '70s: A Selection,* Museum of Fine Arts, Boston, 1972.

John Russell, *Richard Diebenkorn, The Ocean Park Series: Recent Work,* Marlborough Fine Art, London, 1973.

Philip Brookman and Walker Melion, *Richard Diebenkorn: Drawings, 1944–1973,* Mary Porter Sesnon Gallery, University of California, Santa Cruz, 1974.

Linda L. Cathcart, *The Martha Jackson Collection at the Albright-Knox Art Gallery,* Buffalo, New York, 1975.

Robert T. Buck, Jr., Linda L. Cathcart, Gerald Nordland, and Maurice Tuchman, *Richard Diebenkorn: Paintings and Drawings, 1943–1976,* Albright-Knox Art Gallery, Buffalo, New York, 1976.

Jeffrey Hoffeld, *Three Generations of American Painting: Motherwell, Diebenkorn, Edlich,* Gruenebaum Gallery, New York, 1976.

Gerald Nordland, *Richard Diebenkorn: Monotypes,* The Frederick S. Wight Art Gallery, University of California, Los Angeles, 1976.

Budd Hopkins, "Diebenkorn Reconsidered," *Artforum,* vol. 15, no. 7, March 1977, pp. 37–41.

Nancy Marmer, "Richard Diebenkorn: Pacific Extensions," *Art in America,* vol. 66, no. 1, January–February 1978, pp. 95–99.

Robert T. Buck, "Richard Diebenkorn: The Ocean Park Paintings," *Art International,* vol. 22, nos. 5–6, summer 1978, pp. 29–34, 60.

Tom E. Hinson, "Recent Paintings by Richard Diebenkorn and Jack Tworkov," *The Bulletin of the Cleveland Museum of Art,* vol. 48, no. 2, February 1980, pp. 31–40.

Sam Francis

Born in San Mateo, California, 1923; lives in Santa Monica, California.
B.A., University of California, Berkeley, 1949; M.A., 1950.

Selected One-Man Exhibitions

Galerie du Dragon, Paris, 1952.

Galerie Rive Droite, Paris, 1955, 1956.

Martha Jackson Gallery, New York, 1956, 1957, 1958, 1959, 1963, 1964, 1968, 1970.

Gimpel Fils, London, 1957, 1974.

Kornfeld und Klipstein, Bern, Switzerland, 1957, 1959, 1961, 1963, 1965, 1966, 1968, 1973, 1975, 1976.

Galerie Alfred Schmela, Düsseldorf, West Germany, 1958, 1961.

Pasadena Art Museum, California, 1959 (traveled to San Francisco Museum of Art; Seattle Art Museum, Washington).

Kunsthalle Bern, Switzerland, 1960 (traveled to Moderna Museet, Stockholm).

Galerie Jacques Dubourg, Paris, 1961.

Galerie de Seine, Paris, 1961.

Minami Gallery, Tokyo, 1961, 1964, 1966, 1968, 1970, 1974, 1977, 1979.

David Anderson Gallery, New York, 1960, 1961.

Esther Bear Gallery, Santa Barbara, California, 1962.

Kestner-Gesellschaft, Hannover, West Germany 1963.

Arthur Tooth & Sons, London, 1965.

Auslander Gallery, New York, 1965.

Museum of Fine Arts, Houston, 1967 (traveled to University Art Museum, University of California, Berkeley).

Pierre Matisse Gallery, New York, 1967.

The UCLA Art Galleries, Los Angeles, 1967.

Kunsthalle Basel, Switzerland, 1968.

Stedelijk Museum, Amsterdam, 1968.

Centre National d'Art Contemporain, Paris, 1968.

Badischer Kunstverein, Karlsruhe, West Germany, 1968.

André Emmerich Gallery, New York, 1969, 1971, 1973, 1975, 1976, 1979.

Felix Landau Gallery, Los Angeles, 1969.

Los Angeles County Museum of Art, 1970, 1980.

Nicholas Wilder Gallery, Los Angeles, 1970, 1973, 1975, 1978.

Stanford University Museum and Art Gallery, Palo Alto, California, 1972.

Albright-Knox Art Gallery, Buffalo, New York, 1972 (retrospective; traveled to Corcoran Gallery of Art, Washington, D.C.; Whitney Museum of American Art, New York; Dallas Museum of Fine Arts, Texas; The Oakland Museum, California).

Smith Andersen Gallery, Palo Alto, California, 1972, 1973, 1975, 1978, 1980.

Galerie Jean Fournier, Paris, 1973, 1975, 1976, 1979.

Idemitsu Art Gallery, Tokyo, 1974.

Nantenshi Gallery, Osaka, 1974.

Margo Leavin Gallery, Los Angeles, 1974.

Portland Center for the Visual Arts, Oregon, 1974.

Fundación Eugenio Mendoza, Caracas, Venezuela, 1974.

Robert Elkon Gallery, New York, 1974.

Louisiana Museum, Humlebaek, Denmark, 1977.

Honolulu Academy of Arts, Hawaii, 1977.

Centre National d'Art et de Culture Georges Pompidou, Paris, 1978.

Otis Art Institute, Los Angeles, 1978.

Institute of Contemporary Art, Boston, 1979 (retrospective).

Cantor/Lemberg Gallery, Birmingham, Michigan, 1979.

Abbaye de Senanque, Lourdes, France, 1980.

James Corcoran Gallery, Los Angeles, 1980.

Riko Mizuno Gallery, Los Angeles, 1980.

Ace Gallery, Venice, California, 1981.

Selected Group Exhibitions

66th Annual Exhibition of the San Francisco Art Association, Museum of Fine Arts, San Francisco, 1946.

VIe Salon de Mai, Musée d'Art Moderne de la Ville de Paris, 1950; *XVIIe Salon de Mai,* 1961.

Opposing Forces, Institute of Contemporary Arts, London, 1953.

American Painting, The Art Institute of Chicago, 1954.

Tendances actuelles 3, Kunsthalle Bern, Switzerland, 1955.

Art in the 20th Century, San Francisco Museum of Art, 1955.

12 Americans, The Museum of Modern Art, New York, 1956.

Expressionism 1900–1955, Walker Art Center, Minneapolis, Minnesota, 1956.

New Trends in Painting, Arts Council of Great Britain, Cambridge, 1956 (traveled to City Art Gallery, York; Walker Art Gallery, Liverpool; Hatton Gallery, Newcastle).

50 Ans d'Art Moderne, Musées Royaux des Beaux-Arts, Brussels, 1957.

Sam Francis, Kimber Smith, and Shirley Jaffe, Centre Culturel Américain, Paris, 1958.

Jong Amerika Schildert, Stedelijk Museum, Amsterdam, 1958.

The New American Painting, The Museum of Modern Art, New York, 1958–59 (traveled to Kunsthalle, Basel, Switzerland; Galleria Civica d'Arte Moderna, Milan, Italy; Museo Nacional de Arte Contemporanea, Madrid; Hochschule für bildende Künste, Berlin, West Germany; Stedelijk Museum, Amsterdam; Musées Royaux des Beaux-Arts, Brussels; Musée d'Art Moderne de la Ville de Paris; The Tate Gallery, London).

Documenta 2, Kassel, West Germany, 1959; *Documenta 3,* 1964.

Annual Exhibition of Contemporary American Painting, Whitney Museum of American Art, New York, 1959, 1961, 1962, 1963, 1964.

60 American Painters 1960, Walker Art Center, Minneapolis, Minnesota, 1960.

Images at Mid-Century, University of Michigan Museum of Art, Ann Arbor, 1960.

64th American Exhibition of Painting and Sculpture, The Art Institute of Chicago, 1961; *65th American Exhibition,* 1962.

American Abstract Expressionists and Imagists, The Solomon R. Guggenheim Museum, New York, 1961.

The Logic of Modern Art, William Rockhill Nelson Gallery of Art, Kansas City, Missouri, 1961.

Kompas, Schilders uit Parijis 1945–1961, Stedelijk van Abbemuseum, Eindhoven, The Netherlands, 1961–62.

Abstrakte Amerikanische Malerei, Hessisches Landsmuseum, Darmstadt, West Germany, 1962.

Kunst des 20 Jahrhunderts: Developments in Painting V, Haus der Stadt, Kunstsammlung, Bonn, West Germany, 1962.

Kunst von 1900 bis heute, Museum des 20 Jahrhunderts, Vienna, 1962.

Réalités Nouvelles, Musée d'Art Moderne de la Ville de Paris, 1963.

Gesammelt im Ruhrgebiet, Kunsthalle Recklinghausen, West Germany, 1963.

Private Views, The Tate Gallery, London, 1963.

Painting and Sculpture of a Decade 1954–1964, The Tate Gallery, London, 1964.

Post Painterly Abstraction, Los Angeles County Museum of Art, 1964.

International Painting since 1950, Kunsthalle Basel, Switzerland, 1964.

American Drawings, The Solomon R. Guggenheim Museum, New York, 1964.

Venice Biennale, Italy, 1964.

Two American Painters, Abstract and Figurative: Sam Francis, Richard Diebenkorn, Scottish National Gallery of Modern Art, Edinburgh, 1965.

Seven Americans, Arkansas Arts Center, Little Rock, 1965.

Inner and Outer Space, Moderna Museet, Stockholm, 1965.

Two Decades of American Painting, The Museum of Modern Art, New York, 1966.

Contemporary Painters and Sculptors as Printmakers, The Museum of Modern Art, New York, 1966.

Licht Bewegung Farbe, Kunsthalle Nürnberg, West Germany, 1967.

Vom Bauhaus bis zur Gegenwart, Kunstverein, Hamburg, West Germany, 1967 (traveled to Frankfurter Kunstverein, Frankfurt; Kölnischer Kunstverein, Cologne).

Neuerwerbungen 1962–1967, Städtische Kunstmuseum, Bonn, West Germany, 1967.

Kleine Dokumenta (Kunst nach 1950), Overbeck-Gesellschaft, Lübeck, West Germany, 1968.

West Coast 1945–1969, Pasadena Art Museum, California, 1969 (traveled to City Art Museum of St. Louis, Missouri; Art Gallery of Ontario, Toronto; Fort Worth Art Center Museum, Texas).

Color and Field, Albright-Knox Art Gallery, Buffalo, New York, 1970 (traveled to Dayton Art Institute, Ohio; Cleveland Museum of Art, Ohio).

Francis, Kanemitsu, Moses, Wayne, Downey Museum of Art, California, 1970.

32nd Biennial Exhibition of Contemporary American Painting, Corcoran Gallery of Art, Washington, D.C., 1971.

Abstract Expressionism: The First and Second Generations in the Albright-Knox Art Gallery, Buffalo, New York, 1972.

Fresh Air School: Sam Francis, Joan Mitchell, and Walasse Ting, Museum of Art, Carnegie Institute, Pittsburgh, Pennsylvania, 1972.

Twelve American Painters, Virginia Museum, Richmond, 1974.

15 Abstract Artists, Santa Barbara Museum of Art, California, 1974.

Painting and Sculpture in California: The Modern Era, San Francisco Museum of Modern Art, California, 1976 (traveled to National Collection of Fine Arts, Smithsonian Institution, Washington, D.C.).

Paris-New York, Centre National d'Art et de Culture Georges Pompidou, Paris, 1977.

Selected Bibliography

Herbert Read, "An Art of Internal Necessity," *Quadrum,* no. 1, May 1956, pp. 7–22.

K. G. Pontus Hultén, Brion Gysiu, Sinclair Belles, and Yoshiaki Tono, *Sam Francis,* Moderna Museet, Stockholm, 1960.

Franz Meyer, *Sam Francis,* Kunsthalle Bern, Switzerland, 1960.

Franz Meyer, "Sam Francis," *Quadrum,* no. 10, 1961, pp. 119–30.

Makoto Ooka, Yoshiaki Tono, and Shuzo Takiguchi, *Sam Francis: Blue Balls,* Minami Gallery, Tokyo, 1961.

Priscilla Colt, "The Painting of Sam Francis," *The Art Journal,* vol. 22, no. 1, fall 1962, pp. 2–7.

Manuel Gasser, "Sam Francis/ Lithographs by an Action Painter," *Graphis,* vol. 18, no. 104, November–December 1962, pp. 570–73.

Yoshiaki Tono, *Sam Francis,* Tokyo, 1964.

Anneliese Hoyer, *Sam Francis Drawings and Lithographs,* San Francisco Museum of Art, 1966.

James Johnson Sweeney, *Sam Francis,* Museum of Fine Arts, Houston, Texas; University Art Museum, University of California, Berkeley, 1966.

Wieland Schmied, Sam Francis, and Arnold Rudlinger, *Sam Francis,* Kunsthalle Basel, Switzerland, 1968.

J. J. Leveque, "Sam Francis, The Spirit of Vertigo," *Cimaise,* vol. 16, no. 90, 1969, pp. 49–61.

Pierre Schneider, Philipe Hosaisson, Georges Duthuit, Herbert Read, Franz Meyer, and James Johnson Sweeney, *Sam Francis,* Centre National d'Art Contemporain, Paris, 1969.

Gail Scott, *Sam Francis: Recent Paintings,* Los Angeles County Museum of Art, 1970.

Pierre Schneider, *Louvre Dialogues,* New York, 1971.

Robert T. Buck, Jr., Franz Meyer, Wieland Schmied, and Katherine Kline, *Sam Francis,* Albright-Knox Art Gallery, Buffalo, New York, 1972.

Peter Selz, "Sam Francis: The Recent Work," *Art International,* vol. 17, no. 1, January 1973, pp. 14–17.

Carl Betz, "Fitting Sam Francis into History," *Art in America,* vol. 61, no. 1, January–February 1973, pp. 40–45.

Lawrence Alloway, "Sam Francis: From Field to Arabesque," *Artforum,* vol. 11, no. 6, February 1973, pp. 37–41.

Shuzo Takiguchi, Makoto Ooka, and Yoshiaki Tono, *Paintings of Sam Francis in the Idemitsu Collection,* Minami Gallery, Tokyo, 1974.

Peter Selz, *Sam Francis,* New York, 1975.

Sara Giesen, "Sam Francis: His Kaleidoscopic Unfolding," *Arts Magazine,* vol. 50, no. 10, June 1976, pp. 66–69.

Alfred Pacquement, *Sam Francis: Peintures Recentes 1976/1978,* Centre National d'Art et de Culture Georges Pompidou, Paris, 1978.

Jan Butterfield, *Sam Francis: Works on Paper, A Survey, 1948–1979,* Institute of Contemporary Art, Boston, 1979.

Jan Butterfield, "Time Has an Infinite Number of Faces," *Sam Francis,* Los Angeles County Museum of Art, 1980.

Joe Goode

Born in Oklahoma City, Oklahoma, 1937; resident of Los Angeles, 1959–78; lives in Springville, California. Attended Chouinard Art Institute, Los Angeles, 1959–61.

Selected One-Man Exhibitions

Dilexi Gallery, Los Angeles, 1962.

Rolf Nelson Gallery, Los Angeles, 1963.

Nicholas Wilder Gallery, Los Angeles, 1966, 1969, 1970, 1972, 1974, 1975, 1978, 1979.

Rowan Gallery, London, 1967.

Kornblee Gallery, New York, 1968.

Galerie Neuendorf, Cologne, West Germany, 1970, 1972.

Galerie Neuendorf, Hamburg, West Germany, 1970, 1973, 1975.

Pomona College Art Gallery, California, 1971.

Galleria Milano, Italy, 1971.

La Jolla Museum of Contemporary Art, California, 1971.

Mueller Gallery, Düsseldorf, West Germany, 1971.

Minneapolis Institute of Art, Minnesota, 1972.

Corcoran and Corcoran Gallery, Miami, Florida, 1972.

Margo Leavin Gallery, Los Angeles, 1972, 1973.

Felicity Samuel Gallery, London, 1972, 1973, 1975.

Contract Graphics, Houston, Texas, 1972, 1973, 1975.

Fort Worth Art Center Museum, Texas, 1972.

Contemporary Arts Museum, Houston, Texas, 1973.

Cirrus Gallery, Los Angeles, 1973, 1974.

California State College, Northridge, 1974.

Seder/Creigh Gallery, Coronado, California, 1975.

James Corcoran Gallery, Los Angeles, 1976.

Washington University, St. Louis, Missouri, 1976.

Mount St. Mary's College Art Gallery, Los Angeles, 1977.

Texas Gallery, Houston, 1979.

Charles Cowles Gallery, New York, 1980.

Selected Group Exhibitions

War Babies, Huysman Gallery, Los Angeles, 1961.

New Painting of Common Objects, Pasadena Art Museum, California, 1962.

Pop Art USA, Oakland Art Museum, California, 1963.

Six More, Los Angeles County Museum of Art, 1963.

Ten from Los Angeles, Seattle Art Museum, Washington, 1966.

1966 Annual Exhibition of Contemporary American Painting, Whitney Museum of American Art, New York; *1967 Annual Exhibition; 1969 Annual Exhibition.*

Pittsburgh International Exhibition, Carnegie Institute, Pennsylvania, 1967.

West Coast Now, Portland Art Museum, Oregon, 1968.

Ed Ruscha–Joe Goode, The Fine Arts Patrons of Newport Harbor, Balboa Pavilion Gallery, California, 1968.

Contemporary American Drawings, Fort Worth Art Center Museum, Texas, 1969.

Pop Art Redefined, Hayward Gallery, London, 1969.

California Drawings, Ithaca College Art Museum, New York, 1969.

Graphics: Six West Coast Artists, Galleria Milano, Italy, 1969.

West Coast 1945–1969, Pasadena Art Museum, California, 1969 (traveled to City Art Museum of St. Louis, Missouri; Art Gallery of Ontario, Toronto; Fort Worth Art Center Museum, Texas).

Drawings, The Santa Barbara Museum of Art, California, 1970.

Nine Portfolios, The Museum of Modern Art, New York, 1970.

Looking West 1970, Joslyn Art Museum, Omaha, Nebraska, 1970.

Continuing Surrealism, La Jolla Museum of Contemporary Art, California, 1971.

West Coast, The Denver Art Museum, Colorado, 1971.

Oversize Prints, Whitney Museum of American Art, New York, 1971.

Made in California, Grunwald Center for the Graphic Arts, University of California, Los Angeles, 1971.

32nd Biennial Exhibition of Contemporary American Paintings, Corcoran Gallery of Art, Washington, D.C., 1971.

American Pop Art, Whitney Museum of American Art, New York, 1974.

Eight from California, National Collection of Fine Arts, Smithsonian Institution, Washington, D.C., 1974.

Robert Rowan Collection, Mount St. Mary's College Art Gallery, Los Angeles, 1974.

4 Los Angeles Artists, School of Visual Arts, New York, 1975.

Current Concerns: Part I, Los Angeles Institute of Contemporary Art, 1975.

Painting and Sculpture in California: The Modern Era, San Francisco Museum of Modern Art, 1976 (traveled to National Collection of Fine Arts, Smithsonian Institution, Washington, D.C.).

Ed Ruscha, Joe Goode/New Drawings, Laguna Gloria Art Museum, Austin, Texas, 1977.

Black and White Are Colors: Paintings of the 1950s–1970s, Lang Art Gallery, Scripps College, Claremont, California, 1978.

American Painting in the Seventies, Albright-Knox Art Gallery, Buffalo, New York, 1978.

Aspects of Abstract, Crocker Art Museum, Sacramento, California, 1978.

Selected Bibliography

John Coplans, "New Painting of Common Objects," *Artforum,* vol. 1, no. 6, November 1962, pp. 26–29.

Lawrence Alloway, *Six More,* Los Angeles County Museum of Art, 1963.

Claire Wolf, "Los Angeles: Joe Goode, Rolf Nelson Gallery," *Artforum,* vol. 2, no. 11, May 1964, pp. 11–12.

Philip Leider, "The Cool School," *Artforum,* vol. 2, no. 12, summer 1964, pp. 47–52.

Philip Leider, "Joe Goode and the Common Object," *Artforum,* vol. 4, no. 7, March 1966, pp. 24–27.

Fidel Danieli, "Gemini Ltd.: New Lithography Workshop in Los Angeles," *Artforum,* vol. 4, no. 8, April 1966, pp. 20–22.

John Coplans, "Exhibition at Nick Wilder Gallery," *Art News,* vol. 65, no. 57, summer 1966, p. 57.

John Coplans, *Ten from Los Angeles,* Seattle Art Museum, Washington, 1966.

Lucy R. Lippard, *Pop Art,* New York, 1966.

Edward Lucie-Smith, "London: Show at Rowan Gallery," *Studio International,* vol. 173, no. 890, June 1967, p. 312.

Jane Livingston, "Los Angeles," *Artforum,* vol. 6, no. 3, November 1967, p. 67.

Robert Pincus-Witten, "Kornblee Gallery, New York," *Artforum,* vol. 6, no. 7, March 1968, p. 59.

William Wilson, "Four Defectors to L.A.," *Art in America,* vol. 56, no. 2, March 1968, pp. 100–104.

Melinda Terbell, "West Coast Shows," *Arts Magazine,* vol. 42, no. 7, May 1968, p. 61.

Henry T. Hopkins, *Joe Goode and Ed Ruscha,* The Fine Arts Patrons of Newport Harbor, Balboa Pavilion Gallery, California, 1968.

Jane Livingston, "Los Angeles," *Artforum,* vol. 7, no. 5, January 1969, p. 69.

Andrew Rabeneck, "Form Follows Fiction," *Design Quarterly,* no. 73, 1969, p. 31.

John Russell and Suzi Gablik, *Pop Art Redefined,* London, 1969.

Peter Plagens, "Los Angeles: Joe Goode, Nicholas Wilder Gallery," *Artforum,* vol. 9, no. 6, February 1971, p. 91.

Melinda Terbell, "Los Angeles," *Arts Magazine,* vol. 45, no. 4, February 1971, p. 45.

Helene Winer, *Wall Reliefs,* Pomona College Art Gallery, California, 1971.

Bernard Denvir, "London Letter," *Art International,* vol. 16, no. 8, October 1972, p. 46.

Peter Fuller, "Joe Goode," *Arts Review,* vol. 24, no. 20, October 1972, p. 612.

Henry T. Hopkins, *Joe Goode: Work Until Now,* Fort Worth Art Center Museum, Texas, 1972.

William A. Robinson, Perry Walker, and Henry T. Hopkins, "Bengston, Grieger, Goode: Three Interviews," *Art in America,* vol. 61, no. 2, March–April 1973, pp. 48–53.

Nancy Marmer, "Joe Goode," *Art in America,* vol. 62, no. 4, July–August 1974, p. 96.

Lawrence Alloway, *American Pop Art,* Whitney Museum of American Art, New York, 1974.

Peter Plagens, *Sunshine Muse: Contemporary Art on the West Coast,* New York, 1974.

M. Shepherd, "Joe Goode," *Arts Review,* vol. 27, no. 15, July 1975, p. 424.

Peter Winter, "Joe Goode," *Kunstwerk,* vol. 28, no. 4, July 1975, p. 72.

Michele D. De Angelus, "Isolated Imagery: Joe Goode," Los Angeles Institute of Contemporary Art *Journal,* no. 20, October 1978, pp. 34–35.

Ann Schoenfeld, "Paintings under Control: Joe Goode," *Artweek,* vol. 10, no. 20, May 19, 1979, p. 7.

M. Shepherd, "American Painting in the 1970's," *Arts Review,* vol. 31, no. 15, August 1979, p. 399.

David Hockney

Born in Bradford, England, 1937; currently lives in Los Angeles and London. Attended Bradford College of Art, 1953–57; The Royal College of Art, London, 1959–62.

Selected One-Man Exhibitions

Editions Alecto Gallery, The Print Centre, London, 1963.

Kasmin Gallery, London, 1963, 1965, 1966, 1968, 1969, 1970, 1972.

Alan Gallery, New York, 1964.

The Museum of Modern Art, New York, 1964, 1968, 1979.

Stedelijk Museum, Amsterdam, 1966.

Galleria dell'Ariete, Milan, Italy, 1966.

Studio Marconi, Milan, Italy, 1966.

Museés Royaux des Beaux-Arts, Brussels, 1966.

Landau-Alan Gallery, New York, 1967.

Galerie Mikro, Berlin, West Germany, 1968.

Whitworth Art Gallery, Manchester, England, 1969.

André Emmerich Gallery, New York, 1969, 1970, 1971, 1972, 1973, 1977, 1979, 1980, 1981.

Galerie Springer, Berlin, West Germany, 1970.

Kestner-Gesellschaft, Hannover, West Germany, 1970.

Whitechapel Art Gallery, London, 1970 (retrospective; traveled to Hannover, West Germany; Rotterdam, The Netherlands; Belgrade, Yugoslavia).

Lane Gallery, Bradford, England, 1970.

Kunsthalle Bielefeld, West Germany, 1971.

Victoria and Albert Museum, London, 1972.

Holburne Museum, Bath, England, 1973.

M. Knoedler and Company, New York, 1973, 1974, 1980.

Michael Walls Gallery, New York, 1974.

Kinsman Morrison Gallery, London, 1974.

D. M. Gallery, London, 1974.

Musée des Arts Décoratifs, Paris, 1974 (retrospective).

Galerie d'Eendt, Amsterdam, 1974.

La Medusa Graphica, Rome, 1974.

Dayton's Gallery 12, Minneapolis, Minnesota, 1974.

Margo Leavin Gallery, Los Angeles, 1975.

European Gallery, San Francisco, 1975.

Galerie Claude-Bernard, Paris, 1975.

Nishimura Gallery, Tokyo, 1975.

City Art Gallery, Manchester, England, 1975.

City Art Gallery, Bristol, England, 1975.

Dorothy Rosenthal Gallery, Chicago, 1975, 1977.

Nicholas Wilder Gallery, Los Angeles, 1976.

Waddington Graphics, London, 1976.

Robert Self Gallery, London, 1976.

Laing Art Gallery, Newcastle upon Tyne, England, 1976.

Sonnabend Gallery, New York, 1976.

Gallery One, San Jose State University Art Department, California, 1977.

Galerie André Emmerich, Zurich, Switzerland, 1977.

Galerie Neuendorf, Hamburg, West Germany, 1977.

Gemini G.E.L., Los Angeles, 1977, 1979.

Gallery at 24, Miami, Florida, 1978.

Waddington Galleries, Toronto, 1978.

Graphische Sammlung Albertina, Vienna, 1978 (traveled to Tiroler Landesmuseum Ferdinandeum, Innsbruck, Austria; Galerie Bloch, Innsbruck; Kulturhaus de Stadt, Graz, Austria; Künstlerhaus Salzburg, Austria).

L.A. Louver, Venice, California, 1978.

Yale Center for British Art, New Haven, Connecticut, 1978 (traveled to Minneapolis Institute of Arts, Minnesota; Cranbrook Academy of Art, Bloomfield Hills, Michigan; Nelson Gallery-Atkins Museum, Kansas City, Missouri; Hirshhorn Museum and Sculpture Garden, Washington, D.C.; Art Gallery of Ontario, Toronto; Toledo Museum of Art, Ohio; The Fine Arts Museums of San Francisco; The Denver Art Museum, Colorado; Grey Art Gallery and Study Center, New York; The Tate Gallery, London).

M. H. de Young Memorial Museum, San Francisco, 1979.

Foster Goldstrom Fine Arts, San Francisco, 1979.

Frances Aronson Gallery, Ltd., Atlanta, Georgia, 1979.

City Art Gallery and Museum, Bradford, England, 1979.

Petersburg Press, New York, 1980.

Getler/Pall Gallery, New York, 1980.

Selected Group Exhibitions

New Painting 1958–61, The Arts Council of Great Britain, London, 1961 (traveled throughout Great Britain).

Second Paris Biennale of Young Artists, Musée d'Art Moderne de la Ville de Paris, 1961; *Third Paris Biennale,* 1963.

Third International Biennale of Prints, National Museum of Art, Tokyo, 1962.

British Painting in the Sixties, Whitechapel Art Gallery, London, 1963.

Screen Prints, Institute of Contemporary Arts, London, 1964.

Contemporary Painters and Sculptors as Printmakers, The Museum of Modern Art, New York, 1966.

Young British Painters, 1955–1960, Art Gallery of New South Wales, Sydney, Australia, 1964.

Six Young Painters, The Arts Council of Great Britain, London, 1964 (traveled throughout Great Britain).

Pop, etc...., Museum des 20 Jahrhunderts, Vienna, 1964.

Pick of the Pops, National Museum of Wales, Cardiff, 1964.

Painting and Sculpture of a Decade 1954–1964, The Calouste Gulbenkian Foundation, The Tate Gallery, London, 1964.

Nieuwe Realisten, Gemeente Museum, The Hague, The Netherlands, 1964.

London Group Jubilee Exhibition 1914–1964, The Tate Gallery, London, 1964.

British Painters of Today, Kunsthalle Düsseldorf, West Germany, 1964.

London: The New Scene, Walker Art Center, Minneapolis, Minnesota, 1965.

Pop Art, Nouveau Réalisme, etc., Musées Royaux des Beaux-Arts, Brussels, 1965.

IX Bienal de São Paulo, Brazil, 1967.

Drawing Towards Painting, The Arts Council of Great Britain, London, 1967.

European Painters of Today, Musée des Arts Décoratifs, Paris, 1967.

Painting in Britain, Rhode Island School of Design, Providence, 1967.

Documenta 4, Kassel, West Germany, 1968.

Venice Biennale, Italy, 1968.

Young Generation: Great Britain, Akademie der Künste, Berlin, West Germany, 1968.

Pop Art Redefined, Hayward Gallery, London, 1969.

Image/Design: Animation, Recherche, Confrontation, Musée d'Art Moderne de la Ville de Paris, 1970.

British Painting and Sculpture, 1960–1970, National Gallery of Art, Washington, D.C., 1971.

Snap, National Portrait Gallery, London, 1971.

La Peinture Anglaise Aujourd'hui, Musée d'Art Moderne de la Ville de Paris, 1972.

Henry Moore to Gilbert and George: Modern British Art from The Tate Gallery, Musées Royaux des Beaux-Arts, Brussels, 1973.

European Painting in the '70s, Los Angeles County Museum of Art, 1975.

Drawings of Five British Artists, Museum Boymans-van Beuningen, Rotterdam, The Netherlands, 1976.

Art Around 1970, The Ludwig Collection at Aachen, Künstlerhaus, Vienna, 1977.

Künstlerphotographien im XX Jahrhundert, Kestner-Gesellschaft, Hannover, West Germany, 1977.

Printed Art: A View of Two Decades, The Museum of Modern Art, New York, 1980.

Selected Bibliography

Guy Brett, "David Hockney: A Note in Progress," *The London Magazine,* vol. 3, no. 1, April 1963.

David Hockney, *David Hockney: A Rake's Progress and Other Etchings,* London, December 1963.

G. S. Whittet, "David Hockney: His Life and Good Times," *The Studio,* vol. 166, no. 848, December 1963, pp. 252–53.

Gene Baro, "The British Scene," *Arts Magazine,* vol. 38, no. 9, May–June 1964, pp. 94–101.

Larry Rivers and David Hockney, "Beautiful or Interesting," *Art and Literature,* no. 5, summer 1965, pp. 94–117.

Robert Hughes, "Blake and Hockney," *The London Magazine,* vol. 5, no. 10, January 1966, pp. 68–73.

Gene Baro, "Hockney's Ubu," *Art and Artists,* vol. 1, no. 2, May 1966, pp. 8–13.

Gene Baro, "David Hockney's Drawings," *Studio International,* vol. 171, no. 877, May 1966, pp. 184–86.

Gene Baro, *David Hockney,* Stedelijk Museum, Amsterdam, 1966.

Lucy R. Lippard, *Pop Art,* New York, 1966.

Patrick Procktor, *David Hockney,* Galleria dell'Ariete, Milan, Italy, 1966.

Wibke von Bonin, *David Hockney 1968,* Galerie Mikro, Berlin, West Germany, 1968.

David Shapiro, "David Hockney Paints a Portrait," *Art News,* vol. 68, no. 3, May 1969, pp. 28–31, 64–66.

Wibke von Bonin, "Germany: Hockney's Graphic Art," *Arts Magazine,* vol. 43, no. 8, summer 1969, pp. 52–53.

Frank Bowling, "A Shift in Perspective," *Arts Magazine,* vol. 43, no. 8, summer 1969, pp. 24–27.

Mario Amaya, *David Hockney,* Whitworth Art Gallery, Manchester University, England, 1969.

Christopher Finch, *Images as Language: Aspects of British Art 1950–1968,* London, 1969.

T. A. Heinrich, *Graphics by David Hockney,* Rodman Hall Arts Centre, St. Catharines, Ontario, Canada, 1969.

Edward Lucie-Smith, *Late Modern,* New York, 1969.

John Russell and Suzi Gablick, *Pop Art Redefined,* London, 1969.

John Christopher Battye, "Interview with David Hockney," *Art and Artists,* vol. 5, no. 1, April 1970, pp. 50–53.

Edward Lucie-Smith, "The Real David Hockney," *Nova* (London), April 1970.

Mark Glazebrook, *David Hockney,* Kestner-Gesellschaft, Hannover, West Germany, 1970.

Mark Glazebrook, *David Hockney: Paintings, Prints, and Drawings, 1960–1970,* Whitechapel Art Gallery, London, 1970.

John Loring, "David Hockney Drawings," *Arts Magazine,* vol. 49, no. 3, November 1974, pp. 66–67.

John Rothenstein, *Modern British Painters: Wood to Hockney,* vol. 3, London, 1974.

Ellen Lubell, "David Hockney," *Arts Magazine,* vol. 49, no. 6, February 1975, p. 11.

Sarah Fox-Pitt, "David Hockney und The Rake's Progress," *DU* (Zurich), vol. 35, no. 413, July 1975, pp. 71–81.

Marc Fumaroli, *David Hockney: dessins et gravures,* Galerie Claude Bernard, Paris, 1975.

Petra Kipphoff, "Verse in Farben von David Hockney (Line in Color by David Hockney)," *Zeitmagazin,* vol. 1, no. 15, April 1977, pp. 58–65.

Carter Ratcliff, "The Photographs of David Hockney," *Arts Magazine,* vol. 51, no. 8, April 1977, pp. 96–97.

Nigel Gosling, "Things Exactly as They Are," *Horizon,* vol. 20, no. 11, November 1977, pp. 46–51.

Barnaby Conrad, "Mr. Geldzahler Looks at Mr. Hockney," *Art World,* vol. 1, no. 3, November–December 1977.

David Deitcher, "David Hockney: The Recent Work," *Arts Magazine,* vol. 52, no. 4, December 1977, pp. 129–133.

Peter Fuller, "An Interview with David Hockney," *Art Monthly,* December/January 1978, pp. 5–10.

David Hockney, *David Hockney by David Hockney,* ed. Nikos Stangos, intro. by Henry Geldzahler, New York, 1977.

David Conrad, "A Candidate in Search of a Fall," *Times Literary Supplement,* March 10, 1978.

Roy Bongartz, "David Hockney: Reaching the Top with Apparently No Great Effort," *Art News,* vol. 77, no. 3, March 1978, pp. 44–47.

Gene Baro, *David Hockney: Prints and Drawings,* International Exhibitions Foundation, Washington, D.C., 1978.

Edmund Pillsbury, *David Hockney: Travels with Pen, Pencil, and Ink,* New York, 1978.

Peter Weiermair, *Drawings and Prints,* Graphische Sammlung Albertina, Vienna, 1978.

Eric Gibson, "David Hockney," *Art International,* vol. 23, no. 10, March 1979, pp. 48–49.

Anthony Bailey, "Profiles: David Hockney," *The New Yorker,* July 30, 1979, pp. 35–69.

Jan Butterfield, "David Hockney: Blue Hedonistic Pools," *Print Collector's Newsletter,* vol. 10, no. 3, July–August 1979, pp. 73–76.

Stephen Bann, "Where the English Draw the Line," *Artforum,* vol. 28, no. 1, September 1979, pp. 70–72.

Nikos Stangos, *Pictures by David Hockney,* London, 1979.

Henry Geldzahler, "Hockney Abroad: A Slide Show," *Art in America,* vol. 69, no. 2, February 1981, pp. 126–41.

Robert Irwin

Born in Long Beach, California, 1928; lives in Los Angeles. Attended Otis Art Institute, Los Angeles, 1948–50; Jepson Art Institute, Los Angeles, 1951; Chouinard Art Institute, Los Angeles, 1952–54.

Selected One-Man Exhibitions

Ferus Gallery, Los Angeles, 1959, 1960, 1962, 1964.

Pasadena Art Museum, California, 1960, 1968.

Pace Gallery, New York, 1966 1968, 1969, 1971, 1973, 1974.

Museum of Art, Rhode Island School of Design, Providence, 1969.

La Jolla Museum of Art, California, 1969.

Artist's Studio, Venice, California, 1970.

The Museum of Modern Art, New York, 1971.

Ace Gallery, Los Angeles, 1971.

Fogg Art Museum, Cambridge, Massachusetts, 1972.

Galerie Ileana Sonnabend, Paris, 1972.

Riko Mizuno Gallery, Los Angeles, 1972, 1974, 1976.

University Art Galleries, Wright State University, Dayton, Ohio, 1974.

Art Galleries, University of California, Santa Barbara, 1974.

Fort Worth Art Museum, Texas, 1975.

Museum of Contemporary Art, Chicago, 1975.

Walker Art Center, Minneapolis, Minnesota, 1976.

Whitney Museum of American Art, New York, 1977.

San Diego State University Art Gallery, California, 1979.

Selected Group Exhibitions

50 Paintings by 37 Painters of the Los Angeles Area, The UCLA Art Galleries, University of California, Los Angeles, 1960.

Pacific Profile of Young West Coast Painters, Pasadena Art Museum, California, 1962.

Fifty California Artists, Whitney Museum of American Art, New York, 1962.

Seven New Artists, Sidney Janis Gallery, New York, 1964.

Some New Art from Los Angeles, San Francisco Art Institute, 1964.

The Responsive Eye, The Museum of Modern Art, New York, 1965 (traveled to Pasadena Art Museum).

VIII Bienal de São Paulo, Brazil, 1965.

Robert Irwin/Kenneth Price, Los Angeles County Museum of Art, 1966.

Gene Davis, Robert Irwin, Richard Smith, The Jewish Museum, New York, 1968.

Los Angeles 6, Vancouver Art Gallery, British Columbia, 1968.

Faculty '68, Art Gallery, University of California, Irvine, 1968.

6 Artists, 6 Exhibitions, Walker Art Center, Minneapolis, Minnesota, 1968.

Documenta 4, Kassel, West Germany, 1968.

Late Fifties at the Ferus, Los Angeles County Museum of Art, 1968.

Robert Irwin/Doug Wheeler, Fort Worth Art Center Museum, Texas, 1969 (traveled to Corcoran Gallery of Art, Washington, D.C.; Stedelijk Museum, Amsterdam).

Kompas 4: West Coast USA, Stedelijk van Abbemuseum, Eindhoven, The Netherlands, 1969 (traveled to Pasadena Art Museum, California; City Art Museum of St. Louis, Missouri; Art Gallery of Ontario, Toronto; Fort Worth Art Center Museum, Texas).

West Coast 1945–1969, Pasadena Art Museum, California, 1969 (traveled to City Art Museum of St. Louis, Missouri; Art Gallery of Ontario, Toronto; Fort Worth Art Center Museum, Texas).

Bell/Irwin/Wheeler, The Tate Gallery, London, 1970.

Permutations: Light and Color, Museum of Contemporary Art, Chicago, 1970.

Transparency, Reflection, Light, Space: Four Artists, The UCLA Art Galleries, University of California, Los Angeles, 1971.

Art and Technology, Los Angeles County Museum of Art, 1971.

Works for New Spaces, Walker Art Center, Minneapolis, Minnesota, 1971.

11 Los Angeles Artists, Hayward Gallery, London, 1971 (traveled to Musées Royaux des Beaux-Arts, Brussels; Akademie der Künste, Berlin, West Germany).

USA West Coast, Kunstverein, Hamburg, West Germany, 1972 (traveled to Kunstverein, Hannover; Kölnischer Kunstverein, Cologne; Württembergisher Kunstverein, Stuttgart).

Works in Spaces, San Francisco Museum of Art, 1973.

Art in Space: Some Turning Points, The Detroit Institute of Arts, Michigan, 1973.

Illumination and Reflection, Downtown Branch, Whitney Museum of American Art, New York, 1974.

Art Now 74, John F. Kennedy Center for the Performing Arts, Washington, D.C., 1974.

Some Recent American Art, The Museum of Modern Art, New York, 1974.

A View Through, Art Galleries, California State University, Long Beach, 1975.

University of California, Irvine: 1965–75, La Jolla Museum of Contemporary Art, California, 1975.

The Last Time I Saw Ferus: 1957–1966, Newport Harbor Art Museum, Newport Beach, California, 1976.

200 Years of American Sculpture, Whitney Museum of American Art, New York, 1976.

Critical Perspectives in American Art, Fine Arts Center Gallery, University of Massachusetts, Amherst, 1976.

Projects for PCA, Philadelphia College of Art, 1976.

Venice Biennale, Italy, 1976.

Painting and Sculpture in California: The Modern Era, San Francisco Museum of Modern Art, 1976 (traveled to National Collection of Fine Arts, Smithsonian Institution, Washington, D.C.).

American Artists: A New Decade, Fort Worth Art Museum, Texas, 1976.

Andre, Buren, Irwin, Nordman: Space as Support, University Art Museum, University of California, Berkeley, 1979.

Contemporary Art in Southern California, The High Museum of Art, Atlanta, Georgia, 1980.

Selected Bibliography

Lloyd Goodrich and George Culler, *Fifty California Artists,* Whitney Museum of American Art, New York, 1962.

Constance Perkins, *Pacific Profile of Young West Coast Painters,* Pasadena Art Museum, California, 1962.

Jan van der Marck, "The Californians," *Art International,* vol. 7, no. 5, May 1963, pp. 28–31.

John Coplans, "Circle of Styles on the West Coast," *Art in America,* vol. 52, no. 4, June 1964, pp. 24–41.

John Coplans, "Formal Art," *Artforum,* vol. 2, no. 12, summer 1964, pp. 42–46.

Henry T. Hopkins, "Abstract Expressionism," *Artforum,* vol. 2, no. 12, summer 1964, pp. 59–63.

Philip Leider, "The Cool School," *Artforum,* vol. 2, no. 12, summer 1964, pp. 47–52.

John Coplans, "Los Angeles: The Scene," *Art News,* vol. 64, no. 6, March 1965, pp. 29, 56–58.

John Coplans, "The New Abstraction on the West Coast USA," *Studio International,* vol. 169, no. 865, May 1965, pp. 192–99.

Robert Irwin, "Statement," *Artforum,* vol. 3, no. 9, June 1965, p. 23.

William C. Seitz, *The Responsive Eye,* The Museum of Modern Art, New York, 1965.

Barbara Rose, "Los Angeles: The Second City," *Art in America,* vol. 54, no. 1, January–February 1966, pp. 110–15.

Philip Leider, *Robert Irwin/Kenneth Price,* Los Angeles County Museum of Art, 1966.

Robert Irwin, "Letter to Editor," *Artforum,* vol. 6, no. 6, February 1968, p. 4.

Emily Wasserman, "Robert Irwin, Gene Davis, Richard Smith," *Artforum,* vol. 6, no. 9, May 1968, pp. 47–49.

Corrine Robins, "The Circle in Orbit," *Art in America,* vol. 56, no. 6, November–December 1968, p. 65.

John Coplans, *Robert Irwin,* Pasadena Art Museum, California, 1968.

John Coplans, *Gene Davis, Robert Irwin, Richard Smith,* The Jewish Museum, New York, 1968.

Jane Livingston, *Robert Irwin/Doug Wheeler,* Fort Worth Art Center Museum, Texas, 1969.

Melinda Terbell, "Los Angeles," *Arts Magazine,* vol. 45, no. 2, November 1970, p. 53.

Peter Plagens, "Robert Irwin, the Artist's Premises," *Artforum,* vol. 9, no. 4, December 1970, pp. 88–89.

Michael Compton, *Bell/Irwin/Wheeler,* The Tate Gallery, London, 1970.

Elizabeth Baker, "Los Angeles, 1971," *Art News,* vol. 70, no. 5, September 1971, pp. 30–31.

Maurice Tuchman and Jane Livingston, *11 Los Angeles Artists,* Hayward Gallery, London, 1971.

Maurice Tuchman, *A Report on the Art and Technology Program of the Los Angeles County Museum of Art,* Los Angeles, 1971.

Frederick S. Wight, *Transparency, Reflection, Light, Space: Four Artists,* The UCLA Art Galleries, University of California, Los Angeles, 1971.

Alistair Mackintosh, "Robert Irwin: An Interview with Alistair Mackintosh," *Art and Artists,* vol. 6, no. 12, March 1972, pp. 24–27.

Jan Butterfield, "Part I. The State of the Real: Robert Irwin Discusses the Art of an Extended Consciousness," *Arts Magazine,* vol. 46, no. 8, summer 1972, pp. 47–49.

Sam Hunter, *American Art of the Twentieth Century,* New York, 1973.

Jan Butterfield, "An Uncompromising Other Way," *Arts Magazine,* vol. 48, no. 9, June 1974, pp. 52–55.

Peter Plagens, *Sunshine Muse: Contemporary Art on the West Coast,* New York, 1974.

Larry Rosing, "Robert Irwin at Pace," *Art in America,* vol. 63, no. 2, March 1975, p. 87.

Robert Irwin, "Twenty Questions," *Vision,* no. 1, September 1975, pp. 38–39.

Ira Licht, *Robert Irwin,* Museum of Contemporary Art, Chicago, 1975.

Barbara Rose, *American Art since 1900,* New York, 1975.

Jan Butterfield, "Robert Irwin: On the Periphery of Knowing," *Arts Magazine,* vol. 50, no. 6, February 1976, pp. 72–77.

Edward Levine, "Robert Irwin: World Without Frame," *Arts Magazine,* vol. 50, no. 6, February 1976, pp. 72–77.

Janet Kardon, *Projects for PCA,* Philadelphia College of Art, 1976.

Edward Levine, "Robert Irwin's Recent Work," *Artforum,* vol. 16, no. 4, December 1977, pp. 24–29.

Frederick S. Wight, *Los Angeles Art Community Group Portrait: Robert Irwin,* Oral History Program, University of California, Los Angeles, 1977.

"The Image of Nature," *Art Actuel,* Skira Annuel, Switzerland, vol. 4, 1978, pp. 92–127.

Peter Plagens, "Irwin's Bar Paintings," *Artforum,* vol. 17, no. 7, March 1979, pp. 41–43.

Robert Atkins, "Irwin Trips the Light Fantastic: University Art Museum, Berkeley, CA," *Artweek,* vol. 10, no. 15, April 14, 1979, pp. 1, 16.

Clark V. Poling, *Contemporary Art in Southern California,* The High Museum of Art, Atlanta, Georgia, 1980.

Craig Kauffman

Born in Los Angeles, 1932; lives in Los Angeles and New York.
B.A., University of California, Los Angeles, 1955; M.A., 1956.

Selected One-Man Exhibitions

Felix Landau Gallery, Los Angeles, 1953.

Dilexi Gallery, San Francisco, 1958, 1960.

Ferus Gallery, Los Angeles, 1958, 1963, 1965, 1967.

Pace Gallery, New York, 1967, 1969, 1970, 1973.

Irving Blum Gallery, Los Angeles, 1969, 1972.

Pasadena Art Museum, California, 1970.

University of California, Irvine, 1970.

Galerie Darthea Speyer, Paris, 1973, 1976.

Riko Mizuno Gallery, Los Angeles, 1975.

Robert Elkon Gallery, New York, 1976.

Comsky Gallery, Los Angeles, 1976.

Arco Center for Visual Art, Los Angeles, 1978.

Blum-Helman Gallery, New York, 1979.

Janus Gallery, Los Angeles, 1979.

Grapestake Gallery, San Francisco, 1979.

La Jolla Museum of Contemporary Art, California, 1981 (traveling retrospective).

Selected Group Exhibitions

50 Paintings by 37 Painters of the Los Angeles Area, The UCLA Art Galleries, University of California, Los Angeles, 1960.

5 at Pace, Pace Gallery, New York, 1965.

Multiples, The Museum of Modern Art, New York, 1965.

Los Angeles Now, Robert Fraser Gallery, London, 1966.

Ten from Los Angeles, Seattle Art Museum, Washington, 1966.

Form, Color, Image, The Detroit Institute of Arts, 1967.

A New Aesthetic, Washington Gallery of Modern Art, Washington, D.C., 1967.

The 1960s, The Museum of Modern Art, New York, 1967.

The United States of America: V Paris Biennale, 1967 (organized by Pasadena Art Museum, California).

Contemporary American Painting and Sculpture, Krannert Art Museum, University of Illinois, Urbana, 1967.

California, Janie C. Lee Gallery, Dallas, Texas, 1968.

Painting: Out from the Wall, Des Moines Art Center, Iowa, 1968.

Made of Plastic, Flint Institute of Arts, Michigan, 1968.

Los Angeles 6, Vancouver Art Gallery, British Columbia, 1968.

1968 Annual Exhibition: Sculpture, Whitney Museum of American Art, New York; *1979 Biennial Exhibition.*

Late Fifties at the Ferus, Los Angeles County Museum of Art, 1968.

Three from Los Angeles: Irwin, Bell, Kauffman, Dunkelman Gallery, Montreal, 1969.

14 Sculptors: The Industrial Edge, Walker Art Center, Minneapolis, Minnesota, 1969.

Plastic New Art, Institute of Contemporary Art of the University of Pennsylvania, Philadelphia, 1969.

Plastic Presence, Milwaukee Art Center, Wisconsin, 1969.

Contemporary American Master Works, La Jolla Museum of Art, California, 1969.

Kompas 4: West Coast USA, Stedelijk van Abbemuseum, Eindhoven, The Netherlands, 1969.

A Los Angeles Aesthetic, University of California, Irvine, 1969.

A Decade of California Color, Pace Gallery, New York, 1970.

Transparency, Reflection, Light, Space: Four Artists, The UCLA Art Galleries, University of California, Los Angeles, 1971.

The State of California Painting, Govett-Brewster Art Gallery, New Plymouth, New Zealand, 1972.

Spray, The Santa Barbara Museum of Art, California, 1971.

Contemporary American Art: Los Angeles, Fort Worth Art Center Museum, Texas, 1972.

33rd Biennial Exhibition of Contemporary American Painting, Corcoran Gallery of Art, Washington, D.C., 1973.

71st American Exhibition of Painting and Sculpture, The Art Institute of Chicago, 1974.

Illuminations and Reflections, Whitney Museum of American Art, New York, 1974.

Modern and Contemporary Sculpture, Newport Harbor Art Museum, Newport Beach, California, 1974.

Current Concerns, Part I, Los Angeles Institute of Contemporary Art, 1975.

University of California, Irvine: 1965–75, La Jolla Museum of Contemporary Art, California, 1975.

The Last Time I Saw Ferus, 1957–1966, Newport Harbor Art Museum, Newport Beach, California, 1976.

Painting and Sculpture in California: The Modern Era, San Francisco Museum of Modern Art, 1976 (traveled to National Collection of Fine Arts, Smithsonian Institution, Washington, D.C.).

California Abstraction, Sacramento Museum of Art, California, 1979.

Selected Bibliography

John Coplans, "Circle of Styles on the West Coast," *Art in America,* vol. 52, no. 3, June 1964, p. 24.

Clair Wolfe, "Art West," *Arts and Architecture,* vol. 81, no. 7, July 1964, pp. 6, 44.

John Coplans, "Formal Art," *Artforum,* vol. 2, no. 12, summer 1964, pp. 42–46.

Henry T. Hopkins, "Abstract Expressionism," *Artforum,* vol. 2, no. 12, summer 1964, pp. 59–63.

Philip Leider, "The Cool School," *Artforum,* vol. 2, no. 12, summer 1964, pp. 47–52.

Clair Wolfe, "Notes on Craig Kauffman," *Artforum,* vol. 3, no. 5, February 1965, pp. 20–21.

John Coplans, "Los Angeles: The Scene," *Art News,* vol. 64, no. 1, March 1965, p. 28.

John Coplans, "The New Abstraction on the West Coast USA," *Studio International,* vol. 169, no. 865, May 1965, pp. 192–99.

Barbara Rose, "Los Angeles: The Second City," *Art in America,* vol. 54, no. 1, January/February 1966, pp. 110–15.

Robert Smithson, "Entropy and the New Movements," *Artforum,* vol. 4, no. 10, June 1966, pp. 26–31.

Larry Aldrich, "New Talent USA," *Art in America,* vol. 54, no. 4, July/August 1966, p. 22.

Henry T. Hopkins, "West Coast Style," *Art Voices,* vol. 5, no. 4, fall 1966, pp. 60–72.

John Coplans, *Los Angeles Now,* Robert Fraser Gallery, London, 1966.

John Coplans, *Ten from Los Angeles,* Seattle Art Museum, Washington, 1966.

Barbara Rose, *A New Aesthetic,* Washington Gallery of Modern Art, Washington, D.C., 1967 (with statement by Kauffman).

Douglas M. Davis, "Art and Technology," *Art in America,* vol. 56, no. 1, January/February 1968, p. 28.

Jane Livingston, "Recent Works by Craig Kauffman: A New Non-Pictorial Set of Terms," *Artforum,* vol. 6, no. 6, February 1968, pp. 36–39.

Martin Friedman, Barbara Rose, and Christopher Finch, *14 Sculptors: The Industrial Edge,* Walker Art Center, Minneapolis, Minnesota, 1969.

Barbara Rose, *American Painting,* Cleveland, Ohio, 1970.

Craig Kauffman and Robert Morris, *Using Walls,* The Jewish Museum, New York, 1970.

Frederick S. Wight, *Transparency, Reflection, Light, Space: Four Artists,* The UCLA Art Galleries, University of California, Los Angeles, 1971 (interview with Kauffman).

Sam Hunter, *American Art of the Twentieth Century,* New York, 1972.

Peter Plagens, *Sunshine Muse: Contemporary Art on the West Coast,* New York, 1974.

Jan Butterfield, "Craig Kauffman Interviewed by Jan Butterfield," *Art in America,* vol. 64, no. 4, July 1974, pp. 81–82.

Melinda Wortz, "Craig Kauffman's Interiors," *Artweek,* vol. 9, no. 19, May 1978, p. 3.

Peter Frank, "Unslick in L.A.," *Art in America,* vol. 66, no. 5, September/October 1978, pp. 84–91.

Melinda Wortz, *Craig Kauffman,* Arco Center for Visual Art, Los Angeles, 1978.

Robert McDonald, *Craig Kauffman: A Comprehensive Exhibition 1957–1980,* La Jolla Museum of Contemporary Art, California, 1981.

Edward Kienholz

Born in Fairfield, Washington, 1927; resident of Los Angeles, 1953–73; lives in Hope, Idaho, and Berlin, West Germany. Attended Washington State College, 1945.

Selected One-Man Exhibitions

Cafe Galeria, Los Angeles, 1955.

Coronet Louvre, Los Angeles, 1955.

Syndell Studios, Los Angeles, 1956.

Exodus Gallery, San Pedro, California, 1958.

Ferus Gallery, Los Angeles, 1959, 1960, 1961, 1963.

Pasadena Art Museum, California, 1961.

Alexander Iolas Gallery, New York, 1963.

Dwan Gallery, Los Angeles, 1963, 1964, 1965.

Dwan Gallery, New York, 1965, 1967.

Los Angeles County Museum of Art, 1966 (traveled to Institute of Contemporary Art, Boston).

University of Saskatchewan, Regina, Canada, 1966.

Washington Gallery of Modern Art, Washington, D.C., 1967.

Boise Art Museum, Idaho, 1968.

Gallery 669, Los Angeles, 1968.

Eugenia Butler Gallery, Los Angeles, 1969.

Ateneumin Taidemuseo, Helsinki, Finland, 1969.

Wide White Space Gallery, Antwerp, Belgium, 1970, 1971, 1972.

Gallery Michael Werner, Cologne, West Germany, 1970.

Onnasch Gallery, Cologne, West Germany, 1970, 1973.

Moderna Museet, Stockholm, 1970 (retrospective of tableaux; traveled to Stedelijk Museum, Amsterdam; Städtische Kunsthalle Düsseldorf, West Germany; Kunsthaus Zurich, Switzerland; The Museum of Modern Art, New York; Centre National d'Art Contemporain, Paris; Institute of Contemporary Arts, London).

Gemini G.E.L., Los Angeles, 1972, 1980.

Akademie der Künste, Berlin, West Germany, 1973.

Städtische Kunsthalle Düsseldorf, West Germany, 1973.

Galerie Christel, Helsinki, Finland, 1974.

Galleria Bocchi, Milan, Italy, 1974.

Nationalgalerie, Berlin, West Germany, 1977 (traveled to Galerie Maeght, Zurich, Switzerland).

Galleria d'Arte Il Gabbiano, Rome, 1977.

Centre National d'Art et de Culture Georges Pompidou, Paris, 1977.

Städtische Kunsthalle Düsseldorf, West Germany, 1977.

Galerie Apollon Die Insel, Munich, West Germany, 1977.

Akademie der Künste, Berlin, West Germany, 1978.

Galerie Maeght, Paris, 1979.

Louisiana Museum, Humlebaek, Denmark, 1979.

Henry Art Gallery, University of Washington, Seattle, 1979.

University Art Museum, University of California, Berkeley, 1979.

The Douglas Hyde Gallery, Trinity College, Dublin, 1981.

Galerie Maeght, Zurich, Switzerland, 1981.

Selected Group Exhibitions

The Art of Assemblage, The Museum of Modern Art, New York, 1961.

Fifty California Artists, Whitney Museum of American Art, New York, 1962.

My Country 'Tis of Thee, Dwan Gallery, Los Angeles, 1962.

Contemporary California Sculpture, Oakland Art Museum, California, 1963.

Contemporary American Sculpture, Whitney Museum of American Art, New York, 1964.

Boxes, Dwan Gallery, Los Angeles, 1964.

Contemporary Sculpture and Prints, Whitney Museum of American Art, New York, 1966.

68th American Exhibition of Painting and Sculpture, The Art Institute of Chicago, 1966.

American Sculpture of the Sixties, Los Angeles County Museum of Art, 1967.

Protest and Hope, New School Art Center, New York, 1967.

Dada, Surrealism and Their Heritage, The Museum of Modern Art, New York, 1968.

Los Angeles 6, Vancouver Art Gallery, British Columbia, 1968.

The Machine, The Museum of Modern Art, New York, 1968.

Assemblage in California, University of California, Irvine, 1968.

Documenta 4, Kassel, West Germany, 1968; *Documenta 5,* 1972.

Late Fifties at the Ferus, Los Angeles County Museum of Art, 1968.

When Art Becomes Form, Kunsthalle Bern, Switzerland, 1968.

Kunst der Sechziger Jahre, Sammlung Ludwig, Wallraf-Richartz Museum, Cologne, West Germany, 1969.

Human Concern/Personal Torment: The Grotesque in American Art, Whitney Museum of American Art, New York, 1969.

Pop Art Redefined, Hayward Gallery, London, 1969.

Kompas 4: West Coast USA, Stedelijk van Abbemuseum, Eindhoven, The Netherlands, 1969.

Das Ding als Objekt, Kunsthalle Nürnberg, West Germany, 1970.

Continuing Surrealism, La Jolla Museum of Contemporary Art, California, 1971.

Metamorphose van het object, Musées Royaux des Beaux-Arts, Brussels, 1971.

Looking West 1970, Joslyn Art Museum, Omaha, Nebraska, 1970.

Ars 74, Ateneumin Taidemuseo, Helsinki, Finland, 1974.

Word Works, Mt. San Antonio College, Walnut, California, 1974.

8 from Berlin: Erben, Erber, Gosewitz, Hödicke, Kienholz, Koberling, Lakner, Schönebeck, Fruit Market Gallery, Scottish Arts Council, Edinburgh, 1975.

Painting and Sculpture in California: The Modern Era, San Francisco Museum of Modern Art, 1976 (traveled to National Collection of Fine Arts, Smithsonian Institution, Washington, D.C.)

Venice Biennale, Italy, 1977.

Aspekte der 60er Jahre: Aus der Sammlung Reinhard Onnasch, Nationalgalerie, Berlin, West Germany, 1978.

Écouter par les yeux, Musée d'Art Moderne de la Ville de Paris, 1980.

1981 Biennial Exhibition, Whitney Museum of American Art, New York, 1981.

Selected Bibliography

William C. Seitz, *The Art of Assemblage,* The Museum of Modern Art, New York, 1961.

Donald Factor, "Assemblage," *FM and Fine Arts* (Beverly Hills), vol. 3, no. 9, September 1962, pp. 6–9.

Arthur Secunda, "John Bernhardt, Charles Frazier, Edward Kienholz," *Artforum,* vol. 1, no. 5, November 1962, pp. 30–34.

Donald Judd, "Review: Exhibition at Alexander Iolas Gallery," *Arts Magazine,* vol. 37, no. 6, March 1963, pp. 63–64.

Philip Leider, "West Coast Art: Three Images," *Artforum,* vol. 1, no. 12, June 1963, pp. 21–23.

John Coplans, "Sculpture in California," *Artforum,* vol. 2, no. 11, August 1963, pp. 3–6.

Donald Factor, "A Portfolio of California Sculptors: Edward Kienholz," *Artforum,* vol. 2, no. 2, August 1963, pp. 15–59.

Dore Ashton, *Edward Kienholz,* Alexander Iolas Gallery, New York, 1963.

John Coplans, "Circle of Styles on the West Coast," *Art in America,* vol. 52, no. 3, June 1964, pp. 24–41.

John Reuschel, "Los Angeles: Edward Kienholz, Three Tableaux," *Artforum,* vol. 3, no. 1, September 1964, p. 14.

Philip Leider, "Kienholz," *Frontier,* vol. 16, no. 1, November 1964, p. 25.

Walter Hopps, *Boxes,* Dwan Gallery, Los Angeles, 1964.

Barbara Rose, "Looking at American Sculpture," *Artforum,* vol. 3, no. 5, February 1965, pp. 29–36.

John Coplans, "Los Angeles: The Scene," *Art News,* vol. 64, no. 1, March 1965, pp. 28–29, 56–58.

John Coplans, "Assemblage: the Savage Eye of Edward Kienholz," *Studio International,* vol. 170, no. 869, September 1965, pp. 112–15.

Suzi Gablik, "Crossing the Bar," *Art News,* vol. 64, no. 6, October 1965, pp. 22–25.

Henry T. Hopkins, "Edward Kienholz," *Art in America,* vol. 53, no. 5, October–November 1965, p. 73.

Barbara Rose, "Los Angeles: The Second City," *Art in America,* vol. 54, no. 1, January/February 1966, pp. 110–15.

Annette Michelson, "Review: Exhibition at Dwan Gallery," *Art International,* vol. 10, no. 2, February 1966, pp. 60–61.

Michael Blankfort, "Edward Kienholz: A Very Private Report," *Los Angeles Magazine,* April 1966, pp. 48–51.

Sidney Tillim, "The Underground Pre-Raphaelites of Edward Kienholz," *Artforum,* vol. 4, no. 8, April 1966, pp. 38–40.

Maurice Tuchman, "A Decade of Edward Kienholz," *Artforum,* vol. 4, no. 8, April 1966, pp. 41–45.

Lucy R. Lippard, *Pop Art,* New York, 1966.

Maurice Tuchman, *Edward Kienholz,* Los Angeles County Museum of Art, 1966.

Walter Hopps, *Works from the 1960s by Edward Kienholz,* Washington Gallery of Modern Art, Washington, D.C., 1967.

Jo Baer, "Edward Kienholz: A Sentimental Journeyman," *Art International,* vol. 12, no. 4, April 1968, pp. 45–49.

John Coplans, Walter Hopps, Philip Leider, and Hal Glicksman, *Assemblage in California: Works from the late 50's and early 60's,* Art Gallery, University of California, Irvine, 1968.

John Coplans, Barbara Rose, Jane Livingston, and Maurice Tuchman, *Los Angeles 6,* Vancouver Art Gallery, British Columbia, 1968.

K. G. Pontus Hultén, *The Machine,* The Museum of Modern Art, New York, 1968.

Dore Ashton, "Crisis/Violence/Reform: Response to Crisis in American Art," *Art in America,* vol. 57, no. 1, January/February 1969, pp. 24–35.

Charlotte Willard, "Crisis/Violence/Reform: Violence and Art," *Art in America,* vol. 57, no. 1, January/February 1969, pp. 36–43.

Dore Ashton, "A Planned Coincidence," *Art in America,* vol. 57, no. 5, September/October 1969, pp. 36–47.

Robert Doty, *Human Concern/Personal Torment: The Grotesque in American Art,* Whitney Museum of American Art, New York, 1969.

John Russell and Suzi Gablik, *Pop Art Redefined,* London, 1969.

Gilbert Brownstone and Jean Clair, "Edward et Lyn Kienholz" (interview), *Chroniques de l'Art Vivant,* no. 14, October 1970, p. 6.

Art Seidenbaum, "Goodbye Ed Kienholz," *Los Angeles Times West Magazine,* November 22, 1970, pp. 9–13.

Alain Jouffroy, "Edward Kienholz," *Opus International,* no. 21, December 1970, pp. 21–25.

LeRoy Butler, *Looking West 1970,* Joslyn Art Museum, Omaha, Nebraska, 1970.

K. G. Pontus Hultén, *Edward Kienholz: 11 + 11 Tableaux,* Moderna Museet, Stockholm, 1970.

Jürgen Harten and K. G. Pontus Hultén, *Edward Kienholz, 1960–1970,* Städtische Kunsthalle Düsseldorf, West Germany, 1970.

Margit Staber, "Geofrorene Scheinheiligkeiten," *Die Weltwoche,* no. 29, January 1971, p. 37.

Jörg Steiner, "Landschaffen Februar bis Marz 1971," *Tagesanzeiger Magazine,* vol. 7, no. 20, February 1971, pp. 8–12.

K. G. Pontus Hultén, "Edward Kienholz," *Art and Artists,* vol. 6, no. 3, June 1971, pp. 14–19.

Heine Bastian, *Edward Kienholz, 10 Objekte von 1960 bis 1964,* Onnasch Galerie, Cologne, West Germany, 1971.

Dieter Ronte, "Le 'Monument aux Morts Transportable' d'Edward Kienholz," *Oeil,* no. 216, December 1972, pp. 22–29.

Joan Mondale, *Politics in Art,* Minneapolis, Minnesota, 1972.

Willy Rotzler, *Objekt-Kunst: Von Duchamp bis Kienholz,* Cologne, West Germany, 1972.

G. Metken, "Moralische 'Tableau': zum Werk von Edward Kienholz," *Pantheon,* vol. 31, no. 1, January–March 1973, pp. 75–89.

Barbara Catoir, "Interview mit Edward Kienholz," *Kunstwerk,* vol. 26, no. 2, March 1973, pp. 49–50.

John Anthony Thwaites, "Kienholz and Realism," *Art and Artists,* vol. 8, no. 6, September 1973, pp. 22–27.

Salme Savajas-Korte, *Ars 74,* Ateneumin Taidemuseo, Helsinki, Finland, 1974.

Edward Kienholz, Galleria Bocchi, Milan, Italy, 1974.

K. G. Pontus Hultén and F. Minervino, "Che ve ne sembra dell'America?" *Bollaffiarte,* vol. 6, no. 46, January–February 1975, pp. 28–33.

Wayne Andersen, *American Sculpture in Process: 1930/1970,* Boston, 1975.

Edward Kienholz, "Ed Kienholz Tableaux Concepts," *Opus International,* no. 60, July 1976, pp. 18–19.

K. Ruhberg, "Mein Thema ist, dass wir hier sind," *Magazin Kunst,* vol. 16, no. 3, 1976, pp. 40–49.

Paul von Blum, *The Art of Social Conscience,* New York, 1976.

Cynthia Golomb Dettelbach, *In the Driver's Seat: the Automobile in American Literature and Popular Culture,* Westport, Connecticut, 1976.

K. G. Pontus Hultén, *The Art Show, 1963–77: Edward Kienholz,* Centre National d'Art et de Culture Georges Pompidou, Paris, 1977.

Jörn Merkert, *Edward Kienholz: Volksempfängers,* Nationalgalerie, Berlin, West Germany, 1977.

Willy Rotzler, Roland H. Wiegenstein, and Jörn Merkert, *Edward Kienholz: "Volksempfängers,"* Galleria d'Arte Il Gabbiano, Rome, 1977.

Lawrence Weschler, *Los Angeles Art Community Group Portrait: Edward Kienholz,* Oral History Program, University of California, Los Angeles, 1977.

Gerald D. Silk, "Ed Kienholz's 'Back Seat Dodge '38,'" *Arts Magazine,* vol. 52, no. 5, January 1978, pp. 112–18.

Dieter Honisch, *Aspects of the 1960's: From the Collection of Reinhard Onnasch,* Nationalgalerie, Berlin, West Germany, 1978.

Knud W. Jensen, Willy Rotzler, Jörn Merkert, and Karl Ruhrberg, "Kienholz på Louisiana," *Louisiana-Revy,* vol. 19, no. 3, February 1979, pp. 2–25

Ron Glowen, "Kienholz's New Formalism: Sculpture 1976–79," *Artweek,* vol. 10, no. 40, December 1, 1979, p. 7.

Alain Macaire, "Edward Kienholz: Procès de l'Inavouable," *Canal,* no. 34, December 1979, p. 6.

Michael Auping, *Edward Kienholz: The Back Seat Dodge '38,* University Art Museum, University of California, Berkeley, 1979.

Jean Pierre Faye and Jörn Merkert, "Kienholz," *Derrière le Miroir,* Galerie Maeght, Paris, 1979.

Suzanne Page, Frank Popper, René Block, and Helmut Danniger, *Écouter par les yeux,* Musée National d'Art Moderne de la Ville de Paris, 1980.

David Scott, *Edward Kienholz Tableaux, 1961–1979,* Douglas Hyde Gallery, Trinity College, Dublin, 1981.

John McLaughlin

Born in Sharon, Massachusetts, 1898; moved to Dana Point, California, 1946; died in 1976. Self-taught.

Selected One-Man Exhibitions

Felix Landau Gallery, Los Angeles, 1953, 1958, 1962, 1966.

Pasadena Art Museum, California, 1963 (retrospective).

Corcoran Gallery of Art, Washington, D.C., 1969 (retrospective).

University of California, Irvine, 1971.

Nicholas Wilder Gallery, Los Angeles, 1972, 1979.

La Jolla Museum of Contemporary Art, California, 1973.

Whitney Museum of American Art, New York, 1974.

André Emmerich Gallery, New York, 1974, 1979.

Felicity Samuel Gallery, London, 1975.

Galerie André Emmerich, Zurich, Switzerland, 1976, 1981.

University of California, Santa Barbara, 1978.

Annely Juda Fine Art, London, 1981.

Selected Group Exhibitions

III Bienal de São Paulo, Brazil, 1955.

Four Abstract Classicists, Los Angeles County Museum of History, Science and Art, 1959.

Geometrical Abstraction in America, Whitney Museum of American Art, New York, 1962.

The Artist's Environment: West Coast, Amon Carter Museum, Fort Worth, Texas, 1962 (traveled to UCLA Art Galleries, University of California, Los Angeles).

Fifty California Artists, Whitney Museum of American Art, New York, 1962.

California Hard-Edge Painting, The Fine Arts Patrons of Newport Harbor, Balboa Pavilion Gallery, California, 1964.

The Responsive Eye, The Museum of Modern Art, New York, 1955 (traveled to Pasadena Art Museum).

Looking West 1970, Joslyn Art Museum, Omaha, Nebraska, 1970.

11 Los Angeles Artists, Hayward Gallery, London, 1971 (traveled to Musées Royaux des Beaux-Arts, Brussels; Akademie der Künste, Berlin, West Germany).

Painting and Sculpture in California: The Modern Era, San Francisco Museum of Modern Art, 1976 (traveled to National Collection of Fine Arts, Smithsonian Institution, Washington, D.C.).

California: 5 Footnotes to Modern Art History, Los Angeles County Museum of Art, 1977.

Selected Bibliography

Gerald Nordland, "Art," *Frontier,* vol. 11, no. 2, December 1959, p. 23.

Jules Langsner, *Four Abstract Classicists,* Los Angeles County Museum of History, Science and Art, 1959.

Lawrence Alloway, "Classicism or Hard-Edge?" *Art International,* vol. 4, no. 2, February–March 1960, pp. 60–63, 71.

George D. Culler, "California Artists," *Art in America,* vol. 50, no. 3, fall 1962, pp. 84–89.

Philip Leider, "West Coast Art: Three Images," *Artforum,* vol. 1, no. 12, June 1963, p. 21.

John McLaughlin (statement), *John McLaughlin: A Retrospective Exhibition,* Pasadena Art Museum, California, 1963.

John Coplans, "John McLaughlin, Hard-Edge and American Painting," *Artforum,* vol. 2, no. 7, January 1964, p. 28.

Gerald Nordland, "McLaughlin and the Totally Abstract," *Frontier,* vol. 15, no. 3, January 1964, p. 22.

Don Factor, "Southern California Original Hard-Edge Painters," *Artforum,* vol. 3, no. 9, June 1965, p. 12.

John McLaughlin (statement), "Artists on Their Art," *Art International,* vol. 12, no. 5, May 15, 1968, pp. 47–55.

James Harithas, *John McLaughlin: Retrospective Exhibition 1946–1967,* Corcoran Gallery of Art, Washington, D.C., 1969.

Maurice Tuchman and Jane Livingston, *11 Los Angeles Artists,* Hayward Gallery, London, 1971.

"John McLaughlin," interview by Paul Karlstrom, Archives of American Art, Smithsonian Institution, Washington, D.C., July 1974.

Susan C. Larsen, "John McLaughlin," and Donald F. McCallum, "The John McLaughlin Papers in the Archives of American Art," *California: 5 Footnotes to Modern Art History,* Los Angeles County Museum of Art, 1977.

Susan C. Larsen, "John McLaughlin," *Art International,* vol. 22, no. 1, January 1978, p. 8.

Dore Ashton, "Painting Toward: The Art of John McLaughlin," *Arts Magazine,* vol. 54, no. 3, November 1979, pp. 120–21.

Carter Ratcliff, "John McLaughlin's Abstinent Abstraction," *Art in America,* vol. 67, no. 8, December 1979, pp. 100–101.

Sheldon Figoten, "An Appreciation of John McLaughlin," *The Archives of American Art Journal,* vol. 20, no. 4, 1980.

Edward Moses

Born in Long Beach, California, 1926; lives in Venice, California.
B.A., University of California, Los Angeles, 1955; M.A., 1958.

Selected One-Man Exhibitions

Ferus Gallery, Los Angeles, 1958, 1959, 1961, 1963, 1964.

Dilexi Gallery, San Francisco, 1958, 1959, 1960, 1961.

Area Gallery, New York, 1959.

Alan Gallery, New York, 1962, 1965.

Everett Ellin Gallery, Los Angeles, 1965.

Riko Mizuno Gallery, Los Angeles, 1969, 1970, 1980.

Hansen-Fuller Gallery, San Francisco, 1971, 1975.

Ronald Feldman Fine Arts, New York, 1971, 1973.

Pomona College Gallery, Claremont, California, 1971.

Felicity Samuel Gallery, London, 1972, 1975.

Dayton's Gallery 12, Minneapolis, Minnesota, 1972, 1973.

Portland Center for the Visual Arts, Oregon, 1973.

Nicholas Wilder Gallery, Los Angeles, 1973, 1976.

Art in Progress, Zurich, Switzerland, 1973.

Art in Progress, Munich, West Germany, 1974.

André Emmerich Gallery, New York, 1974, 1975.

The Frederick S. Wight Gallery, University of California, Los Angeles, 1976.

Los Angeles County Museum of Art, 1976.

Margo Leavin Gallery, Los Angeles, 1977, 1978.

Daniel Weinberg Gallery, San Francisco, 1977.

Dorothy Rosenthal Gallery, Chicago, 1977.

Municipal Art Gallery, Davenport, Iowa, 1978.

Dorothy Gates Gallery, Kansas City, Missouri, 1978.

Smith Andersen Gallery, Palo Alto, California, 1978.

Texas Gallery, Houston, 1978, 1979.

James Corcoran Gallery, Los Angeles, 1979, 1980.

Sidney Janis Gallery, New York, 1979.

Selected Group Exhibitions

Objects on the Landscape Demanding of the Eye, Ferus Gallery, Los Angeles, 1957.

Fifty California Artists, Whitney Museum of American Art, New York, 1962.

Late Fifties at the Ferus, Los Angeles County Museum of Art, 1968.

West Coast 1945–1969, Pasadena Art Museum, California, 1969 (traveled to City Art Museum of St. Louis, Missouri; Art Gallery of Ontario, Toronto; Fort Worth Art Center Museum, Texas).

Graphics: Six West Coast Artists, Galleria Milano, Italy, 1969.

A Decade of California Color, Pace Gallery, New York, 1970.

32nd Biennial Exhibition of Contemporary American Painting, Corcoran Gallery of Art, Washington, D.C., 1971; *34th Biennial,* 1975.

Documenta 5, Kassel, West Germany, 1972.

70th American Exhibition of Painting and Sculpture, The Art Institute of Chicago, 1973.

Art Now 74, The John F. Kennedy Center for the Performing Arts, Washington, D.C., 1974.

The Last Time I Saw Ferus: 1957–1966, Newport Harbor Art Museum, Newport Beach, California, 1976.

Painting and Sculpture in California: The Modern Era, San Francisco Museum of Modern Art, 1976 (traveled to National Collection of Fine Arts, Smithsonian Institution, Washington, D.C.).

Selections from the Frederick R. Weisman Company Collection of California Art, Corcoran Gallery of Art, Washington, D.C., 1979.

A Painting Installation, Baxter Art Gallery, California Institute of Technology, Pasadena, 1979.

Contemporary Art in Southern California, The High Museum of Art, Atlanta, Georgia, 1980.

Selected Bibliography

Jules Langsner, "Los Angeles: Moses in Abstraction," *Art News,* vol. 58, no. 4, summer 1959, p. 59.

Regina Bogat, "Fifty California Artists," *Artforum,* vol. 1, no. 7, November 1962, pp. 23–26.

Lloyd Goodrich and George Culler, *Fifty California Artists,* Whitney Museum of American Art, New York, 1962.

Donald Factor, "Assemblage," *Artforum,* vol. 2, no. 12, summer 1964, pp. 38–41.

Fidel A. Danieli, "Los Angeles," *Artforum,* vol. 3, no. 1, September 1964, pp. 16–18.

Henry T. Hopkins, "West Coast Style: Ed Moses," *Art Voices,* vol. 5, no. 4, fall 1966, p. 69.

James Monte, *Late Fifties at the Ferus,* Los Angeles County Museum of Art, 1968.

Jane Livingston, "Two Generations in Los Angeles," *Art in America,* vol. 57, no. 1, January 1969, pp. 92–97.

Thomas Garver, "Los Angeles: Mizuno," *Artforum,* vol. 7, no. 10, summer 1969, p. 67.

Peter Plagens, "Los Angeles: Edward Moses, Mizuno Gallery," *Artforum,* vol. 9, no. 1, September 1970, p. 82.

Melinda Terbell, "Los Angeles: Mizuno Gallery," *Arts,* vol. 45, no. 2, November 1970, p. 53.

Peter Plagens, "West Coast Blues," *Artforum,* vol. 9, no. 6, February 1971, pp. 52–57.

Melinda Terbell, "Edward Moses: Mizuno Gallery, Los Angeles," *Arts,* vol. 45, no. 4, February 1971, p. 45.

Helene Winer, *Ed Moses: Some Early Work, Some Recent Work and Some Work in Progress,* Pomona College Gallery, Claremont, California, 1971.

Peter Plagens, "Ed Moses: The Problem of Regionalism," *Artforum,* vol. 10, no. 7, March 1972, pp. 83–85.

Peter Plagens, "From School Painting to a School of Painting in Los Angeles," *Art in America,* vol. 61, no. 2, March/April 1973, pp. 36–41.

Paul Stitelman, "Notes on the Absorption of the Avant-Garde into the Culture," *Arts Magazine,* vol. 47, no. 7, May/June 1973, p. 55.

John Loring, "Print as Surface," *Arts Magazine,* vol. 48, no. 1, September–October 1973, p. 48.

Jeremy Gilbert-Rolfe, "Ed Moses, André Emmerich Gallery Uptown," *Artforum,* vol. 12, no. 9, May 1974, p. 69.

Peter Plagens, *Sunshine Muse: Contemporary Art on the West Coast,* New York, 1974.

Joseph Masheck, "Ed Moses and the Problem of 'Western' Tradition," *Arts Magazine,* vol. 50, no. 4, December 1975, pp. 56–61.

Melinda Wortz, "Field Flowers, Plexiglas Horizons," *Art News,* vol. 75, no. 8, October 1976, p. 94.

Nancy Marmer, "Ed Moses' Absolutist Abstractions," *Art in America,* vol. 64, no. 6, November–December 1976, pp. 94–95.

Stephanie Barron, *Ed Moses: New Paintings,* Los Angeles County Museum of Art, 1976.

Henry T. Hopkins, *Painting and Sculpture in California: The Modern Era,* San Francisco Museum of Modern Art, 1976.

Joseph Masheck, *Ed Moses: Drawings 1958–1976,* The Frederick S. Wight Art Gallery, University of California, Los Angeles, 1976.

Betty Turnbull, *The Last Time I Saw Ferus: 1957–1966,* Newport Harbor Art Museum, Newport Beach, California, 1976.

Susan C. Larsen, "Los Angeles—Inside Jobs," *Art News,* vol. 77, no. 1, January 1978, p. 110.

David S. Rubin, "Ed Moses," *Arts Magazine,* vol. 52, no. 5, January 1978, p. 12.

Jeff Perrone, "Ed Moses at Sidney Janis," *Artforum,* vol. 17, no. 10, summer 1979, p. 70.

"Edward Moses," interview by Sheldon Figoten, Archives of American Art, Smithsonian Institution, Washington, D.C., July 1980 (restricted access).

Clark V. Poling, *Contemporary Art in Southern California,* The High Museum of Art, Atlanta, Georgia, 1980.

Bruce Nauman

Born in Fort Wayne, Indiana, 1941; resident of Pasadena, 1969–78; lives in Pecos, New Mexico.
B.S., University of Wisconsin, Madison, 1960–64; M.A., University of California, Davis, 1964–66.

Selected One-Man Exhibitions

Nicholas Wilder Gallery, Los Angeles, 1966, 1969, 1970, 1973, 1977.

Leo Castelli Gallery, New York, 1968, 1969, 1971, 1973, 1975, 1976, 1978, 1980.

Galerie Konrad Fischer, Düsseldorf, West Germany, 1968, 1970, 1971, 1974, 1975, 1978.

Art Gallery, Sacramento State College, California, 1968.

Galerie Ileana Sonnabend, Paris, 1969, 1971.

20–20 Gallery, London, Ontario, Canada, 1969.

Galleria Sperone, Turin, Italy, 1970.

Art Gallery, San Jose State College, California, 1970.

Galerie Ricke, Cologne, West Germany, 1970.

Gallery Reese Palley, San Francisco, 1970.

Galerie Bischofberger, Zurich, Switzerland, 1971.

Helman Gallery, St. Louis, Missouri, 1971.

Betty Gold Fine Modern Prints, Los Angeles, 1971.

Ace Gallery, Vancouver, British Columbia, 1971, 1974, 1976.

Galleria Françoise Lambert, Milan, Italy, 1971.

Projection Gallery, Cologne, West Germany, 1972.

Los Angeles County Museum of Art, 1972–73 (retrospective; traveled to Whitney Museum of American Art, New York; Kunsthalle Bern, Switzerland; Städtische Kunsthalle Düsseldorf, West Germany; Stedelijk van Abbemuseum, Eindhoven, The Netherlands; Palazzo Reale, Milan, Italy; Contemporary Arts Museum, Houston, Texas; San Francisco Museum of Art).

Fine Arts Gallery, University of California, Irvine, 1973.

Cirrus Gallery, Los Angeles, 1974.

Art in Progress, Munich, West Germany, 1974.

Wide White Space Gallery, Antwerp, Belgium, 1974.

Santa Ana College Art Gallery, California, 1974.

Gemini G.E.L., Los Angeles, 1975.

Albright-Knox Art Gallery, Buffalo, New York, 1975.

Art Gallery, University of Nevada, Las Vegas, 1976.

Ace Gallery, Los Angeles, 1976.

Sperone Westwater Fischer, New York, 1976.

Sonnabend Gallery, New York, 1976.

Bruna Soletti, Milan, Italy, 1977.

Minneapolis College of Art and Design, Minnesota, 1978.

InK, Zurich, Switzerland, 1978.

Art Gallery, California State University, San Diego, 1978.

Galerie Schmela, Düsseldorf, West Germany, 1979.

Marianne Deson Gallery, Chicago, 1979.

Portland Center for the Visual Arts, Oregon, 1979.

Hester van Royen Gallery, London, 1979.

Hill's Gallery of Contemporary Art, Santa Fe, New Mexico, 1980.

Selected Group Exhibitions

New Directions, San Francisco Museum of Art, California, 1966.

American Sculpture of the Sixties, Los Angeles County Museum of Art, 1967.

Documenta 4, Kassel, West Germany, 1968.

Three Young Americans, Allen Memorial Art Museum, Oberlin, Ohio, 1968.

31st Annual Exhibition of Contemporary American Painting, Corcoran Gallery of Art, Washington, D.C., 1969.

Square Pegs in Round Holes, Stedelijk Museum, Amsterdam, 1969.

When Attitude Becomes Form, Kunsthalle Bern, Switzerland, 1969.

Anti-Illusion: Procedures/Materials, Whitney Museum of American Art, New York, 1969.

Nine Young Artists, Theodoron Awards, The Solomon R. Guggenheim Museum, New York, 1969.

Kompas 4: West Coast USA, Stedelijk van Abbemuseum, Eindhoven, The Netherlands, 1969.

Art by Telephone, Museum of Contemporary Art, Chicago, 1969.

Contemporary American Drawings, Fort Worth Art Center Museum, Texas, 1969.

Conceptual Art and Conceptual Aspects, New York Cultural Center, 1970.

N Dimensional Space, Finch College Art Museum, New York, 1970.

American Art since 1960, Princeton University Art Museum, New Jersey, 1970.

Information, The Museum of Modern Art, New York, 1970.

Holograms and Lasers, Museum of Contemporary Art, Chicago, 1970.

Against Order: Chance and Art, Institute of Contemporary Art of the University of Pennsylvania, Philadelphia, 1970.

1970 Annual Exhibition: Sculpture, Whitney Museum of American Art, New York; *1977 Biennial Exhibition.*

Body, New York University, 1971.

Projected Art: Artists at Work, Finch College Museum of Art, New York, 1971.

Air, Stedelijk Museum, Amsterdam, 1971.

Prospect 71, Städtische Kunsthalle Düsseldorf, West Germany, 1971.

11 Los Angeles Artists, Hayward Gallery, London, 1971 (traveled to Musées Royaux des Beaux-Arts, Brussels; Akademie der Künste, Berlin, West Germany).

Modern Painting, Drawing, and Sculpture Collected by Louise and Joseph Pulitzer, Fogg Art Museum, Cambridge, Massachusetts, 1971.

Diagrams and Drawings, Kroller-Muller, Otterloo, The Netherlands, 1972.

USA West Coast, Kunstverein, Hamburg, West Germany, 1972 (traveled to Kunstverein, Hannover; Kölnischer Kunstverein, Cologne; Württembergisher Kunstverein, Stuttgart).

American Art–Third Quarter Century, The Seattle Art Museum, Washington, 1973.

Idea and Image in Recent Art, The Art Institute of Chicago, 1974.

Art Now 74, The John F. Kennedy Center for the Performing Arts, Washington, D.C., 1974.

Painting and Sculpture Today: 1974, Indianapolis Museum of Art, Indiana (traveled to The Contemporary Art Center, The Taft Museum, Cincinnati, Ohio).

Prints from Gemini G.E.L., Walker Art Center, Minneapolis, Minnesota, 1974.

Art/Voir, Centre National d'Art Contemporain, Paris, 1974.

Light/Sculpture, William Hayes Ackland Memorial Art Center, University of North Carolina, Chapel Hill, 1975.

Menace, Museum of Contemporary Art, Chicago, 1975.

Zeichnungen 3, USA, Städtiches Museum Leverkusen, West Germany, 1975.

Language and Structure in North America, Kensington Art Association Gallery, Toronto, 1975.

Body Works, Museum of Contemporary Art, Chicago, 1975.

Sculpture, American Directions 1945–1975, National Collection of Fine Arts, Smithsonian Institution, Washington, D.C., 1975.

Drawing Now, The Museum of Modern Art, New York, 1975.

Autogeography, Downtown Branch, Whitney Museum of American Art, New York, 1976.

72nd American Exhibition of Painting and Sculpture, The Art Institute of Chicago, 1976; *73rd American Exhibition,* 1979.

200 Years of American Sculpture, Whitney Museum of American Art, New York, 1976.

Rooms P.S. 1, P.S. 1, Long Island City, New York, 1976.

American Artists: A New Decade, The Detroit Institute of Arts, Michigan, 1976.

The Artist and the Photograph, Israel Museum, Jerusalem, 1976.

Words at Liberty, Museum of Contemporary Art, Chicago, 1977.

Painting and Sculpture in California: The Modern Era, San Francisco Museum of Modern Art, 1976 (traveled to National Collection of Fine Arts, Smithsonian Institution, Washington, D.C.).

A View of a Decade, Museum of Contemporary Art, Chicago, 1977.

Drawings for Outdoor Sculpture: 1946–1977, John Weber Gallery, New York, 1977.

Made by Sculptors, Stedelijk Museum, Amsterdam, 1978.

The Broadening of the Concept of Reality in the Art of the '60s and '70s, Museum Haus Lange, Krefeld, West Germany, 1979.

Great Big Drawing Show, Institute for Art and Urban Resources, P.S. 1, Long Island City, New York, 1979.

Artists and Books: The Literal Use of Time, Ulrich Museum of Art, Wichita State University, Kansas, 1979.

The New American Filmmakers Series, Whitney Museum of American Art, New York, 1980.

Contemporary Art in Southern California, The High Museum of Art, Atlanta, Georgia, 1980.

Selected Bibliography

Lucy R. Lippard, "Eccentric Abstraction," *Art International,* vol. 10, no. 9, November 1966, pp. 28, 34–40.

Fidel A. Danieli, "The Art of Bruce Nauman," *Artforum,* vol. 6, no. 4, December 1967, pp. 15–19.

Maurice Tuchman, *American Sculpture of the Sixties,* Los Angeles County Museum of Art, 1967.

John Perreault, "Art," *The Village Voice,* February 8, 1968.

Robert Pincus-Witten, "New York," *Artforum,* vol. 6, no. 8, April 1968, pp. 63–65.

Rachel Griffin and Henry T. Hopkins, *The West Coast Now,* Portland Art Museum, Oregon, 1968.

Ellen H. Johnson and Athena T. Spear, *Three Young Americans,* Allen Memorial Art Museum, Oberlin, Ohio, 1968.

David Whitney, *Bruce Nauman,* Leo Castelli Gallery, New York, 1968.

Max Kozloff, "9 in a Warehouse," *Artforum,* vol. 7, no. 6, February 1969, pp. 38–42.

Scott Burton, "Time on Their Hands," *Art News,* vol. 68, no. 4, summer 1969, pp. 40–43.

James Harithas, *31st Biennial Exhibition of Contemporary American Painting,* Corcoran Gallery of Art, Washington, D.C., 1969.

Jean Leering, *Kompas 4: West Coast USA,* Stedelijk van Abbemuseum, Eindhoven, The Netherlands, 1969.

Thomas M. Messer and Diane Waldman, *Nine Young Artists,* The Solomon R. Guggenheim Museum, New York, 1969.

James Monte and Marcia Tucker, *Anti-Illusion: Materials/Procedures,* Whitney Museum of American Art, New York, 1969.

Peter Plagens, *Contemporary American Drawings,* Fort Worth Art Center Museum, Texas, 1969.

Harold Szeeman, Scott Burton, Gregoire Muller, and Tommaso Trini, *Attitude Becomes Form,* Kunsthalle Bern, Switzerland, 1969.

Germano Celant, "Bruce Nauman," *Casabella 345,* vol. 34, February 1970, pp. 38–41.

Willoughby Sharp, "Body Works," *Avalanche,* no. 1, fall 1970, pp. 14–17.

Marcia Tucker, "PheNAUMANology," *Artforum,* vol. 9, no. 4, December 1970, pp. 38–44.

Donald Karshan, *Conceptual Art and Conceptual Aspects,* New York Cultural Center, New York, 1970.

Kynaston L. McShine, *Information,* The Museum of Modern Art, New York, 1970.

Robert Pincus-Witten, *Against Order: Chance and Art,* Institute of Contemporary Art of the University of Pennsylvania, Philadelphia, 1970.

Elayne H. Varian, *N Dimensional Space,* Finch College Art Museum, New York, 1970.

Cindy Nemser, "Subject-Object Body Art," *Arts Magazine,* vol. 46, no. 1, September–October 1971, p. 38.

Emily S. Rauh, "Bruce Nauman," *Modern Painting, Drawing, and Sculpture Collected by Louise and Joseph Pulitzer,* Fogg Art Museum, Cambridge, Massachusetts, 1971.

Maurice Tuchman and Jane Livingston, *11 Los Angeles Artists,* Hayward Gallery, London, 1971.

Robert Pincus-Witten, "Bruce Nauman: Another Kind of Reasoning," *Artforum,* vol. 10, no. 6, February 1972, pp. 30–37.

Bruce Kurtz, "Interview with Giuseppe Panza di Biumo," *Arts Magazine,* vol. 46, no. 5, March 1972, pp. 40–43.

Carter Ratcliff, "Adversary Spaces," *Artforum,* vol. 11, no. 2, October 1972, pp. 40–44.

Jane Livingston and Marcia Tucker, *Bruce Nauman: Work from 1965 to 1972,* Los Angeles County Museum of Art, 1972.

Helmut Heissenbüttel and Helene Winer, *USA West Coast,* Kunstverein, Hamburg, West Germany, 1972.

Peter Plagens, "Roughly Ordered Thoughts on the Occasion of the Bruce Nauman Retrospective in Los Angeles," *Artforum,* vol. 11, no. 7, March 1973, pp. 57–59.

Paul Stitelman, "Bruce Nauman at the Whitney Museum," *Arts Magazine,* vol. 47, no. 7, May 1973, pp. 54–55.

Kim Levin, "Bruce Nauman: Stretching the Truth," *Opus International,* no. 46, September 1973, pp. 44–46.

Hein Reedijk, "Bruce Nauman: Kunst voor navelstaarders?" *Museumjournal,* vol. 18, no. 4, September 1973, pp. 154 59.

Jürgen Harten, "T for Technics, B for Body," *Art and Artists,* vol. 8, no. 8, November 1973, pp. 28–33.

Barbara Catoir, "Uber den subjektivismus bei Bruce Nauman," *Kunstwerk,* vol. 26, no. 6, November 1973, pp. 3–12.

Jean Marc Poinsot, "Bruce Nauman: La problématique du nonsens," *Art Press,* no. 10, March–April 1974, pp. 12–15.

Philip Larson, "Words in Print," *Print Collector's Newsletter,* vol. 5, no. 3, July–August 1974, pp. 53–56.

M. Schneckenburger, "Wahrnehmung, Dingfest Gemacht: ein Problemkreis um Chuck Close und Bruce Nauman in der Ausstellung 'Projekt 74,' " *Museen in Köln,* vol. 13, no. 8, August 1974, pp. 262–63.

Philip Larson, *Prints from Gemini G.E.L.: Johns, Kelly, Lichtenstein, Motherwell, Nauman, Rauschenberg, Serra, Stella,* Walker Art Center, Minneapolis, Minnesota, 1974.

François Pluchart, "L'art corporel," *Artitudes International,* vol. 18, no. 20, January–March 1975, pp. 49–96.

Jan Butterfield, "Bruce Nauman: the Center of Yourself," *Arts,* vol. 49, no. 6, February 1975, pp. 53–55.

Tom Marioni, "Out Front," *Vision,* no. 1, September 1975, pp. 8–11.

Bruce Nauman, "False Silences," *Vision,* no. 1, September 1975, pp. 44–45.

R. Goldberg, "Space as Praxis," *Studio International,* vol. 190, no. 977, September–October 1975, pp. 130–35.

N. Calas, *Mirrors of the Mind,* Multiples, Inc., Castelli Graphics, 1975.

Trudy Zandee, "Kunstkritiek en de veelzijde lijfelijkheid van Body Art," *Museumjournal,* vol. 21, no. 1, February 1976, pp. 97–106.

Carter Ratcliff, "Notes on Small Sculpture," *Artforum,* vol. 14, no. 8, April 1976, pp. 35–42.

I. Wiegand, "Video Shock," *Print,* vol. 30, no. 4, July–August 1976, pp. 63–69.

A. McIntyre, "L'Art corporel (Body Art)," *Art and Australia,* vol. 14, no. 1, July–September 1976, pp. 74–78.

M. Bloem, "La photographie, lieu d'une expérience artistique nouvelle," *Art Actuel: Skira Annuel,* vol. 2, 1976, pp. 147-A.

Germano Celant, *Senza titolo 1974,* Rome, 1976.

Jeff Perrone, "Reviews," *Artforum,* vol. 15, no. 5, January 1977, pp. 58–62.

Jeff Perrone, "Words: When Art Takes a Rest," *Artforum,* vol. 15, no. 10, summer 1977, p. 37.

Robert Pincus-Witten, *Postminimalism,* New York, 1977.

Marc Treib, "Architecture Versus Architecture: Is an Image a Reality?" *Architectural Association Quarterly,* vol. 9, no. 4, 1977, pp. 3–14.

Eric Cameron, "On Painting and Video (Upside Down)," *Parachute,* summer 1978, pp. 14–17.

Jürgen Schilling, "Zur Entwicklungsgeschichte der Performance," *Heute Kunst,* no. 25, March–April 1979, pp. 22–23.

"Bruce Nauman," interview by Michelle D. De Angelus, Archives of American Art, Smithsonian Institution, Washington, D.C., May 1980.

Kenneth Price

Born in Los Angeles, 1935; moved to Taos, New Mexico, 1971; lives in Taos.

Studied at Chouinard Art Institute, Los Angeles, 1956; Los Angeles City College, 1956; B.F.A., University of Southern California, 1956; M.F.A., State University of New York, Alfred, 1959.

Selected One-Man Exhibitions

Ferus Gallery, Los Angeles, 1960, 1961, 1964.

Kasmin Gallery, London, 1968, 1970.

Riko Mizuno Gallery, Los Angeles, 1969, 1971.

Whitney Museum of American Art, New York, 1969.

Gemini G.E.L., Los Angeles, 1970, 1972.

David Whitney Gallery, New York, 1971.

Galerie Neuendorf, Cologne, West Germany, 1971.

Galerie Neuendorf, Hamburg, West Germany, 1973.

Nicholas Wilder Gallery, Los Angeles, 1973.

Felicity Samuel Gallery, London, 1974.

Willard Gallery, New York, 1974, 1979.

Ronald Greenberg Gallery, St. Louis, Missouri, 1976.

James Corcoran Gallery, Los Angeles, 1976, 1980.

Los Angeles County Museum of Art, 1978.

Gallery of Contemporary Art, Taos, New Mexico, 1978.

Texas Gallery, Houston, 1979, 1980.

Hansen Fuller Goldeen Gallery, San Francisco, 1979.

Contemporary Arts Museum, Houston, Texas, 1980.

Visual Arts Museum, New York, 1980.

Selected Group Exhibitions

Fifty California Artists, Whitney Museum of American Art, New York, 1962.

Sculpture of California, Oakland Art Museum, California, 1963.

Boxes, Dwan Gallery, Los Angeles, 1964.

New American Sculpture, Pasadena Art Museum, California, 1964.

Robert Irwin/Kenneth Price, Los Angeles County Museum of Art, 1966.

Ten from Los Angeles, Seattle Art Museum, Washington, 1966.

Five Los Angeles Sculptors and Sculptors' Drawings, University of California, Irvine, 1966.

Abstract Expressionist Ceramics, University of California, Irvine, 1966.

American Sculpture of the Sixties, Los Angeles County Museum of Art, 1967.

Late Fifties at the Ferus, Los Angeles County Museum of Art, 1968.

Kompas 4: West Coast USA, Stedelijk van Abbemuseum, Eindhoven, The Netherlands, 1969.

Contemporary American Drawings, Fort Worth Art Center Museum, Texas, 1969.

West Coast 1945–1969, Pasadena Art Museum, California, 1969 (traveled to City Art Museum of St. Louis, Missouri; Art Gallery of Ontario, Toronto; Fort Worth Art Center Museum, Texas).

Graphics: Six West Coast Artists, Galleria Milano, Italy, 1969.

Bengston/Price, Janie C. Lee Gallery, Dallas, Texas, 1970.

Contemporary American Sculpture, Whitney Museum of American Art, New York, 1970.

A Decade of California Color, Pace Gallery, New York, 1970.

Contemporary Ceramic Art, National Museum of Modern Art, Kyoto, Japan, 1971.

11 Los Angeles Artists, Hayward Gallery, London, 1971 (traveled to Musées Royaux des Beaux-Arts, Brussels; Akademie der Künste, Berlin, West Germany).

USA West Coast, Kunstverein, Hamburg, West Germany, 1972 (traveled to Kunstverein, Hannover; Kölnischer Kunstverein, Cologne; Württembergisher Kunstverein, Stuttgart).

Contemporary American Art: Los Angeles, Fort Worth Art Center Museum, Texas, 1972.

Joe Goode, Kenneth Price, Edward Ruscha, Museum Boymans-van Beuningen, Rotterdam, The Netherlands, 1972.

Clay, Whitney Museum of American Art, New York, 1974.

Sculpture: American Directions, 1945–1975, National Collection of Fine Arts, Smithsonian Inst., Washington, D.C., 1975.

200 Years of American Sculpture, Whitney Museum of American Art, New York, 1976.

Painting and Sculpture in California: The Modern Era, San Francisco Museum of Modern Art, 1976 (traveled to National Collection of Fine Arts, Smithsonian Institution, Washington, D.C.).

The Last Time I Saw Ferus: 1957–1966, Newport Harbor Art Museum, Newport Beach, California, 1976.

Nine West Coast Clay Sculptors, Everson Museum of Art, Syracuse, New York, 1978.

One Hundred Years of American Ceramics, Everson Museum of Art, Syracuse, New York, 1979.

Contemporary Sculpture, The Museum of Modern Art, New York, 1979.

Directions, Hirshhorn Museum and Sculpture Garden, Washington, D.C., 1979.

West Coast Clay, Stedelijk Museum, Amsterdam, 1979.

One Space/Three Visions, Albuquerque Museum, New Mexico, 1979.

The Vessel, Delahunty Gallery, Dallas, Texas, 1980.

1981 Biennial Exhibition, Whitney Museum of American Art, New York.

Selected Bibliography

Jules Langsner, "Painting and Sculpture: the Los Angeles Season," *Craft Horizons*, vol. 22, no. 41, July/August 1962, pp. 40–41.

John Coplans, "Los Angeles: The Scene," *Art News*, vol. 64, no. 57, March 1965, p. 28.

John Coplans, *Ten from Los Angeles*, Seattle Art Museum, Washington, 1966.

John Coplans, *Abstract Expressionist Ceramics*, University of California, Irvine, 1966.

Lucy R. Lippard, *Robert Irwin/Kenneth Price*, Los Angeles County Museum of Art, 1966.

David Thompson, "London Commentary: Kenneth Price at Kasmin," *Studio International*, vol. 175, no. 899, April 1968, pp. 199–200.

Jane Livingston, "Two Generations in Los Angeles," *Art in America*, vol. 57, no. 1, January/February 1969, pp. 92–97.

Dore Ashton, "New York Commentary," *Studio International*, vol. 178, no. 177, November 1969, pp. 176–77.

Jean Leering, *Kompas 4: West Coast USA*, Stedelijk van Abbemuseum, Eindhoven, The Netherlands, 1969.

Maurice Tuchman and Jane Livingston, *11 Los Angeles Artists*, Hayward Gallery, London, 1971.

Carter Ratcliff, "Notes on Small Sculpture," *Artforum*, vol. 14, no. 38, April 1976, pp. 35–42.

Sandy Ballatore, "California Clay Rush," *Art in America*, vol. 64, no. 84, July/August 1976, pp. 84–88.

Betty Turnbull, *The Last Time I Saw Ferus: 1957–1966*, Newport Harbor Art Museum, Newport Beach, California, 1976.

Maurice Tuchman, *Ken Price: Happy's Curios*, Los Angeles County Museum of Art, 1978.

Addison Parks, "Ken Price," *Arts Magazine*, vol. 54, no. 5, January 1980, p. 40.

Joan Simon, "An Interview with Ken Price," *Art in America*, vol. 68, no. 1, January 1980, pp. 98–104.

"Kenneth Price," interview by Michele D. De Angelus, Archives of American Art, Smithsonian Institution, Washington, D.C., May 1980.

Edward Ruscha

Born in Omaha, Nebraska, 1937; moved to Los Angeles, 1956; lives in Los Angeles. Attended Chouinard Art Institute, Los Angeles, 1956–60.

Selected One-Man Exhibitions

Ferus Gallery, Los Angeles, 1963, 1964, 1965.

Alexander Iolas Gallery, New York, 1967, 1970.

Irving Blum Gallery, Los Angeles, 1968, 1969.

Rudolf Zwirner, Cologne, West Germany, 1968.

Alexander Iolas Gallery, Paris, 1970.

Heiner Friedrich, Munich, West Germany, 1970.

Nigel Greenwood, London, 1970, 1973.

University of California, Santa Cruz, 1972.

Janie C. Lee Gallery, Dallas, Texas, 1972.

Corcoran & Corcoran Gallery, Miami, Florida, 1972.

Minneapolis Institute of Arts, Minnesota, 1972.

Leo Castelli Gallery, New York, 1973, 1974, 1980.

University of California, San Diego, 1973.

Galleria Françoise Lambert, Milan, Italy, 1973, 1974.

John Berggruen Gallery, San Francisco, 1973.

Ace Gallery, Los Angeles, 1973, 1975, 1977.

The Texas Gallery, Houston, 1974, 1979.

H. Peter Findlay/Works of Art, New York, 1974.

Galerie Ricke, Cologne, West Germany, 1975, 1978.

Sable-Castelli Gallery Ltd., Toronto, 1975, 1976.

University of North Dakota, Grand Forks, 1975.

The Arts Council of Great Britain (traveled throughout Great Britain), 1975–76.

Ace Gallery, Vancouver, British Columbia, 1976.

Los Angeles Institute of Contemporary Art, 1976.

Wadsworth Athenaeum, Hartford, Connecticut, 1976.

Stedelijk Museum, Amsterdam, 1976.

Albright-Knox Art Gallery, Buffalo, New York, 1976.

Institute of Contemporary Art, London, 1976.

University of Lethbridge, Alberta, Saskatchewan, 1977.

Fort Worth Art Museum, Texas, 1977.

MTL Gallery, Brussels, 1978.

Rudiger Schottle, Munich, West Germany, 1978.

University of Redlands, California, 1978.

Auckland City Art Gallery, New Zealand, 1978.

Getler/Pall, New York, 1978.

Richard Hines Gallery, Seattle, Washington, 1979.

InK, Zurich, Switzerland, 1979.

Portland Center for the Visual Arts, Oregon, 1980.

Arco Center for Visual Art, Los Angeles, 1981.

Selected Group Exhibitions

New Painting of Common Objects, Pasadena Art Museum, California, 1962.

Six More, Los Angeles County Museum of Art, 1963.

Pop Art USA, Oakland Art Museum, California, 1963.

Word and Image, The Solomon R. Guggenheim Museum, New York, 1965.

Pop Art and the American Tradition, Milwaukee Art Center, Wisconsin, 1965.

5 at Pace, Pace Gallery, New York, 1965.

Ten from Los Angeles, Seattle Art Museum, Washington, 1966.

Los Angeles Now, Robert Fraser Gallery, London, 1966.

IX Bienal de São Paulo, Brazil, 1967.

V Paris Biennale, Musée d'Art Moderne de la Ville de Paris, 1967.

Ed Ruscha–Joe Goode, The Fine Arts Patrons of Newport Harbor, Balboa Pavilion Gallery, California, 1968.

40 Now California Painters, Tampa Bay Art Center, Tampa, Florida, 1968.

West Coast Now, Portland Art Museum, Oregon, 1968.

Three Modern Masters: Billy Al Bengston, Edward Ruscha, Frank Lloyd Wright, Gallery Reese Palley, San Francisco, 1969.

Kompas 4: West Coast USA, Stedelijk van Abbemuseum, Eindhoven, The Netherlands, 1969.

Pop Art Redefined, Hayward Gallery, London, 1969.

West Coast 1945–1969, Pasadena Art Museum, California, 1969 (traveled to City Art Museum of St. Louis, Missouri; Art Gallery of Ontario, Toronto; Fort Worth Art Center Museum, Texas).

Graphics: Six West Coast Artists, Galleria Milano, Italy, 1969.

Superlimited: Books, Boxes, and Things, The Jewish Museum, New York, 1969.

The Highway, Institute of Contemporary Art of the University of Pennsylvania, Philadelphia, 1970.

The Word as Image, The Jewish Museum, New York, 1970.

Information, The Museum of Modern Art, New York, 1970.

Venice Biennale, Italy, 1970.

Looking West 1970, Joslyn Art Museum, Omaha, Nebraska, 1970.

A Decade of California Color, Pace Gallery, New York, 1970.

32nd Biennial Exhibition of Contemporary American Painting, Corcoran Gallery of Art, Washington, D.C., 1971.

Made in California, Grunwald Center for the Graphic Arts, University of California, Los Angeles, 1971.

Continuing Surrealism, La Jolla Museum of Contemporary Art, California, 1971.

11 Los Angeles Artists, Hayward Gallery, London, 1971 (traveled to Musées Royaux des Beaux-Arts, Brussels; Akademie der Künste, Berlin, West Germany).

Joe Goode, Kenneth Price en Edward Ruscha: Grafiek en Boeken, Museum Boymans-van Beuningen, Rotterdam, The Netherlands, 1972.

Artists' Books, Moore College of Art, Philadelphia, 1973.

American Drawing, 1970–1973, Yale University Art Gallery, New Haven, Connecticut, 1973.

American Pop Art, Whitney Museum of American Art, New York, 1974.

California Images, Whitney Museum of American Art, New York, 1976.

The Last Time I Saw Ferus, 1957–1966, Newport Harbor Art Museum, Newport Beach, California, 1976.

The Artist and the Photograph, Israel Museum, Jerusalem, 1976.

Painting and Sculpture in California: The Modern Era, San Francisco Museum of Modern Art, San Francisco, 1976 (traveled to National Collection of Fine Arts, Smithsonian Institution, Washington, D.C.).

Thirty Years of American Printmaking, The Brooklyn Museum, New York, 1976.

Ed Ruscha, Joe Goode/New Drawings, Laguna Gloria Art Museum, Austin, Texas, 1977.

The Dada/Surrealist Heritage, Sterling and Francine Clark Art Institute, Williamstown, Massachusetts, 1977.

Bookworks, The Museum of Modern Art, New York, 1977.

Words Words, Museum Bochum, West Germany, 1978.

Mirrors and Windows: American Photography since 1960, The Museum of Modern Art, New York, 1978.

American Painting of the 1970s, Albright-Knox Art Gallery, Buffalo, New York, 1978.

Graphicstudio U.S.F., The Brooklyn Museum, New York, 1978.

73rd American Exhibition of Painting and Sculpture, The Art Institute of Chicago, 1979.

The Decade in Review: Selections from the 1970s, Whitney Museum of American Art, New York, 1979.

Reflections of Realism, Albuquerque Museum, New Mexico, 1979.

Artists and Books: The Literal Use of Time, Edwin A. Ulrich Museum of Art, Wichita State University, Kansas, 1979.

Contemporary Art in Southern California, The High Museum of Art, Atlanta, Georgia, 1980.

Selected Bibliography

John Coplans, "The New Painting of Common Objects," *Artforum*, vol. 1, no. 6, December 1962, pp. 26–29.

Lawrence Alloway, *Six More*, Los Angeles County Museum of Art, 1963.

John Coplans, *Pop Art USA*, Oakland Art Museum, California, 1963.

Philip Leider, "Revealing Juxtapositions," *Frontier*, vol. 16, no. 2, December 1964, pp. 25–26.

John Coplans, "An Interview with Edward Ruscha," *Artforum*, vol. 3, no. 5, February 1965, pp. 24–25.

John Coplans, *Ten from Los Angeles*, Seattle Art Museum, Washington, 1966.

Lucy R. Lippard, *Pop Art*, New York, 1966.

Christopher Finch, "Scanning the Strip," *Art and Artists*, vol. 1, no. 10, January 1967, p. 67.

Lawrence Alloway, "Hi-Way Culture: Man at the Wheel," *Arts Magazine*, vol. 41, no. 1, February 1967, pp. 28–33.

Henry T. Hopkins, *Joe Goode and Edward Ruscha*, The Fine Arts Patrons of Newport Harbor, Balboa Pavilion Gallery, California, 1968.

Carol Lynsley, *Three Modern Masters: Edward Ruscha, Billy Al Bengston, Frank Lloyd Wright*, Gallery Reese Palley, San Francisco, 1969.

John Russell and Suzi Gablik, *Pop Art Redefined*, London, 1969.

Christopher Fox, "Ed Ruscha Discusses His Latest Work with Christopher Fox," *Studio International*, vol. 180, no. 923, May–June 1970, p. 281, 287.

Robert Venturi and Denise Scott Brown, *The Highway*, Institute of Contemporary Art of the University of Pennsylvania, Philadelphia, 1970.

David Bourdon, "A Heap of Words about Ed Ruscha," *Art International*, vol. 15, no. 9, November 1971, p. 25.

Robert Colaciello, "Art: Interview with Ed Ruscha," *Interview*, no. 20, March 1972, p. 42.

David Bourdon, "Ruscha as Publisher (or All Booked Up)," *Art News*, vol. 71, no. 2, April 1972, pp. 32–36.

Ursula Meyer, *Conceptual Art*, New York, 1972.

Eleanor Antin, "Reading Ruscha," *Art in America*, vol. 61, no. 6, November–December 1973, pp. 64–71.

Carl R. Baldwin, "On the Nature of Pop," *Artforum*, vol. 12, no. 10, June 1974, pp. 34–37.

Lawrence Alloway, *American Pop Art*, Whitney Museum of American Art, 1974.

Reyner Banham, *Edward Ruscha Prints and Publications 1962–1974*, The Arts Council of Great Britain, 1975–76.

Nancy Foote, "The Anti-Photographers," *Artforum*, vol. 15, no. 1, September 1976, pp. 46–54.

Linda L. Cathcart, *Paintings, Drawings, and Other Work by Edward Ruscha*, Albright-Knox Art Gallery, Buffalo, New York, 1976.

Hugh M. Davies, *Critical Perspectives in American Art*, University of Massachusetts, Amherst, 1976.

Howardena Pindell, *Edward Ruscha* (interview), Stedelijk Museum, Amsterdam, 1976.

Diane Spodarek, "Feature Interview: Edward Ruscha," *Detroit Artists Monthly*, vol. 2, no. 4, April 1977, pp. 1–5.

Jeff Perrone, "'Words': When Art Takes a Rest," *Artforum*, vol. 15, no. 10, summer 1977, p. 36.

Sam Hunter, *The Dada/Surrealist Heritage*, Sterling and Francine Clark Art Institute, Williamstown, Massachusetts, 1977.

Jonathan Crary, "Edward Ruscha's 'Real Estate Opportunities,'" *Arts Magazine*, vol. 52, no. 5, January 1978, pp. 119–21.

Gene Baro, *Graphicstudio U.S.F.*, The Brooklyn Museum, New York, 1978.

Andrew Bogle, *Graphic Works by Edward Ruscha*, Auckland City Art Gallery, New Zealand, 1978.

Trina Mitchum, "A Conversation with Ed Ruscha," *Journal*, Los Angeles Institute of Contemporary Art, no. 21, January–February 1979, pp. 21–24.

Susan B. Laufer, "Ruscha's Books and Seriality," *L=A=N=G=U=A=G=E*, no. 7, March 1979.

Judith L. Dunham, "Ed Ruscha's Paintings," *Artweek*, vol. 10, no. 16, April 1979, p. 4.

Edward Ruscha, *Guacamole Airlines and Other Drawings*, New York, 1980.

"Ed Ruscha on V-Various S-Subjects" (interview), *Stuff Magazine*, no. 24, June 1980, pp. 20–21.

"Edward Ruscha," interview by Paul Karlstrom, Archives of American Art, Smithsonian Institution, Washington, D.C., October 1980.

Peter Voulkos

Born in Bozeman, Montana, 1924; resident of Los Angeles, 1954–59; lives in Berkeley, California.
B.S., Montana State College, Bozeman, 1951; M.F.A., California College of Arts and Crafts, Oakland, 1952.

Selected One-Man Exhibitions

America House, New York, 1952.

Gump's Gallery, San Francisco, 1952, 1954.

University of Florida, Gainesville, 1953.

Oregon Ceramic Studio, Portland, 1953.

Scripps College, Claremont, California, 1954.

Felix Landau Gallery, Los Angeles, 1956, 1958, 1959.

University of Southern California, Los Angeles, 1957.

Bonniers, New York, 1957.

The Art Institute of Chicago, 1957.

Pasadena Art Museum, California, 1958.

Penthouse Gallery, The Museum of Modern Art, New York, 1960.

Primus-Stuart Galleries, Los Angeles, 1961.

Art Unlimited Gallery, Los Angeles, 1964.

Los Angeles County Museum of Art, 1965.

David Stuart Galleries, Los Angeles, 1967.

Quay Gallery, San Francisco, 1968, 1974.

San Francisco Museum of Art, 1972.

Pasadena City College, California, 1973.

Kemper Gallery, Kansas City Art Institute, Missouri, 1975.

Helen Drutt Gallery, Philadelphia, 1975.

Fendrick Gallery, Washington, D.C., 1975.

Braunstein/Quay Gallery, New York, 1975.

Yaw Gallery, Birmingham, Michigan, 1976.

Exhibit A Gallery of American Ceramics, Evanston, Illinois, 1976, 1979.

Contemporary Crafts Association, Portland, Oregon, 1977.

Braunstein/Quay Gallery, San Francisco, 1978.

The Museum of Contemporary Crafts of the American Crafts Council, New York, 1978 (retrospective; traveled to San Francisco Museum of Modern Art; Contemporary Arts Museum, Houston, Texas; Milwaukee Art Center, Wisconsin).

Foster/White Gallery, Seattle, Washington, 1979.

Hill's Gallery of Contemporary Art, Santa Fe, New Mexico, 1979.

Okun-Thomas Gallery, St. Louis, Missouri, 1980.

Morgan Gallery, Kansas City, Missouri, 1980.

Charles Cowles Gallery, New York, 1981.

Selected Group Exhibitions

Exposition Universelle et Internationale de Bruxelles, Brussels, 1958.

Amerikanische Keramik 1960/1962, Third International Ceramic Exhibition, Prague, 1962.

Molten Image: 7 Sculptors, San Francisco Museum of Art, 1962.

Creative Casting, Museum of Contemporary Crafts, New York, 1963.

International Exhibition of Contemporary Ceramic Art, National Museum of Modern Art, Tokyo, 1964.

Abstract Expressionist Ceramics, Art Gallery, University of California, Irvine, 1966.

American Sculpture of the Sixties, Los Angeles County Museum of Art, 1967.

Kompas 4: West Coast USA, Stedelijk van Abbemuseum, Eindhoven, The Netherlands, 1969.

Expo 70, San Francisco Pavilion, Osaka, Japan, 1970.

A Decade of Ceramic Art, 1962–1972, from the Collection of Professor and Mrs. R. Joseph Monsen, San Francisco Museum of Art, 1972.

Painting and Sculpture in California: The Modern Era, San Francisco Museum of Modern Art, 1976 (traveled to National Collection of Fine Arts, Smithsonian Institution, Washington, D.C.).

200 Years of American Sculpture, Whitney Museum of American Art, New York, 1976.

Turner/Voulkos, Illinois State University, Normal, 1978.

Selected Bibliography

Conrad Brown, "Peter Voulkos, Southern California's Top Potter," *Craft Horizons,* vol. 16, no. 5, September/October 1956, pp. 12–18.

Dore Ashton, "New Talent Exhibition at The Museum of Modern Art," *Craft Horizons,* vol. 20, no. 2, March/April 1960, p. 42.

Rose Slivka, "The New Ceramic Presence," *Craft Horizons,* vol. 21, no. 4, July/August 1961, p. 31.

Jules Langsner, "Abstract Sculptures at the Primus-Stuart Galleries in Los Angeles," *Craft Horizons,* vol. 22, no. 1, January/February 1962, pp. 39–40.

Philip Leider, "West Coast Art: Three Images," *Artforum,* vol. 1, no. 12, June 1963, pp. 21–25.

John Coplans, "Sculpture in California," *Artforum,* vol. 2, no. 2, August 1963, pp. 3–6.

Joanna Magloff, "Peter Voulkos," *Artforum,* vol. 2, no. 2, August 1963, p. 29.

John Coplans, "Out of Clay: West Coast Ceramic Sculpture Emerges as a Strong Regional Trend," *Art in America,* vol. 51, no. 6, December 1963, p. 40.

Bernard Pyron, "The Tao and Dada of Recent American Ceramic Art," *Artforum,* vol. 2, no. 9, March 1964, pp. 41–42.

John Coplans, "Circle of Styles on the West Coast," *Art in America,* vol. 52, no. 3, June 1964, p. 24.

Thomas B. Hess, "The Disrespectful Handmaiden," *Art News,* vol. 63, no. 9, January 1965, pp. 38–39, 57–58.

Nancy Marmer, "Peter Voulkos," *Artforum,* vol. 3, no. 9, June 1965, pp. 9–11.

John Coplans, "Voulkos: Redemption through Ceramics," *Art News,* vol. 64, no. 4, summer 1965, pp. 33–39, 64–65.

Maurice Tuchman and L. Clarice Davis, *Peter Voulkos, Sculpture,* Los Angeles County Museum of Art, 1965.

Peter Voulkos and Paul Soldner, "West Coast Ceramics," *Craft Horizons,* vol. 26, no. 3, June/July 1966, pp. 25–28.

John Coplans, *Abstract Expressionist Ceramics,* University of California, Irvine, 1966.

James Melchert, "Peter Voulkos: a Return to Pottery," *Craft Horizons,* vol. 28, no. 5, September/October 1968, p. 20.

Peter Selz and Brenda Richardson, "California Ceramics," *Art in America,* vol. 57, no. 3, May/June 1969, pp. 104–105.

Suzanne Foley, *A Decade of Ceramic Art, 1962–1972, from the Collection of Professor and Mrs. R. Joseph Monsen,* San Francisco Museum of Art, 1972.

Gerald Nordland, *Peter Voulkos, Bronze Sculpture,* San Francisco Museum of Art, 1972.

Joseph Pugliese, "The Decade: Ceramics," *Craft Horizons,* vol. 33, no. 1, January/February 1973, p. 50.

Sandy Ballatore, "The California Clay Rush," *Art in America,* vol. 64, no. 4, July–August 1976, p. 84.

Hal Fischer, "The Art of Peter Voulkos," *Artforum,* vol. 17, no. 3, November 1978, pp. 41–47.

Rose Slivka, *Peter Voulkos: A Dialogue with Clay,* New York, 1978.

Chronology of Exhibitions: 1959–70

1959

Exhibitions in Los Angeles

California Painters and Sculptors, Thirty-Five and Under
UCLA Art Galleries
January 19–February 22
Catalog with introduction by Jules Langsner

Billy Al Bengston and Edward Kienholz
Ferus Gallery
February 17–March 14

Sam Francis
Pasadena Art Museum
March 3–April 10
Traveled to San Francisco Museum of Art; Seattle Art Museum, Washington.

Robert Irwin
Ferus Gallery
March 23–April 18

Prints and Drawings by June Wayne
Los Angeles County Museum of History, Science and Art
April 1–May 17
Catalog with text by Ebria Feinblatt

Edward Branco Moses
Ferus Gallery
April 27–May 23

Adolph Gottlieb
Paul Kantor Gallery
April 27–May 23

ADOLPH
GOTTLIEB
APRIL 27-MAY 23, 1959
PAUL KANTOR GALLERY
348 NORTH CAMDEN DRIVE • BEVERLY HILLS, CALIFORNIA

Peter Voulkos
Felix Landau Gallery
May 4–23

Arthur Dove Retrospective
UCLA Art Galleries
May–June
Catalog with text by Frederick S. Wight

Joan Miró
Los Angeles County Museum of History, Science and Art
June 10–July 21
Organized in cooperation with The Museum of Modern Art, New York

Annual Exhibition of Artists of Los Angeles and Vicinity (juried by Elmer Bischoff, Kenneth Sawyer, David Smith)
Los Angeles County Museum of History, Science and Art
August 4–September 6
Catalog
Yearly exhibitions; entries limited to 125-mile radius; began 1920, ended 1962

LAICA Journal

Four Abstract Classicists (Karl Benjamin, Lorser Feitelson, Frederick Hammersley, John McLaughlin)
Los Angeles County Museum of History, Science and Art
September 16–October 18
Catalog with foreword by James Elliott, text by Jules Langsner
Jointly organized by Los Angeles County Museum of History, Science and Art and San Francisco Museum of Art.
Traveled to Institute of Contemporary Art, London

UCLA

Lee Mullican
UCLA Art Galleries
October 5–November 1

Helen Lundeberg
Paul Rivas Gallery
October 5–30

Hassel Smith
Ferus Gallery
October 12–November 7

Aristide Maillol
Los Angeles County Museum of History, Science and Art
November 4–December 20
Organized by The Museum of Modern Art, New York

1959

European Art Today (35 artists)
Los Angeles County Museum of History, Science and Art
November 11–December 20
Catalog edited by Sam Hunter; essays by Lawrence Alloway, Umbro Appollonio, Friedrich Bayl, Juan-Edwardo Cirlot, James Fitzsimmons
Organized by The Minneapolis Institute of Arts, Minnesota; traveled to San Francisco Museum of Art; North Carolina Museum of Art, Raleigh; The National Gallery of Canada, Ottawa; French & Company, Inc., New York; The Baltimore Museum of Art, Maryland

Exhibitions outside of Los Angeles

Edward Branco Moses
(first New York one-man show)
Area Gallery, New York
January 2–23

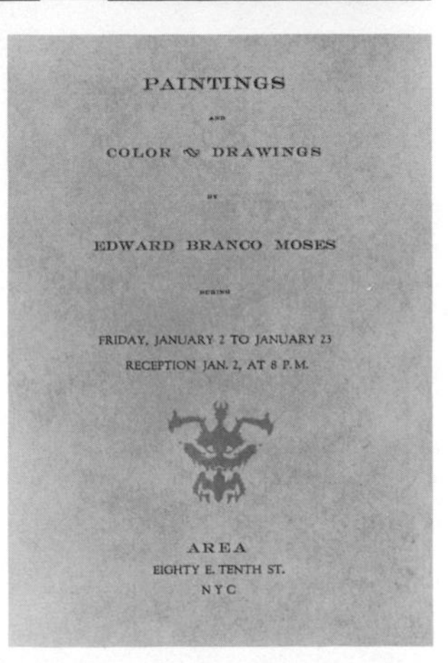

1960

Exhibitions in Los Angeles

Fourteen New York Artists
(Brooks, de Kooning, Gorky, Guston, Hofmann, Kline, Mitchell, Motherwell, Nevelson, Newman, Pollock, Resnick, Rothko, Tworkov)
Ferus Gallery
January 18–February 13

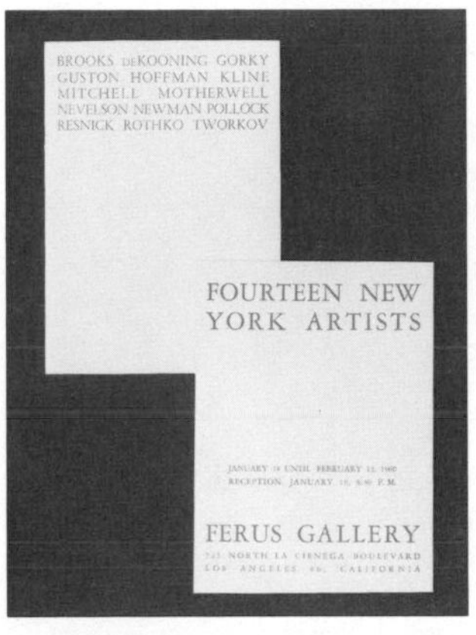

James Jarvaise (Hudson River Series)
Felix Landau Gallery
January 25–February 13
Brochure with introduction by Gerald Nordland

Mark Tobey Retrospective
Pasadena Art Museum
February 7–March 9

Billy Al Bengston
Ferus Gallery
February 15–March 12

East-West (Lester Johnson, Leland Bell, Robert De Niro, William Brim, John Paul Jones, Paul Wonner)
Felix Landau Gallery
February 15–March 15

David Smith
Paul Kantor Gallery
February

50 Paintings by 37 Artists of the Los Angeles Area (includes Bengston, Irwin, Kauffman, Kienholz, Moses, McLaughlin, Voulkos)
UCLA Art Galleries
March 20–April 10
Catalog with text by Henry T. Hopkins

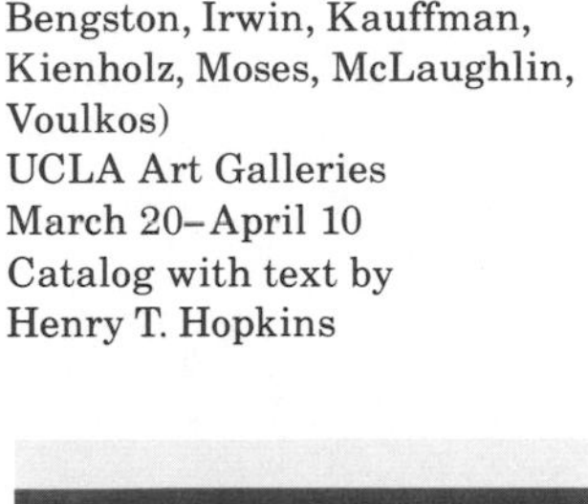

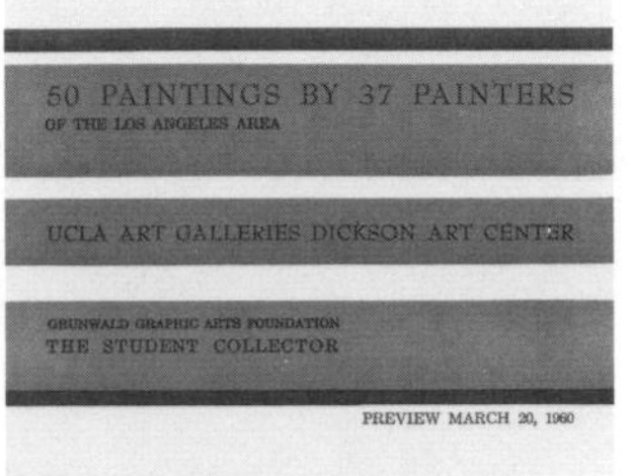

J. DeFeo
Ferus Gallery
March 21–April 16

Sculpture in Our Time–Hirshhorn Collection
Los Angeles County Museum of History, Science and Art
April 12–May 15
Catalog with text by E. P. Richardson, Abram Lerner, Addison Franklin Page
Organized by The Detroit Institute of Arts

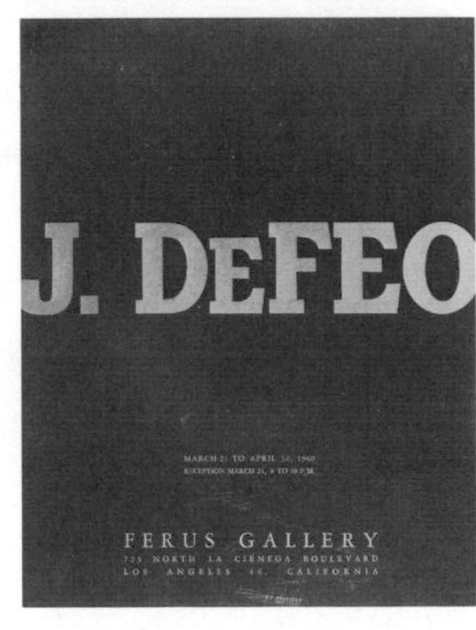

1960

Connor Everts
Pasadena Art Museum
April 13–May 18
Catalog with text by Gerald Nordland

Georges Braque
Pasadena Art Museum
April 20–June 5
Catalog with introduction by Thomas W. Leavitt

Kenneth Price
Ferus Gallery
May 16–June 11

John Mason
Pasadena Art Museum
May 31–July 6

Man Ray: Drawings and Watercolors
Esther Robles Gallery
June 27–July 16

Robert Irwin
Pasadena Art Museum
July 12–August 31

Jasper Johns and Kurt Schwitters
Ferus Gallery
September 6–30

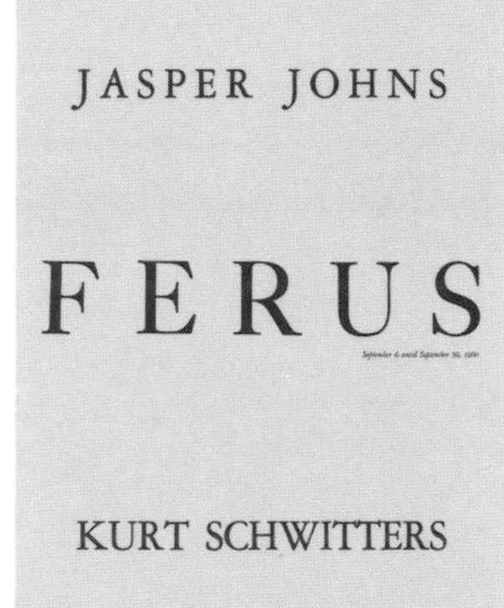

Richard Diebenkorn
Pasadena Art Museum
September 6–October 5
Catalog with text by Thomas W. Leavitt

15 of New York (Bluhm, Brach, Goodnough, Guston, Hartigan, Jenkins, Kanemitsu, Kline, de Kooning, Parker, Pollock, Richenburg, Rivers, Twardovicz, Yunkers)
Dwan Gallery
October 10–

Bob Bucknam

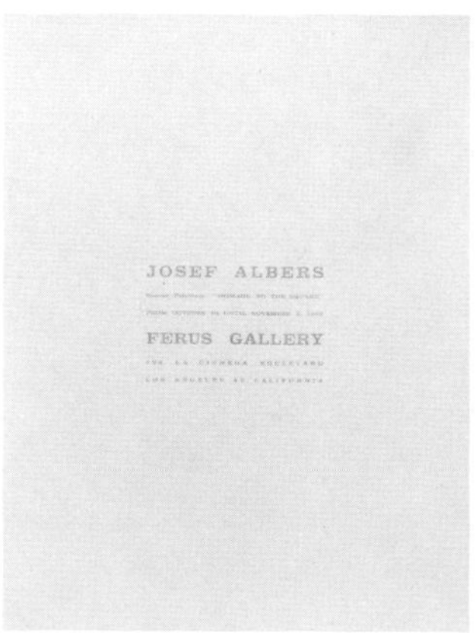

Josef Albers
Ferus Gallery
October 10–November 5

Seymour Rosen

Thirty California Artists
Pasadena Art Museum
November

Hudson River School
Pasadena Art Museum
November 30–June 4

1960

Seymour Rosen

Edward Kienholz
Ferus Gallery
December 5–31

David Smith and Joan Jacobs
Everett Ellin Gallery
Winter

Exhibitions outside of Los Angeles

Peter Voulkos
The Museum of Modern Art, New York
–March 13

1961

Exhibitions in Los Angeles

Larry Aldrich Collection
Los Angeles Municipal Art Gallery, Barnsdall Park
January 5–29

German Expressionist Paintings from the Morton D. May Collection
UCLA Art Galleries
January 8–February 19

John Altoon
Ferus Gallery
January 9–February 11

Larry Rivers
Dwan Gallery
February 6–March 4

Bob Bucknam

Giorgio Morandi
Ferus Gallery
February 13–March 11

The Object Makers: Attitude—West Coast
Pomona College Art Gallery
February 16–March 26

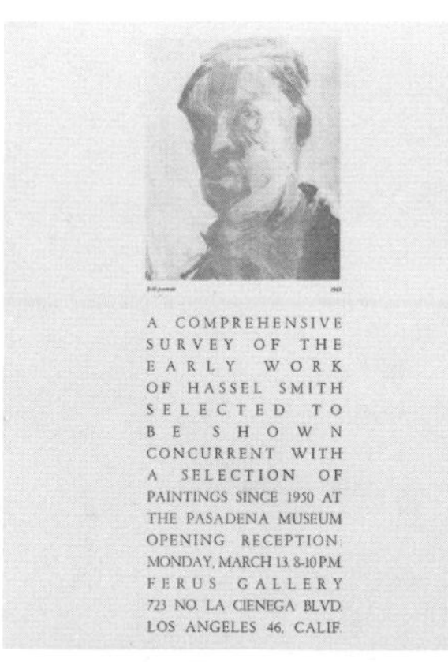

Hassel Smith
Pasadena Art Museum
March 13–April 16
Catalog with text by
Walter Hopps

Cross Section, 1961: Los Angeles–San Francisco
Los Angeles Municipal Art Gallery, Barnsdall Park
March 14–April 9
Works from Northern California selected by San Francisco Museum of Art

Helen Frankenthaler
Everett Ellin Gallery
March 20–April 15

Emerson Woelffer
Primus-Stuart Galleries
April 2–29

Willem de Kooning
Paul Kantor Gallery
April 3–29
Brochure with text by
Clifford Odets

Philip Guston, Franz Kline
Dwan Gallery
April 3–29

John Mason
Ferus Gallery
May 15–June 24

1961

Seymour Rosen

Edward Kienholz
Pasadena Art Museum
May 16–June 21

War Babies
Huysman Gallery
May 29–June 17

Llyn Foulkes
Ferus Gallery
July 31–August 26

1961

Kenneth Price
Ferus Gallery
October 16–November 4

VOULKOS
OCTOBER 16 THROUGH NOVEMBER 11, 1961
PRIMUS • STUART GALLERIES
807 N LA CIENEGA · LOS ANGELES 69 · OL 2-7422

Peter Voulkos
Primus-Stuart Galleries
October 16–November 11

AN EXHIBITION OF RECENT WORK BY BILLY AL BENGSTON
MONDAY NOVEMBER 13th UNTIL SATURDAY DECEMBER 2nd
AT THE FERUS GALLERY 723 NORTH LA CIENEGA BOULEVARD
LOS ANGELES 69 CALIF • OPENING NOVEMBER 13th 8 UNTIL 10 PM
LEBARD
13

Billy Al Bengston
Ferus Gallery
November 13–December 2

Lee Mullican
Pasadena Art Museum
November 21–December 27

Edward Moses
Ferus Gallery
December 4–30

Exhibitions outside of Los Angeles

Richard Diebenkorn
The Phillips Collection,
Washington, D.C.
May 19–June 26

The Art of Assemblage
The Museum of Modern Art,
New York
October 4–November 12
Catalog with text by
William C. Seitz
Traveled to Dallas Museum of
Contemporary Arts, Texas;
San Francisco Museum of Art

The Museum of Modern Art, N.Y.

1962

Exhibitions in Los Angeles

Tamarind Lithographs
UCLA Art Galleries
January 7–February 11
Catalog with introduction by Frederick S. Wight

Futurism
Los Angeles County Museum of Art
January 14–February 19
Catalog with text by Joshua C. Taylor
Organized by The Museum of Modern Art, New York

John McLaughlin
Felix Landau Gallery
January 29–February 17

Ad Reinhardt
Dwan Gallery
February 5–March 3

Robert Motherwell Retrospective (first American retrospective)
Pasadena Art Museum
February 18–March 11

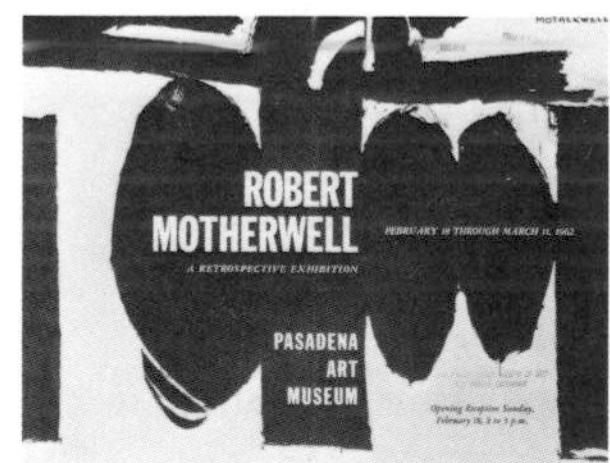

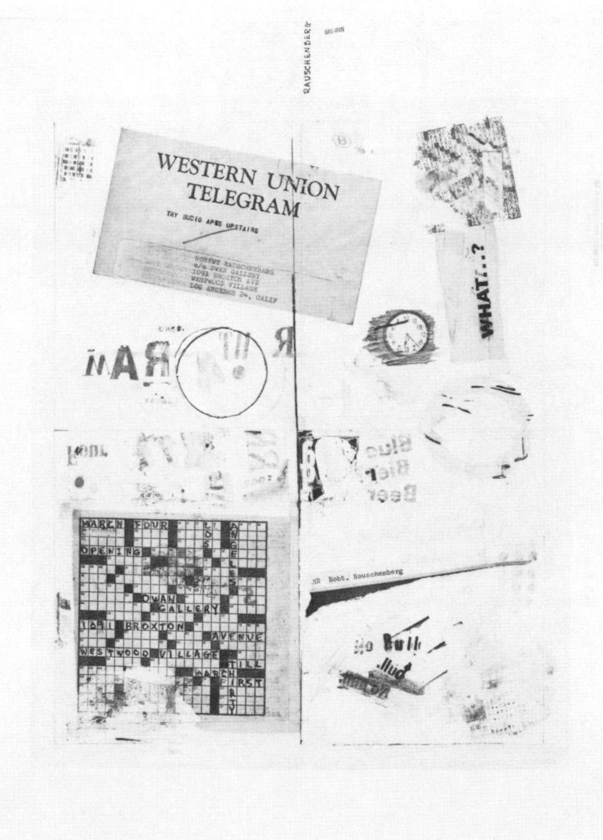

Jean Tinguely and *Niki de St. Phalle*
Everett Ellin Gallery
March 3–4

Robert Rauschenberg
Dwan Gallery
March 4–31

Seymour Rosen

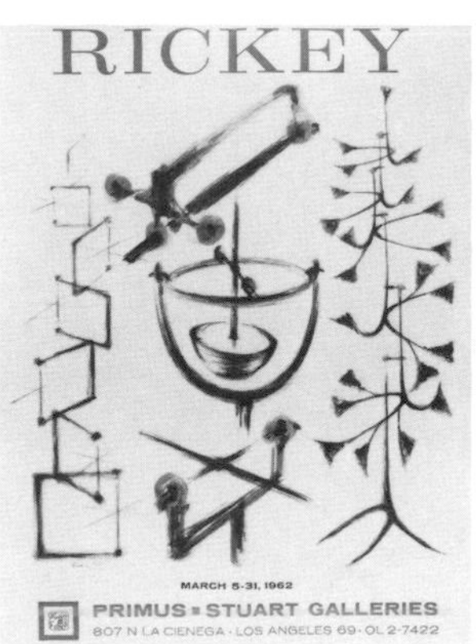

George Rickey
Primus-Stuart Galleries
March 5–31

Edward Kienholz Presents a Tableau at the Ferus Gallery
Ferus Gallery
March 6–24

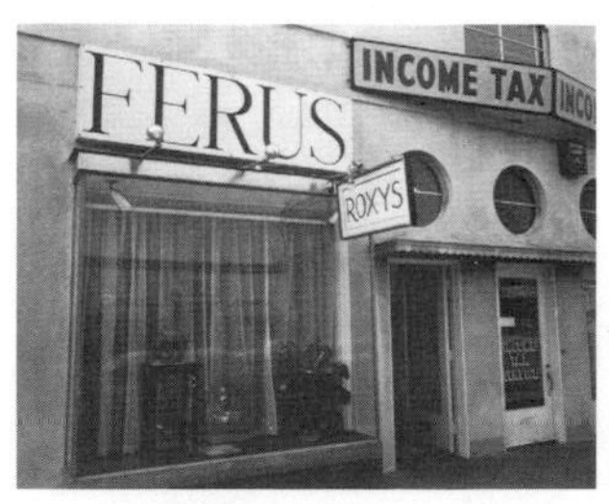

William Claxton

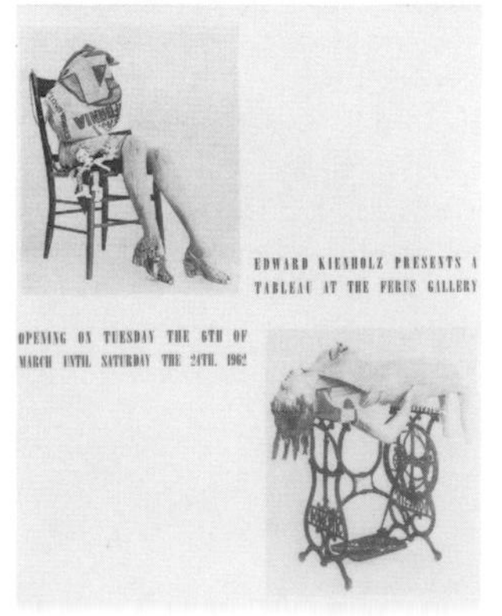

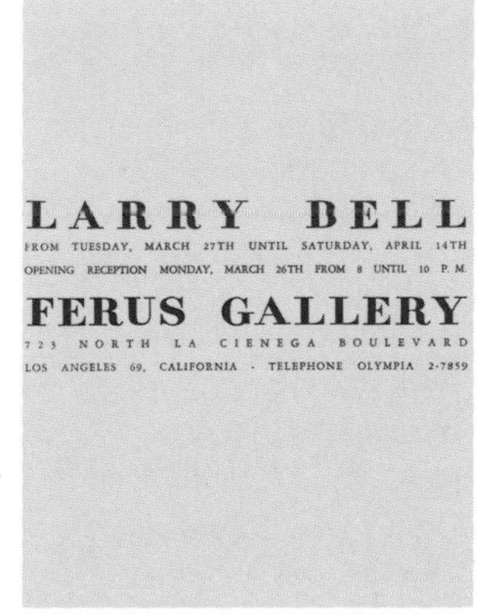

Larry Bell (first one-man show)
Ferus Gallery
March 27–April 14

Arshile Gorky
Everett Ellin Gallery
April 2–28

Frank Lobdell
Ferus Gallery
April 16–May 5

Charles Frazier
Everett Ellin Gallery
May 1–26

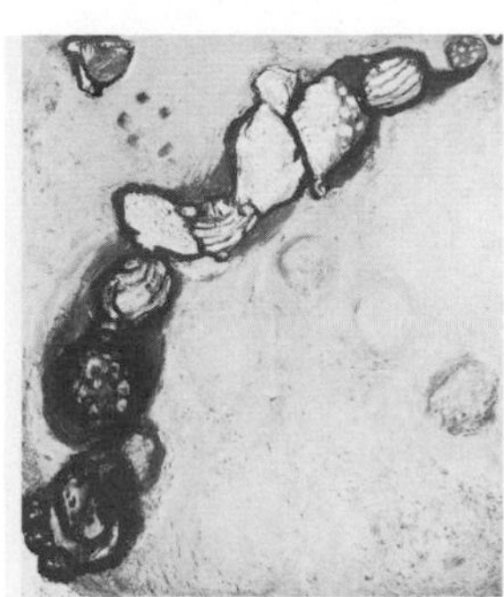

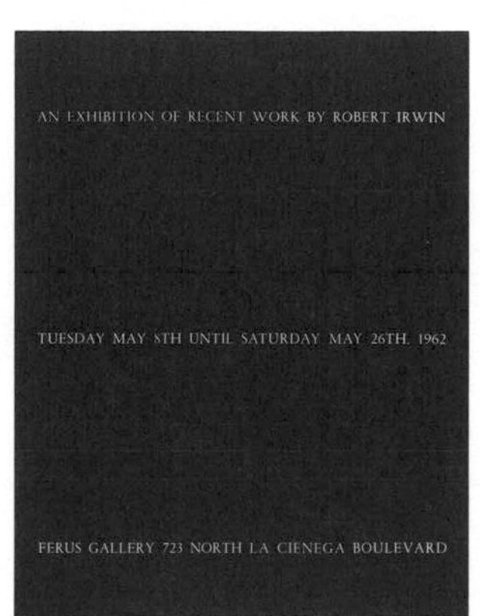

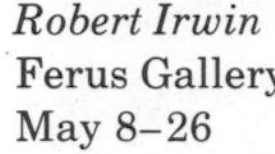

Robert Irwin
Ferus Gallery
May 8–26

John Altoon
Pasadena Art Museum
May 15–June 20

Reuben Nakian (first American retrospective)
Los Angeles County Museum of Art
May 16–June 24
Catalog with text by
Robert W. Goldwater
Organized for the VI Bienal de São Paulo, Brazil; circulated by The Museum of Modern Art, New York

Simon Rodia's Towers in Watts: Photographs by Seymour Rosen
Los Angeles County Museum of Art
May 16–June 24
Catalog with foreword by
William Osmun, text by
Paul Laporte

Bruce Conner
Ferus Gallery
June 4–

A Pacific Profile of Young West Coast Painters
Pasadena Art Museum
June 11–July 19
Catalog with text by
Constance Perkins

Directions in Collage
Pasadena Art Museum
June 19–July 20

Kurt Schwitters: A Retrospective Exhibition
Pasadena Art Museum
June 20–July 17
Catalog with text by
William C. Seitz
Organized by The Museum of Modern Art, New York; traveled to the Currier Gallery of Art, Manchester, New Hampshire; The Phillips Collection, Washington, D.C.; University of Minnesota, Minneapolis; Busch-Reisinger Museum, Harvard University, Cambridge, Massachusetts

Some Hard-Edge Painters
Los Angeles Art Association
June

Louise Nevelson
Los Angeles County Museum of Art
June–July

Andy Warhol
(first commercial show)
Ferus Gallery
July 9–August 4

Seymour Rosen

William Claxton

Jean Dubuffet
Los Angeles County Museum of Art
July 11–August 12
Catalog with text by Peter Selz, and statement by the artist
Organized by The Museum of Modern Art, New York

The Mr. and Mrs. Ben Heller Collection of 20th-Century Paintings
Los Angeles County Museum of Art
August 15–September 30
Catalog with text by Alfred H. Barr, Jr.; Ben Heller; William C. Seitz
Organized by The Museum of Modern Art, New York

Return to the Figure (Carillo, Chavez, Garabedian, Lunetta)
Ceeje Gallery
Fall

1962

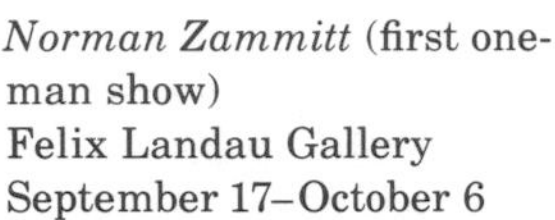

Norman Zammitt (first one-man show)
Felix Landau Gallery
September 17–October 6

Norman Zammitt

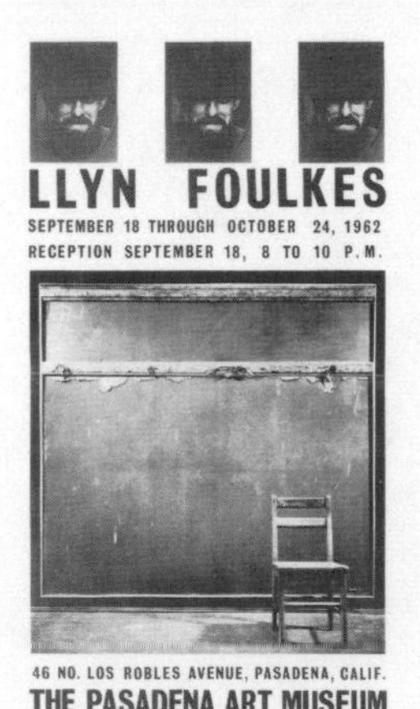

Llyn Foulkes
Pasadena Art Museum
September 18–October 24

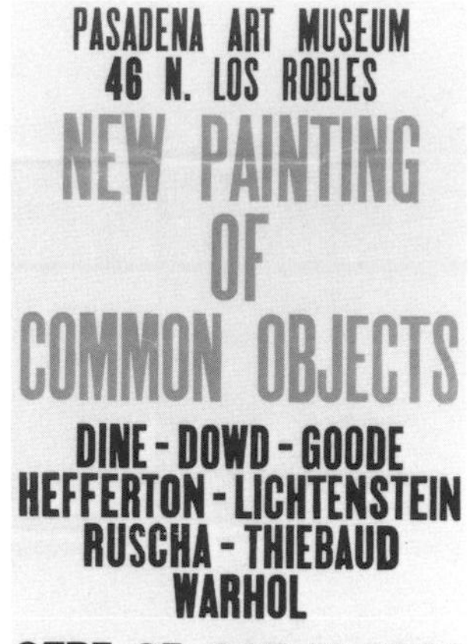

New Painting of Common Objects (Dine, Dowd, Goode, Hefferton, Lichtenstein, Ruscha, Thiebaud, Warhol)
Pasadena Art Museum
September 25–October 19

20th-Century Sculpture
Pasadena Art Museum
September 26–October 30

U.S. Abstract Expressionism
Pasadena Art Museum
September 26–October 19

Lorser Feitelson
Ankrum Gallery
October 15–November 3

Emerson Woelffer: Work from 1946 to 1962
Pasadena Art Museum
October 24–November 18
Catalog with text by Gerald Nordland

1962

The Gifford and Joann Phillips Collection
UCLA Art Galleries
November 4–December 9
Catalog with introduction by Frederick S. Wight

Billy Al Bengston
Ferus Gallery
November 12–December 9

My Country 'Tis of Thee
Dwan Gallery
November 18–December 15

William Claxton

Jasper Johns
Everett Ellin Gallery
November 19–December 15

UCLA

Sam Francis
Esther Bear Gallery, Santa Barbara
November 25–December 31

Craig Kauffman
Ferus Gallery
December 2–

Joseph Cornell
Ferus Gallery
December 10–January 5

Claire Falkenstein
Esther Robles Gallery
December 17–January 7

Seymour Rosen

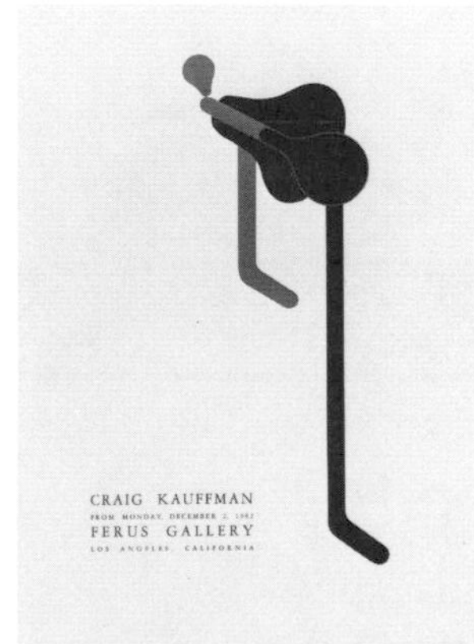

William Claxton

Exhibitions outside of Los Angeles

Edward Moses
Alan Gallery, New York
March

Billy Al Bengston (first New York show)
Martha Jackson Gallery, New York
May 1–26

Fifty California Artists
Whitney Museum of American Art, New York
October 23–December 2
Catalog with text by Lloyd Goodrich, George D. Culler
Jointly organized by San Francisco Museum of Art; Los Angeles County Museum of Art; Whitney Museum of American Art, New York

1963

Exhibitions in Los Angeles

Martial Raysse
Dwan Gallery
January 6–28

The Artist's Environment: The West Coast
UCLA Art Galleries
January 7–February 10
Catalog with introduction by Frederick S. Wight
Organized by Amon Carter Museum of Western Art, Fort Worth, Texas; traveled to Oakland Art Museum, California

Charles Garabedian
Ceeje Gallery
January 28–February 23

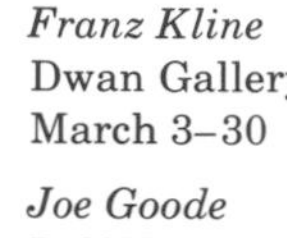

Dealer's Choice
Dwan Gallery
February 10–

Frank Stella
Ferus Gallery
February 18–March 31

Franz Kline
Dwan Gallery
March 3–30

Joe Goode
Rolf Nelson Gallery
March 8–30

John Mason
Ferus Gallery
March 11–30

AN EXHIBITION OF RECENT WORK BY JOHN MASON
MONDAY, MARCH 11th UNTIL SATURDAY, MARCH 30, 1963
AT THE FERUS GALLERY 723 NORTH LA CIENEGA BOULEVARD
LOS ANGELES 69, CALIF. OPENING MARCH 11th 8 UNTIL 10 P.M.

Antoni Tapies
Pasadena Art Museum
March 20–April 25
Catalog with text by Lawrence Alloway
Organized by Museo de Bellas Artes, Caracas, Venezuela; traveled to Phoenix Art Center, Arizona; Felix Landau Gallery, Los Angeles

Seymour Rosen

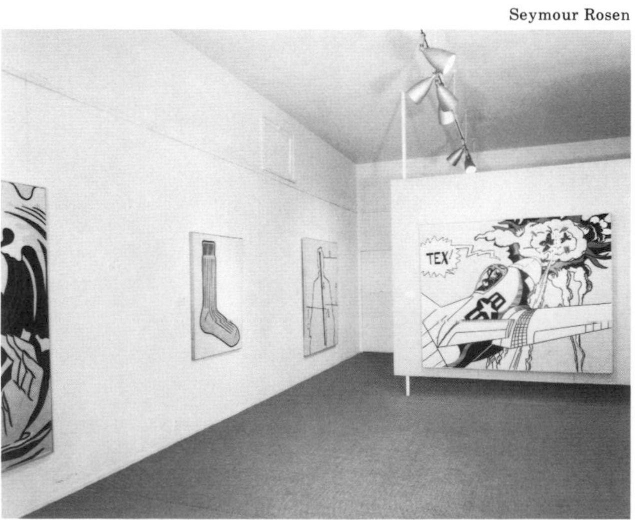

Roy Lichtenstein
Ferus Gallery
April 1–27

Larry Rivers
Dwan Gallery
April 15–May 11

Anthony Berlant
David Stuart Galleries
April 27–May 25

Edward Moses
Ferus Gallery
April 29–May 18

1963

H. C. Westermann
Dilexi Gallery
Spring

Jean Tinguely
Dwan Gallery
May 13–

Edward Ruscha
Ferus Gallery
May 20–June 15

Philip Guston
Los Angeles County Museum of Art
May 22–June 30
Catalog with text by H. H. Arnason
Organized by The Solomon R. Guggenheim Museum, New York

Niki de St. Phalle
Dwan Gallery
May 25–June 22

RUSCHA
EDWARD
OPENING ON MONDAY, MAY 20TH, 1963 FROM 8 UNTIL 10 P.M. AT THE FERUS GALLERY 723 N. LA CIENEGA BLVD., LOS ANGELES 69

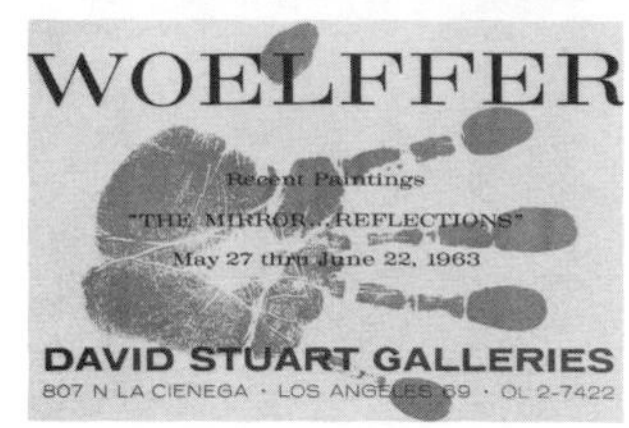

Emerson Woelffer
David Stuart Galleries
May 27–June 22

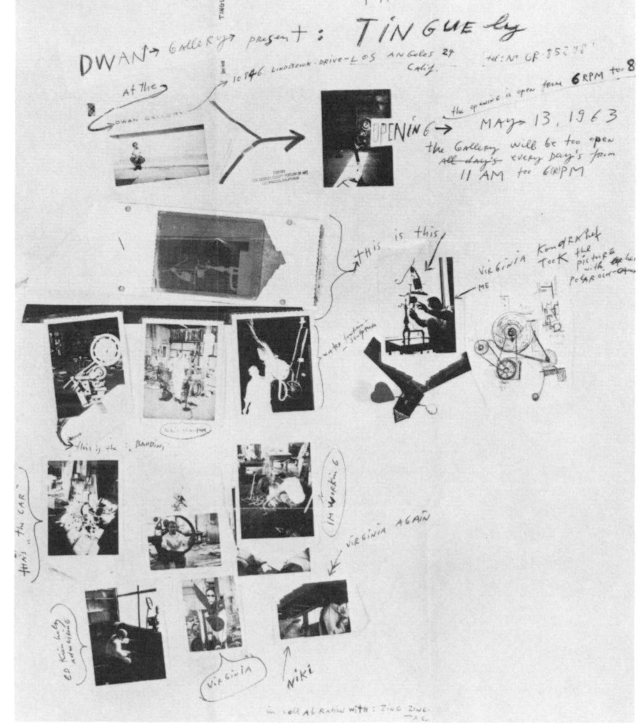

Altoon, Bell, Bengston, DeFeo, Irwin, Kauffman, Lobdell, Mason, Moses, Price, Ruben, Ruscha
Ferus Gallery
June 17–

Six Painters and the Object
(Jim Dine, Jasper Johns, Roy Lichtenstein, Robert Rauschenberg, James Rosenquist, Andy Warhol)
Los Angeles County Museum of Art
July 24–August 25
Catalog with text by Lawrence Alloway
Organized by The Solomon R. Guggenheim Museum, New York

Six More (Billy Al Bengston, Joe Goode, Philip Hefferton, Mel Ramos, Edward Ruscha, Wayne Thiebaud)
Los Angeles County Museum of Art
July 24–August 25
Catalog with foreword by James Elliott, text by Lawrence Alloway
(Shown simultaneously with *Six Painters and the Object*)

LACMA

© 1980 Julian Wasser

Andy Warhol
Ferus Gallery
September 30–October 26

by or of
Marcel Duchamp
or
Rrose Sélavy

Marcel Duchamp Retrospective
Pasadena Art Museum
October 8–November 3
Catalog with introduction by Walter Hopps

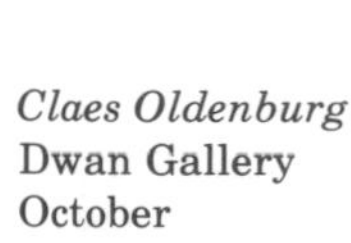
Claes Oldenburg
Dwan Gallery
October

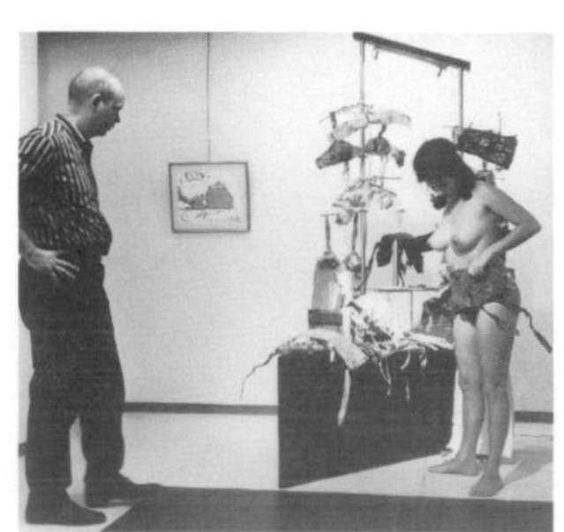

1963

Larry Bell
Ferus Gallery
November 4–

Frank J. Thomas

John McLaughlin
(retrospective)
Pasadena Art Museum
November 12–December 12
Catalog with foreword by Walter Hopps, and statement by the artist

Artforum

Exhibitions outside of Los Angeles

Edward Kienholz
Alexander Iolas Gallery, New York
February 5–23

California Sculpture
Kaiser Center, Oakland, California
August 4–September 15
Jointly organized by Oakland Art Museum, California; Pasadena Art Museum, California; *Artforum*

Open Air (includes Voulkos)
Battersea Park, London
August–September
Catalog

Pop Art USA
Oakland Art Museum and California College of Arts & Crafts, California
September 7–29
Organized by John Coplans

Richard Diebenkorn
M. H. de Young Museum, San Francisco
September 7–October 13

Monday night art walk.

Frank J. Thomas

Peter Voulkos
David Stuart Galleries
November 11–December 7

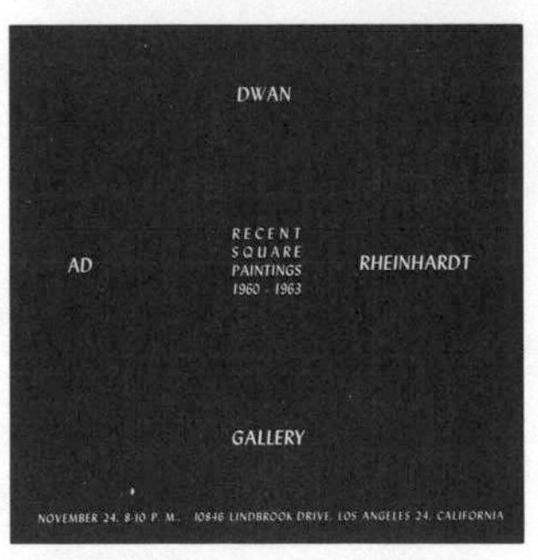

Ad Reinhardt
Dwan Gallery
November 24–January 4

George Herms—Nativity '63
Rolf Nelson Gallery
December 3–28

Craig Kauffman
Ferus Gallery
December

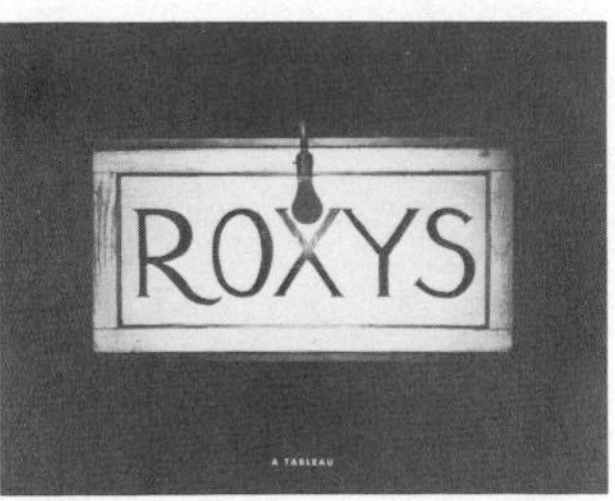

1964

Exhibitions in Los Angeles

Hassel Smith
David Stuart Galleries
January 6–February 1

Philip Hefferton
Rolf Nelson Gallery
January 7–February 1

Boxes (Brecht, Cornell, Frazier, Samaras, Schwitters, Warhol)
Dwan Gallery
February 2–29
Catalog with text by Walter Hopps

LACMA

Kenneth Price
Ferus Gallery
March 3

Lloyd Hamrol
Rolf Nelson Gallery
April 6–May 2

Robert Irwin
Ferus Gallery
April 7–

Post Painterly Abstraction
Los Angeles County Museum of Art
April 23–June 7
Catalog with foreword by James Elliott, text by Clement Greenberg
Traveled to Walker Art Center, Minneapolis, Minnesota; The Art Gallery of Toronto

Arakawa
Dwan Gallery
April

Martial Raysse
Dwan Gallery
May 4–30

Jack Tworkov
Pasadena Art Museum
July 14–August 16

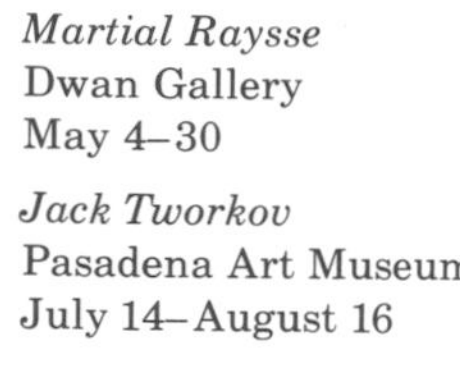

Sterling Holloway Collection
UCLA Art Galleries
September 20–October 25
Catalog with introduction by Henri Dorra

UCLA

Edward Kienholz (tableaux, including *The Back Seat Dodge '38*)
Dwan Gallery
September 29–October 24

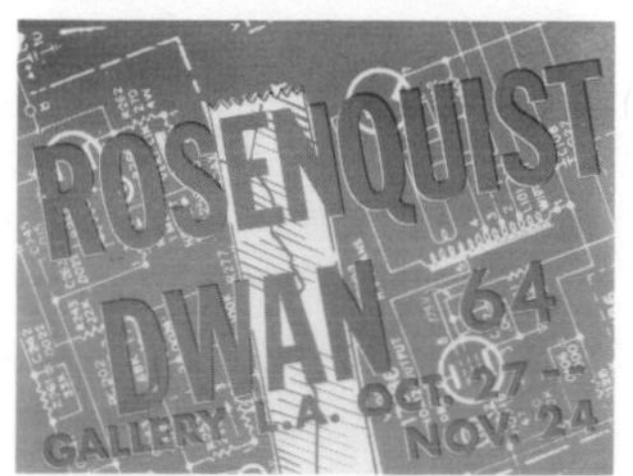

James Rosenquist
Dwan Gallery
October 27–November 24

1964

Roy Lichtenstein
Ferus Gallery
November 24–

Artforum

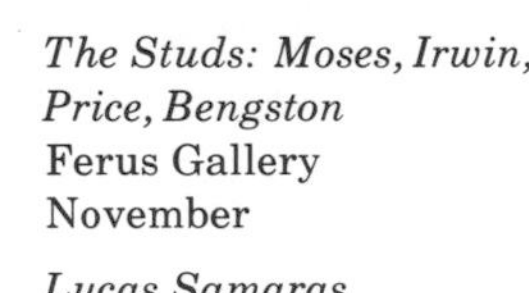

The Studs: Moses, Irwin, Price, Bengston
Ferus Gallery
November

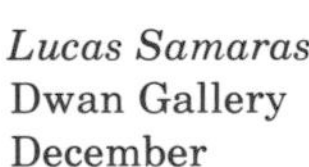

Lucas Samaras
Dwan Gallery
December

Exhibitions outside of Los Angeles

Seven New Artists (includes Bell, Irwin)
Sidney Janis Gallery, New York
May 5–29
Catalog

Richard Diebenkorn (retrospective)
Washington Gallery of Modern Art, Washington, D.C.
November 6–December 31
Catalog with text by Gerald Nordland
Traveled to The Jewish Museum, New York; The Fine Arts Patrons of Newport Harbor, Balboa Pavilion Gallery, California

1965

Artforum

Exhibitions in Los Angeles

Philip Rich
Ferus Gallery
January 1–25

The Arena of Love
Dwan Gallery
January 5–February 1

Piet Mondrian Retrospective
(from American collections)
Santa Barbara Museum of Art
January 12–February 21

Frank Stella
Ferus Gallery
January 26–February 22

Ellsworth Kelly
Ferus Gallery
March 9–

Kurt Schwitters (retrospective)
UCLA Art Galleries
March 21–April 25
Catalog with introduction by Werner Schmalenbach, text by Kate Steinitz, and statements by the artist
Jointly organized by UCLA and Marlborough-Gerson Gallery

Craig Kauffman
Ferus Gallery
March 30–

Edward Avedisian
Nicholas Wilder Gallery
April 5–30

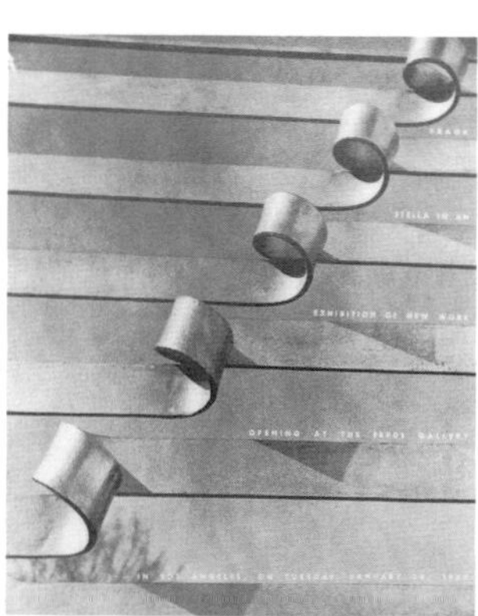

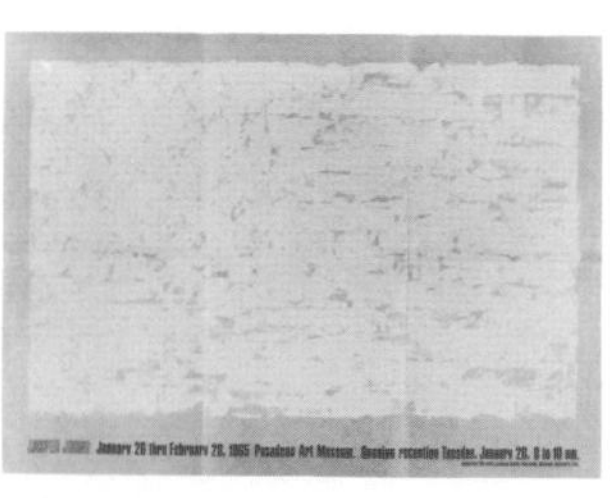

UCLA

Jasper Johns
Pasadena Art Museum
January 26–February 28

Robert Rauschenberg
Dwan Gallery
April 13–May 8

1965

Peter Voulkos
Los Angeles County Museum of Art
April 14–June 20
Catalog

Charles Frazier
Dwan Gallery
May 11–June 5

Lee Mullican
Silvan Simone Gallery
June 7–26

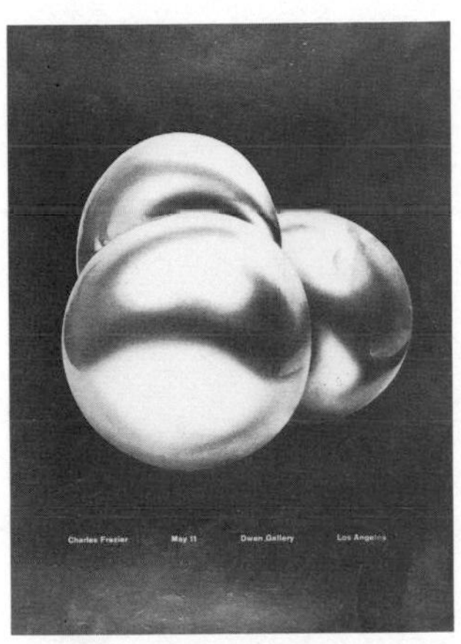

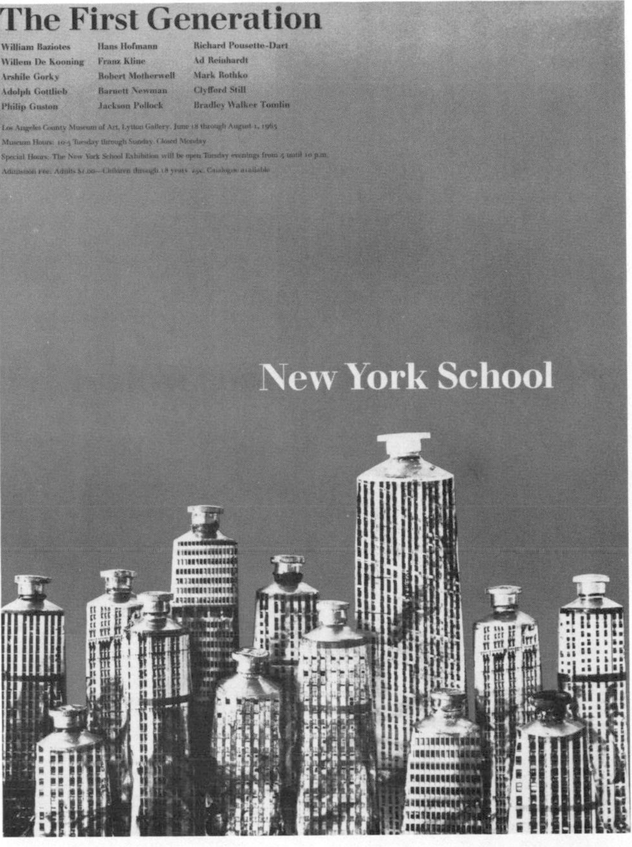

New York School: The First Generation–Paintings of the 1940s and 1950s (Baziotes, de Kooning, Gorky, Gottlieb, Guston, Hofmann, Kline, Motherwell, Newman, Pollock, Pousette-Dart, Reinhardt, Rothko, Still, Tomlin)
Los Angeles County Museum of Art
June 18–August 1
Catalog edited by Maurice Tuchman, texts by Lawrence Alloway, Robert Goldwater, Clement Greenberg, Harold Rosenberg, William S. Rubin, Meyer Schapiro, and statements by each artist

LACMA

Three American Painters: Kenneth Noland, Frank Stella, Jules Olitski
Pasadena Art Museum
July 7–August 1
Catalog with text by Michael Fried
Organized by Fogg Art Museum, Cambridge, Massachusetts

Larry Rivers
Pasadena Art Museum
August 10–September 5
Catalog with text by Sam Hunter, Frank O'Hara
Organized by Rose Art Museum, Brandeis University, Waltham, Massachusetts, in collaboration with The Detroit Institute of Arts; The Jewish Museum, New York; Minneapolis Institute of Arts, Minnesota; Pasadena Art Museum, California

R. B. Kitaj: Paintings and Prints
Los Angeles County Museum of Art
August 11–September 12
Catalog with text by Maurice Tuchman

LACMA

Virginia Dwan Collection
UCLA Art Galleries
September 27–October 24
Catalog with introduction by
Frederick S. Wight

The Responsive Eye
Pasadena Art Museum
September 28–November 7
Catalog with text by
William C. Seitz
Organized by The Museum of Modern Art, New York; traveled to City Art Museum of St. Louis, Missouri; Seattle Art Museum, Washington; Baltimore Museum of Art, Maryland

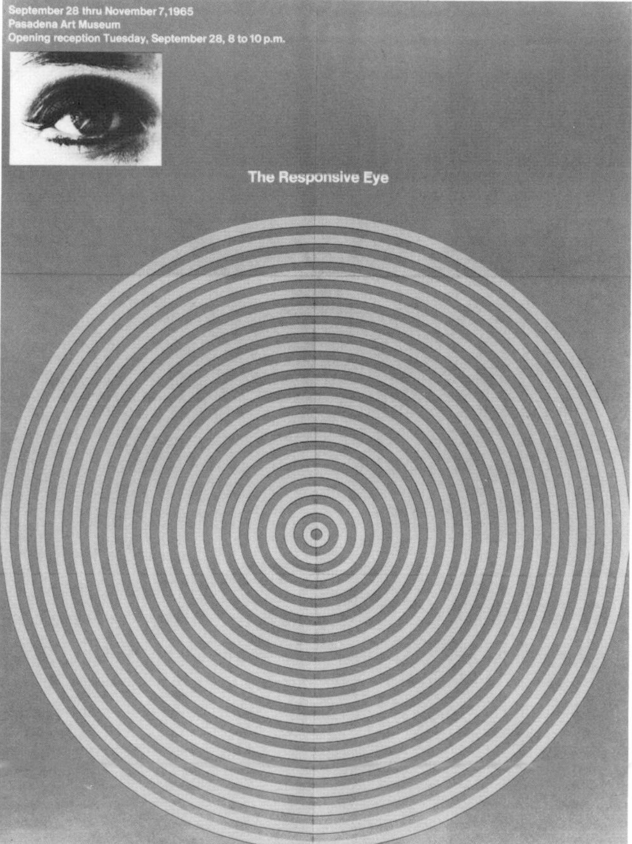

September 28 thru November 7,1965
Pasadena Art Museum
Opening reception Tuesday, September 28, 8 to 10 p.m.
The Responsive Eye

MEL
RAMOS
Opening Tues. Eve Oct. 12, 8-10 pm
Continuing Thru November 6, 1965
DAVID STUART GALLERIES
807 N LA CIENEGA · LOS ANGELES 69 · OL 2-7422

Mel Ramos
David Stuart Galleries
October 12–November 6

Larry Poons
Ferus Gallery
October 15–November 15

Ronald Davis
(first one-man show)
Nicholas Wilder Gallery
October 16–November 13

Artforum

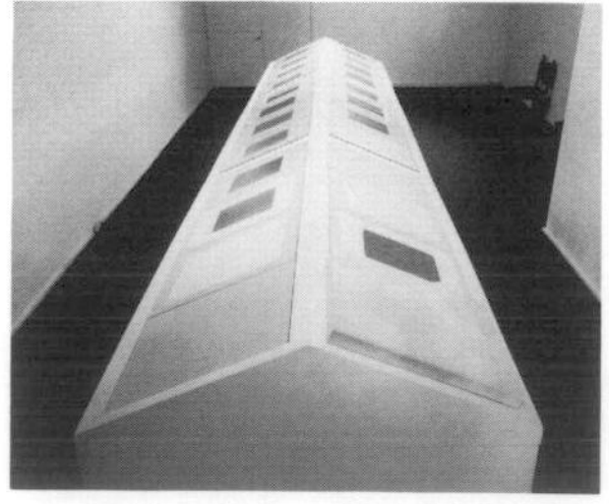

Frank J. Thomas

Bridget Riley
Feigen/Palmer Gallery
September 28–October 25

Mark di Suvero
Dwan Gallery
September 29–November 2

Barnett Newman: XVIII Cantos
Nicholas Wilder Gallery
September

Larry Bell
Ferus Gallery
October 26–

Stuart Davis Memorial Exhibition
UCLA Art Galleries
November 1–28
Catalog with foreword by David W. Scott and introduction by H. H. Arnason

Twentieth Century Sculpture (Archipenko, Arp, Brancusi, Braque, Calder, Cornell, De Rivera, Duchamp, Ernst, Giacometti, Gonzalez, Lachaise, Lehmbruck, Lipchitz, Matisse, Miró, Moore, Pevsner, Picasso, David Smith)
Art Gallery, University of California, Irvine
October–November

Stanton Macdonald-Wright, Herbert Bayer
Esther Robles Gallery
November 15–December 3

Frank J. Thomas

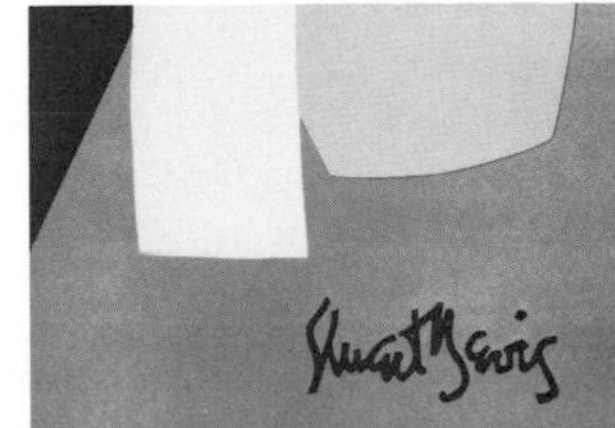

Frank J. Thomas

UCLA

1965

Edward Ruscha
Ferus Gallery
November 16–

5 Younger L.A. Artists (recipients of the New Talent Purchase Award: Melvin Edwards, Anthony Berlant, Lloyd Hamrol, Llyn Foulkes, Philip Rich)
Los Angeles County Museum of Art
November 26–December 26
Catalog with foreword by Maurice Tuchman

LACMA

Maxwell Hendler
Ceeje Galleries
November 29–December 18

David Smith
Los Angeles County Museum of Art
November 30–January 30
Catalog with text by Hilton Kramer

Non-Art Objects
Dwan Gallery
December 1–January 4

Agnes Martin
Nicholas Wilder Gallery
December 11–January 8

1965

Exhibitions outside of Los Angeles

Pop Art and the American Tradition (includes Bengston, Ruscha)
Milwaukee Art Center, Wisconsin
April 9–May 9
Catalog

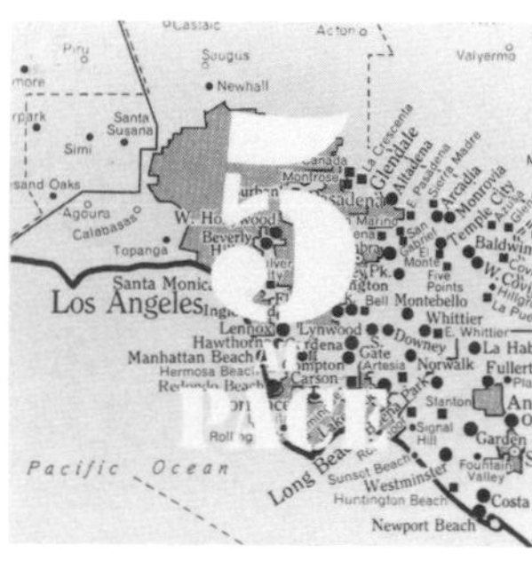

5 at Pace (Bell, DeLap, Kauffman, Reynolds, Ruscha)
Pace Gallery, New York
July–September
Catalog with text by John Coplans

Exhibition of the United States of America VIII Bienal de São Paulo, Brazil (Bell, Bengston, Irwin, Judd, Newman, Poons, Stella)
Museu de Arte Moderna
September 4–November 28
Catalog with text by Walter Hopps
Organized by Pasadena Art Museum for the United States Information Agency
Traveled to Pasadena Art Museum, California; National Collection of Fine Arts, Washington, D.C.

Selections from the Work of California Artists
Witte Memorial Museum, San Antonio, Texas
October 10–November 14

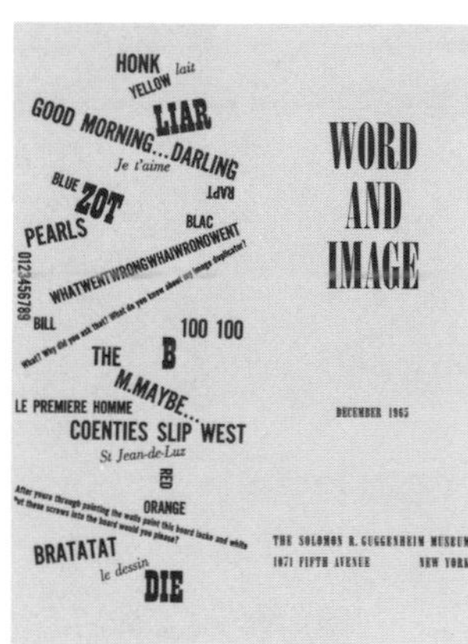

Word and Image (de Kooning, Dine, Frankenthaler, Indiana, Johns, Lichtenstein, Motherwell, Ruscha, Trova)
The Solomon R. Guggenheim Museum, New York
December
Brochure with essay by Lawrence Alloway

Larry Bell
Pace Gallery, New York
Winter

1966

Exhibitions in Los Angeles

Norman Zammitt
Felix Landau Gallery
January 3–29

Henri Matisse Retrospective
UCLA Art Galleries
January 4–March 28
Catalog with text by Jean Leymarie, Herbert Read, William S. Lieberman
Traveled to The Art Institute of Chicago; Museum of Fine Arts, Boston

Five Los Angeles Sculptors and Sculptors' Drawings (Bell, DeLap, Gray, McCracken, Price)
Art Gallery, University of California, Irvine
January 7–February 6
Catalog with introduction by John Coplans

Alberto Giacometti Retrospective
Los Angeles County Museum of Art
January 14–February 20
Catalog with introduction by Peter Selz, and statement by the artist
Organized by The Museum of Modern Art, New York

Artforum

Judith Gerowitz
Rolf Nelson Gallery
January

Robert Graham
Nicholas Wilder Gallery
February 5–March 5

John Marin
La Jolla Museum of Art
February 12–March 27

1966

Seymour Rosen

Artists Protest Tower
(Mark di Suvero)
Corner of La Cienega and
Sunset Boulevards
Dedication February 26

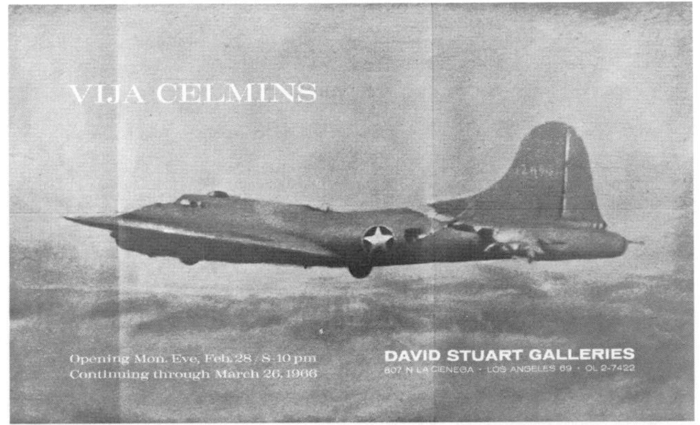

Vija Celmins
David Stuart Galleries
February 28–March 26

John McLaughlin
Felix Landau Gallery
March 1–26

Jawlensky and the Serial Image
Art Gallery, University of California, Irvine
March 4–April 5
Catalog with text by Shirley Hopps, John Coplans
Traveled to Art Gallery, University of California, Riverside

Robert Morris
Dwan Gallery
March 8–April 2

Artforum

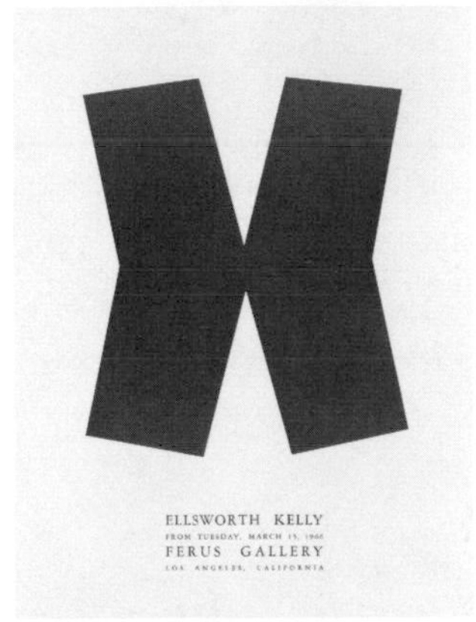

Ellsworth Kelly
Ferus Gallery
March 15–

Joe Goode
Nicholas Wilder Gallery
March 15–April 8

Frank Lobdell
Pasadena Art Museum
March 15–April 10
Catalog with text by
Walter Hopps
Traveled to Stanford University Museum and Art Gallery

Frank J. Thomas

LACMA

Edward Kienholz
Los Angeles County Museum of Art
March 30–May 15
Catalog with text by Maurice Tuchman
Traveled to Institute of Contemporary Art, Boston

Los Angeles Times*

Los Angeles Times

LARGEST CIRCULATION IN THE WEST. 839,735 DAILY, 1,165,396 SUNDAY

VOL. LXXXV † SIX PARTS—PART ONE CC WEDNESDAY MORNING, MARCH 23, 1966 102 PAGES

HIS ART CAUSED A ROW—Edward Kienholz, whose exhibition at County Museum of Art drew the ire of the County Board of Supervisors. He is leaning on one of his works, an animal skull on a human form.

Supervisors Urge Removal of Modern Exhibit at Museum

Assail Art Works by Edward Kienholz as 'Pornographic' but Executive Committee of Institute Rejects Appeal

BY HARRY TRIMBORN
Times Staff Writer

The Board of Supervisors Tuesday urged—but did not order—removal from the County Museum of Art of what it called a "revolting . . . and pornographic" exhibition by modern artist Edward Kienholz.

The appeal was rejected by the executive committee of the museum's board of trustees as an infringement on the museum's obligation to present works "that represent an honest statement by a serious artist."

The display will open next Wednesday and continue through May 14, without any of its originally scheduled presentations removed.

The supervisors' action, taken by unanimous vote, was approval of a letter by Supervisor Warren M. Dorn to trustee president Edward W. Carter, objecting to the display.

Although they vehemently criticized the display, the supervisors stopped short of actually ordering the removal of the works although County Counsel Harold W. Kennedy said they had full authority to order such removal from a county facility.

'Tantamount to Order'

However, Kennedy said after the supervisors' meeting that the action was "tantamount to an order" for removal. But the museum officials interpreted the supervisors' action as a request, not an order.

The supervisors' action touched off a new controversy centering on former museum director Dr. Richard F. Brown, now director of the Kimbell Foundation in Fort Worth.

Dorn declared the exhibition was ordered by Brown as "recrimination" against being fired. It was, he said, a display prompted by "spite."

Brown, supported by his successor, Kenneth Donahue, vehemently denied the charge and the allegation he was fired.

Brown told The Times from Ft. Worth the first proposal to display

Please Turn to Page 31, Col. 1

Assembly OKs Tax for Transit Study

Senate Gets Bill Offering County Alternative Levies

BY JERRY GILLAM
Times Staff Writer

SACRAMENTO—Legislation authorizing temporarily increased taxes to finance preliminary studies for construction of a Southern California mass rapid transit system was approved Tuesday by the Assembly.

A 61-2 vote sent the legislation, authored by Assemblyman Tom C. Carrell (D-San Fernando), to the Senate.

It probably will be referred to the Senate Transportation Committee, headed by Sen. Randolph Collier (D-Yreka). Collier told The Times late Tuesday night he has not read the bill and does not know what his committee might decide to do with it.

The measure would permit Los Angeles County supervisors to adopt one or a combination of three alternative taxes for one year only to raise a total of $3.9 million.

This money would be utilized by the Southern California Rapid Transit District to plan for the proposed system.

The three alternatives open to the supervisors would be:

1—A $1 per vehicle fee.

2—A parking lot tax on up to 5% of gross receipts.

3—A property tax increase.

It is estimated a property tax in-

Please Turn to Page 30, Col. 1

Johnson Backs Wider Contacts With Red China

But He Imposes Condition That Peking Must Soften Its Attitude Toward West

BY RICHARD RESTON
Times Staff Writer

WASHINGTON — President Johnson Tuesday endorsed wider American contacts with Communist China if Peking will soften its belligerent posture toward the West.

His remarks were viewed as a further administration attempt to relax the current harsh dialogue between Washington and Peking.

"We are very anxious to try to have more contact with her (China) and more exchanges with her," the President told an impromptu press conference.

But he noted that "she (China) hangs up the phone" every time the United States proposes moves which would bring about a relaxation of cold war tension.

New Mission to Vietnam

Meanwhile, the President announced the departure of another high-level mission to Vietnam. The fact-finding group will leave Tuesday and will be headed by White House press secretary Bill D. Moyers, Undersecretary of Defense Cyrus R. Vance and Robert Komer, a new special Presidential assistant for "peaceful reconstruction in Vietnam."

Komer's appointment was announced at the press conference.

On the question of improved relations with Peking, Mr. Johnson suggested that it is not the conduct of American policy in Southeast Asia "that creates problems with China. It is China's own position."

Views on China Hearings

He also made the following observations about the China hearings by the Senate Foreign Relations Committee and the House Foreign Affairs Committee:

"We think that it is very good to have the opinion of these professors and experts and ambassadors and other people . . . Until there is some change on China's part, I doubt that these academic discussions will do much more than satisfy people's yearning for information."

Mr. Johnson said the administration

Please Turn to Page 13, Col. 1

Four New Quakes Rock North China

TOKYO (AP) — Four earthquakes, one of great intensity, shook North China Tuesday apparently not far from the city of Singtai, already hit hard by two earth shocks this month. Seismologists in Moscow recorded it as one of the strongest quakes in history.

The shock waves rolled northward to Peking, sending people fleeing into the streets, Japanese correspondents in the Red Chinese capital reported.

In Africa, new earth shocks hit in western Uganda, blocking with rocks the only access road to Kampala, the capital. An earthquake Sunday killed at least 79 persons.

Five similar earthquakes struck around Yugoslavia's Bosnian capital

Please Turn to Page 18, Col. 3

President Cautions Premature Raise ir

AN APOLOGY—James M. Roche, right, president of General Motors, sits with attorney, Theodore C. Sorenson, at Senate hearing at which Roche expressed regrets over any harassment of auto critic Ralph Nader.
UPI Telephoto

GM President Apologizes for Any Harassment of Car Critic

But Denies That Company's Use of Private Detectives to Investigate Author Involved Girls as Sex Lures

BY RONALD J. OSTROW
Times Staff Writer

WASHINGTON—General Motors president James M. Roche apologized Tuesday to a Senate subcommittee for any harassment in a GM-sponsored investigation of an auto safety critic and then hours later repeated his public apology to the critic.

Roche denied that GM's use of private detectives to investigate Ralph Nader involved girls as sex lures, telephone calls at odd hours or other means of intimidation alleged by Nader.

But testimony before the subcommittee revealed that detectives asked questions about such wide-ranging mat and whethe

Nader is t Any Speed," industry safe ticularly crit

On March off (D-Conn. government tee, invited reports were was being ir by private c statement M vestigation c

Concerne

The subco ings on auto pressed conc tion of Nade witness befo Federal Bur is looking in ther harassn witness, a volved.

In their M Tuesday's h sisted the i learn if Nad

Wilson Hit in Eye at Campaign Rally

LONDON (UPI)—Prime Minister Ha-

*Reprinted with permission

© 1966 Los Angeles Times*

"It's awful! . . . Close the door!!"

LACMA

1966

John Baldessari
La Jolla Museum of Art
March 30–April 24

Arakawa
Dwan Gallery
April 12–May 7

Artforum

Bruce Nauman
(first one-man show)
Nicholas Wilder Gallery
May 10–June 2

MAY 10 - JUNE 2 AT THE
NICHOLAS WILDER GALLERY
LOS ANGELES CALIFORNIA

Five Europeans: Bacon, Balthus, Dubuffet, Giacometti, and Morandi
Art Gallery, University of California, Irvine
May 17–June 12
Catalog with text by John Coplans

Jules Olitski
Nicholas Wilder Gallery
June 2–July 1

Self Service, A Happening by Allan Kaprow
Pasadena Art Museum
June–September

Robert Irwin, Kenneth Price
Los Angeles County Museum of Art
July 7–September 4
Catalog with texts by Philip Leider, Lucy R. Lippard

LACMA

René Magritte
Pasadena Art Museum
August 1–September 4

Anthony Magar, Forrest Myers
Dwan Gallery
October 4–29

Artforum

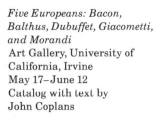

Frank Stella
Pasadena Art Museum
October 17–November 20

Josef Albers: White Line Squares (two lithographic series)
Los Angeles County Museum of Art
October 26–January 29
Catalog with foreword by Kenneth E. Tyler, text by Henry T. Hopkins, and statement by the artist

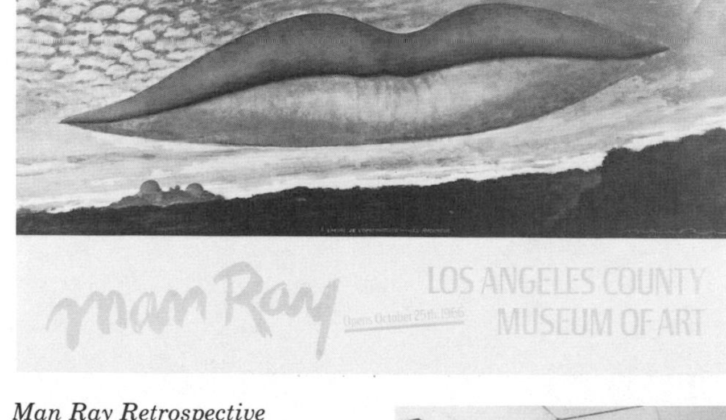

Man Ray Retrospective
Los Angeles County Museum of Art
October 25–January 1
Catalog with foreword by Jules Langsner, statements by the artist and by Paul Eluard, Marcel Duchamp, André Breton, Rrose Selavy, Tristan Tzara, Hans Richter, Carl I. Belz

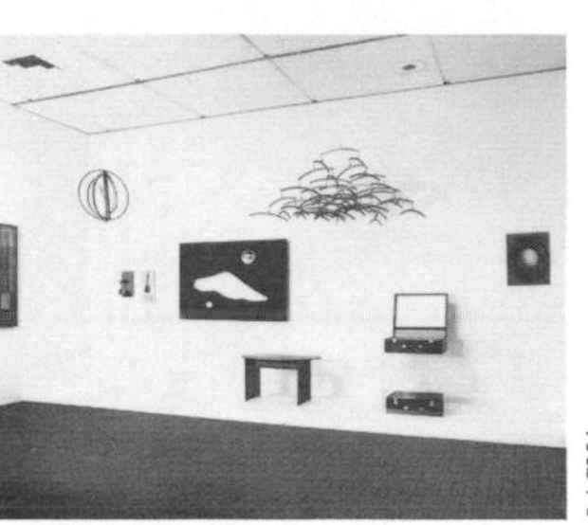
LACMA

Abstract Expressionist Ceramics (Bengston, Frimkess, Mason, McClain, Melchert, Nagle, Neri, Price, Takemoto, Voulkos)
Art Gallery, University of California, Irvine
October 28–November 27
Catalog with text by John Coplans

Gifford Phillips: Some Continuing Trends
The Fine Arts Patrons of Newport Harbor, Balboa Pavilion Gallery
November 6–December 4

John Mason
Los Angeles County Museum of Art
November 16–February 1
Catalog with text by John Coplans

1966

Frank J. Thomas

Dan Flavin (first West Coast show)
Nicholas Wilder Gallery
November 20–December 9

Kenneth Noland
Nicholas Wilder Gallery
November

John Altoon
David Stuart Galleries
December 6–

Jerry McMillen
Pasadena Art Museum
December 13–January 15

Joseph Cornell (retrospective)
Pasadena Art Museum
December 27–February 11
Catalog with text by
Fairfield Porter

ALTOON
DAVID STUART GALLERIES
807 N LA CIENEGA · LOS ANGELES 69 · OL 2-7422

Frank J. Thomas

Exhibitions outside of Los Angeles

Los Angeles Now (Bell, Berman, Collins, Conner, Foulkes, Hopper, Kauffman, Ruscha)
Robert Fraser Gallery, London
January 31–February 19
Catalog with text by
John Coplans

Primary Structures (includes Bell)
The Jewish Museum, New York
April 27–June 12

Ten from Los Angeles (Bell, Bengston, DeLap, Gray, Goode, Kauffman, Mattox, McCracken, Price, Ruscha)
Seattle Art Museum, Washington
July 15–September 5

William Geis and Bruce Nauman
San Francisco Art Institute
September 26–October 22

Ronald Davis
Tibor de Nagy Gallery, New York
October 11–29

Robert Irwin
Pace Gallery, New York
November 12–December 10

1967

Exhibitions in Los Angeles

Tom Holland
Nicholas Wilder Gallery
January 3–21

John Battenberg
Esther Robles Gallery
January 9–27

Kenneth Snelson
Dwan Gallery
January 10–February 4

Artforum

Robert Graham
Nicholas Wilder Gallery
January 24–February 11

Craig Kauffman
Ferus/Pace Gallery
January

Drawings by Frank Stella
Art Gallery, University of California, Irvine
January–February

LACMA

Morris Louis
Los Angeles County Museum of Art
February 15–March 26
Catalog with text by Michael Fried
Organized by Museum of Fine Arts, Boston

Paul Klee Retrospective
Pasadena Art Museum
February 20–April 2
Catalog with text by Will Grohmann

Roy Lichtenstein
Ferus/Pace Gallery
February

Carl Andre
Dwan Gallery
March 8–April 1

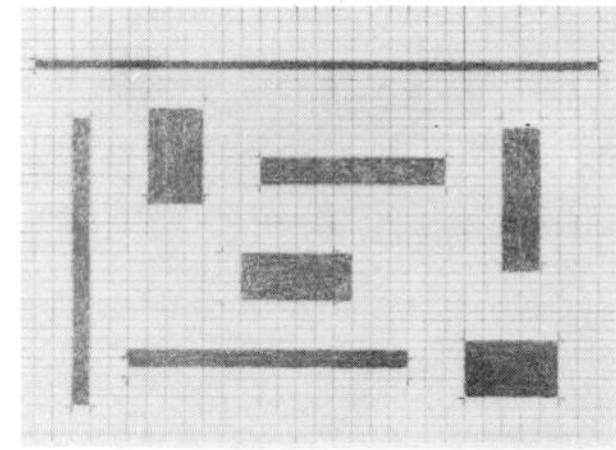

Donald Judd
Ferus/Pace Gallery
March

Helen Frankenthaler, John McCracken
Nicholas Wilder Gallery
March

Sol LeWitt
Dwan Gallery
April 4–29

Roy Lichtenstein
Pasadena Art Museum
April 18–May 28
Catalog with introduction by John Coplans, interview with Lichtenstein
Traveled to Walker Art Center, Minneapolis, Minnesota

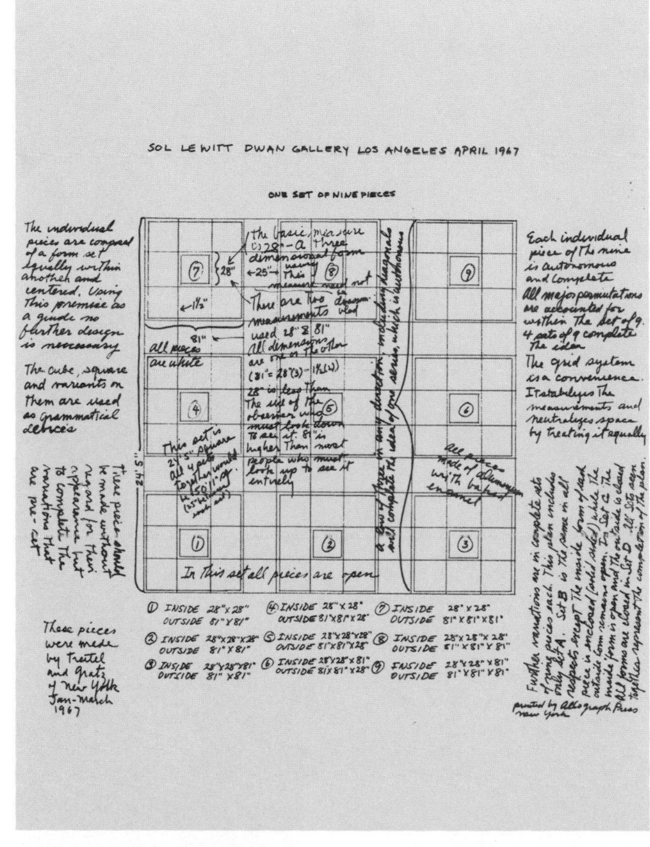

LACMA

American Sculpture of the Sixties (165 works by 80 artists)
Los Angeles County Museum of Art
April 28–June 25
Catalog with introduction by Maurice Tuchman, texts by Lawrence Alloway, Wayne Andersen, Dore Ashton, John Coplans, Clement Greenberg, Max Kozloff, Lucy R. Lippard, James Monte, Barbara Rose, Irving Sandler

1967

Ten (Andre, Baer, Flavin, Judd, LeWitt, Martin, Morris, Reinhardt, Smithson, Steiner)
Dwan Gallery
May 2–27

Dennis Oppenheim
Comara Gallery
May

Robert Rauschenberg
Gemini G.E.L.
May

Vasa
Herbert Palmer Gallery
May

Frank J. Thomas

Peter Voulkos
David Stuart Galleries
May

Selections from the Charles Cowles Collection
Pasadena Art Museum
June 20–July 16

Jackson Pollock Retrospective
Los Angeles County Museum of Art
July 18–September 3
Catalog with text by Francis V. O'Conner
Organized by The Museum of Modern Art, New York

Jules Olitski
Pasadena Art Museum
July 25–August 27
Catalog with text by Michael Fried

Joe Goode, Edward Ruscha
Nicholas Wilder Gallery
August 8–September 2

Mason Williams Bus
Pasadena Art Museum
August 29–September 7

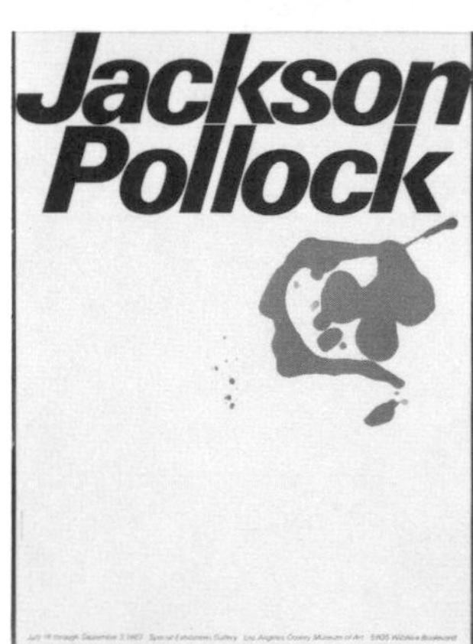

Allan Kaprow
Pasadena Art Museum
September 15–October 22
Catalog with introduction by James Demetrion, text by Allan Kaprow, Kaprow interview by Barbara Berman
Traveled to Washington University, St. Louis, Missouri; University of Texas, Austin

Robert Hudson: Recent Sculpture
Nicholas Wilder Gallery
September 26–October 14

James Turrell
Pasadena Art Museum
September 9–October 9
Catalog with text by John Coplans

Mel Ramos
David Stuart Galleries
October 10–November 4

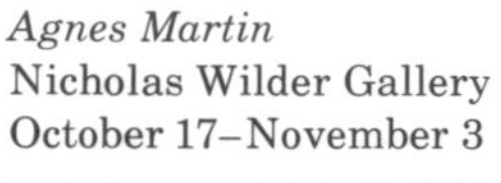

Agnes Martin
Nicholas Wilder Gallery
October 17–November 3

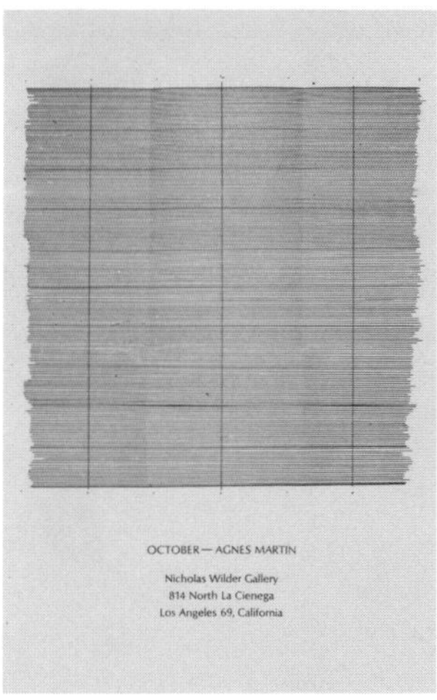

1967

Sam Francis
UCLA Art Galleries
October 30–December 17
Catalog with introduction by Anneliese Hoyer
Organized by San Francisco Museum of Art

UCLA

Ronald Davis
Nicholas Wilder Gallery
November 4–25

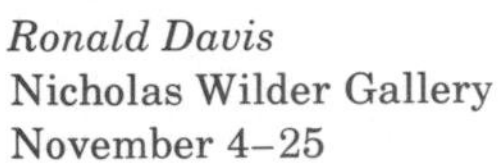

Dry Ice (environment created by Eric Orr, Lloyd Hamrol, Judy Chicago)
Century City
December 14–16

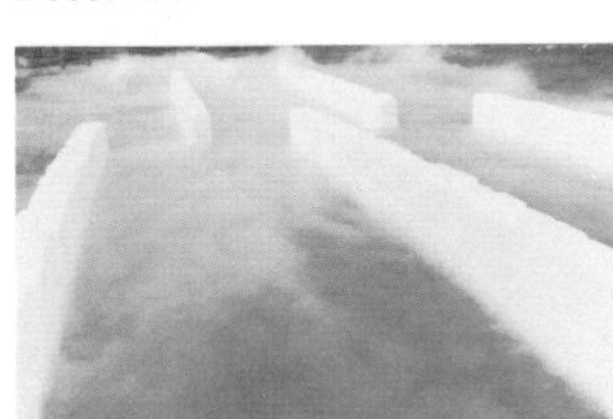

Seymour Rosen

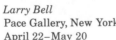

Exhibitions outside of Los Angeles

Ninety-Four Works from the Collection of Sterling Holloway
Portland Art Museum, Oregon
January 24–February 12

Edward Kienholz
Dwan Gallery, New York
January

Craig Kauffman
Pace Gallery, New York
February 18–March 18

The West—80 Contemporaries
The University of Arizona Art Gallery, Tucson
March 19–April 30

Funk (includes Price, Voulkos; 26 artists, most from Northern California)
University Art Museum, University of California, Berkeley
April 18–May 29
Catalog with text by Peter Selz

Larry Bell
Pace Gallery, New York
April 22–May 20

A New Aesthetic (Bell, Davis, Flavin, Judd, Kauffman, McCracken)
Washington Gallery of Modern Art, Washington, D.C.
May 6–June 25
Catalog with text by Barbara Rose

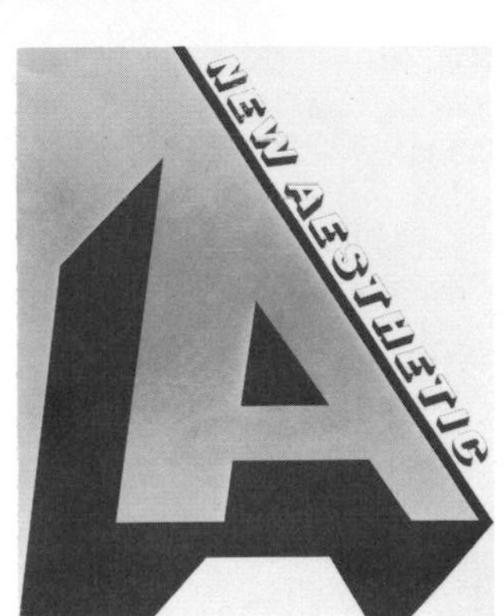

Joe Goode
Rowan Gallery, London
Summer

United States of America V Paris Biennale (Llyn Foulkes, Craig Kauffman, John McCracken, Edward Ruscha)
Musée d'Art Moderne de la Ville de Paris
September 30–November 5
Catalog
Organized by and traveled to Pasadena Art Museum

Sam Francis
Museum of Fine Arts, Houston, Texas
October 12–December 3
Traveled to University Art Museum, University of California, Berkeley

Edward Ruscha (first New York one-man show)
Alexander Iolas Gallery, New York
December 12–January 13

Exhibitions in Los Angeles

UCLA

New British Painting and Sculpture
UCLA Art Galleries
January 8–February 11
Catalog with texts by Sir Herbert Read, Bryan Robertson, Ian Dunlop, David Thompson, Robert Hughes, Frederick S. Wight
Organized by Whitechapel Art Gallery, London

John Altoon
Pasadena Art Museum
January 9–February 4
Catalog with text by Gerald Nordland
Organized by San Francisco Museum of Art; traveled to Art Gallery, University of California, San Diego

Robert Irwin: New Paintings
Pasadena Art Museum
January 16–February 18
Catalog with text by John Coplans

Chaim Soutine, 1893–1943, Retrospective
Los Angeles County Museum of Art
February 20–April 14
Catalog with text by Maurice Tuchman

Dennis Hopper: Bomb Drop
Pasadena Art Museum
February 24–March 17

Frank J. Thomas

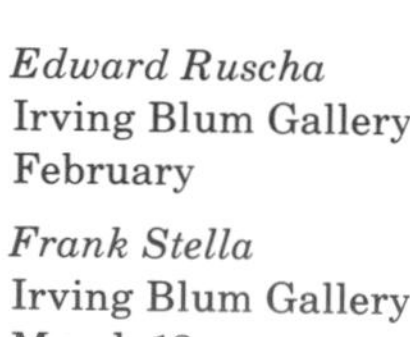

Edward Ruscha
Irving Blum Gallery
February

Frank Stella
Irving Blum Gallery
March 12–

Bruce Nauman
Nicholas Wilder Gallery
March 17–April 17

Ed Ruscha–Joe Goode
The Fine Arts Patrons of Newport Harbor, Balboa Pavilion Gallery
March 27–April 21
Catalog with text by Henry T. Hopkins

Walter de Maria
Nicholas Wilder Gallery
April 9–26

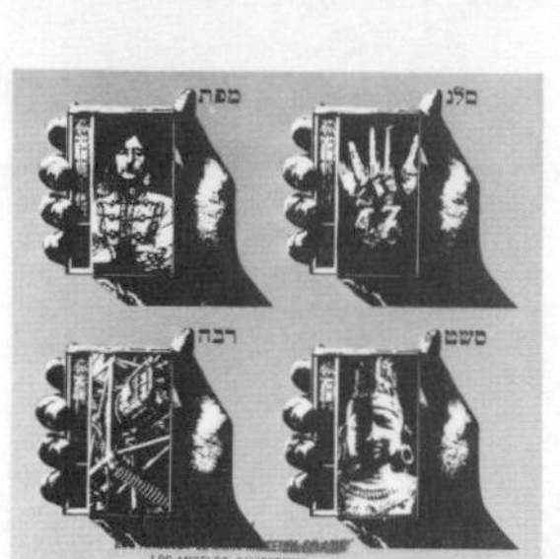

LACMA

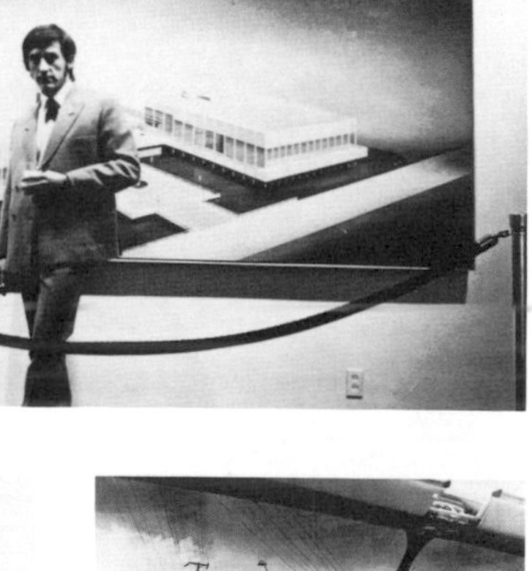

Wallace Berman
Los Angeles County Museum of Art
April 30–June 2
Brochure with text by Gail Scott, statement by Jack Hirschman
Traveled to The Jewish Museum, New York; separate publication with text by James Monte

Donald Judd
Irving Blum Gallery
May 7–26

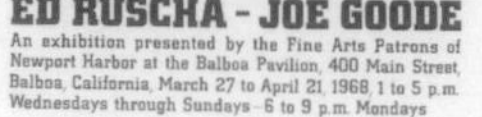

ED RUSCHA - JOE GOODE
An exhibition presented by the Fine Arts Patrons of Newport Harbor at the Balboa Pavilion, 400 Main Street, Balboa, California, March 27 to April 21, 1968, 1 to 5 p.m. Wednesdays through Sundays · 6 to 9 p.m. Mondays

Douglas Wheeler
Pasadena Art Museum
May 28–June 30
Catalog with text by
John Coplans

Claes Oldenburg
Irving Blum Gallery
June 4–

Frank J. Thomas

Assemblage in California
(Berman, Kienholz, Herms,
Conner, F. Mason, Talbert)
Art Gallery, University of
California, Irvine
October 15–November 24
Catalog with texts by John
Coplans, Walter Hopps, Philip
Leider, Hal Glicksman

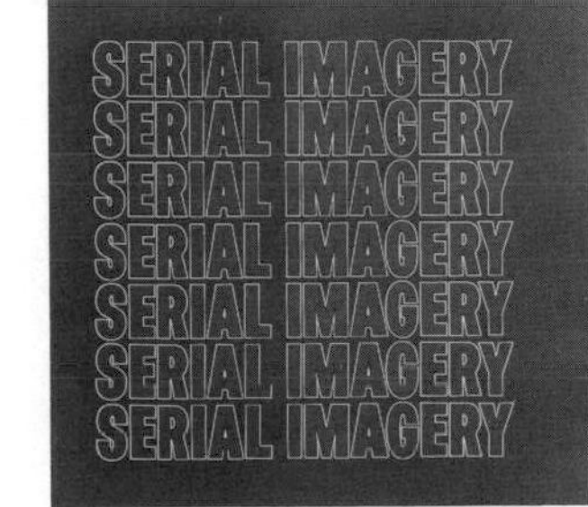

Dada, Surrealism, and Their Heritage
Los Angeles County Museum
of Art
July 16–September 8
Catalog with text by William
S. Rubin
Organized by The Museum of
Modern Art, New York;
traveled to The Art Institute
of Chicago

David Hockney and William Pettet
Nicholas Wilder Gallery
July

Serial Imagery
Pasadena Art Museum
September 17–October 27
Catalog with text by
John Coplans
Traveled to Henry Art Gallery,
University of Washington,
Seattle; Santa Barbara
Museum of Art, California

John Baldessari
Molly Barnes Gallery
October 6–28

LACMA

LACMA

Transparency/Reflection
California State College,
Fullerton
October 18–November 17

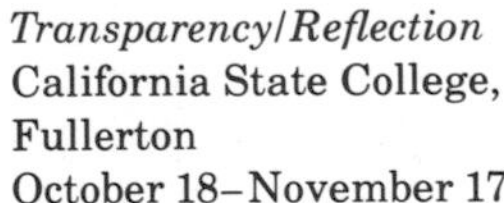

1968

Late Fifties at the Ferus

Late Fifties at the Ferus
(19 artists)
Los Angeles County Museum of Art
November 12–December 17
Catalog with text by James Monte

LACMA

H. C. Westermann
Los Angeles County Museum of Art
November 23–January 12
Catalog with text by James Monte

LACMA

Billy Al Bengston (retrospective)
Los Angeles County Museum of Art
November 26–January 12
Catalog with text by James Monte
Traveled to Corcoran Gallery of Art, Washington, D.C.; Vancouver Art Gallery, British Columbia

Sol LeWitt
Ace Gallery
December 2–January 11

Carl Andre
Irving Blum Gallery
December 3–

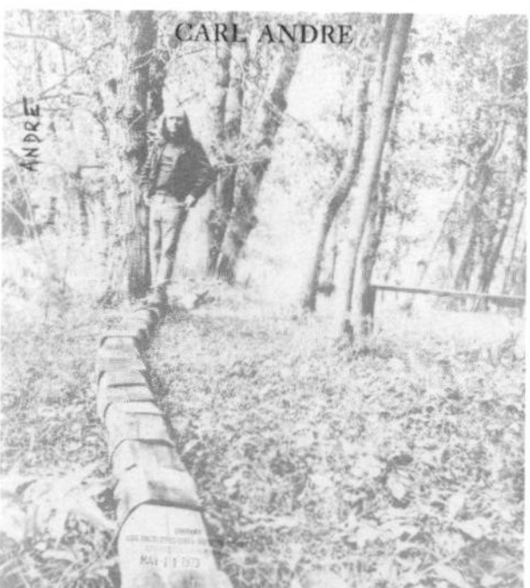

Exhibitions outside of Los Angeles

David Hockney
Kasmin Limited, London
January 19–

Edward Ruscha
Alexander Iolas Gallery, New York
January

The West Coast Now (62 artists)
Portland Art Museum, Oregon
February 9–March 6
Catalog with foreword by Rachel Griffin, texts by Henry T. Hopkins, Gerald Nordland
Traveled to Seattle Art Museum, Washington; M. H. de Young Memorial Museum, San Francisco; Los Angeles Municipal Art Gallery, Barnsdall Park

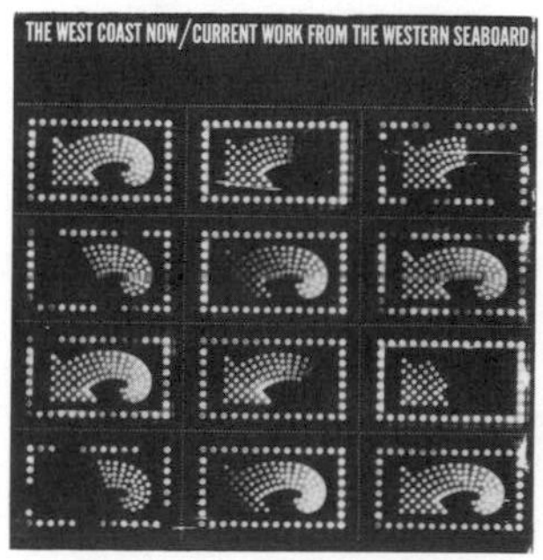

1968

Larry Bell
Stedelijk Museum, Amsterdam
February

Joe Goode
Kornblee Gallery, New York
February

Kenneth Price
Kasmin Gallery, London
March 1–

Robert Irwin
Pace Gallery, New York
March 15–April 11

Gene Davis, Robert Irwin, Richard Smith
The Jewish Museum, New York
March 20–May 12
Separate catalogs for each artist

Los Angeles 6 (Bell, Davis, Irwin, Kauffman, Kienholz, McCracken)
The Vancouver Art Gallery, British Columbia
March 31–May 5
Catalog with text by John Coplans

Archives of American Art

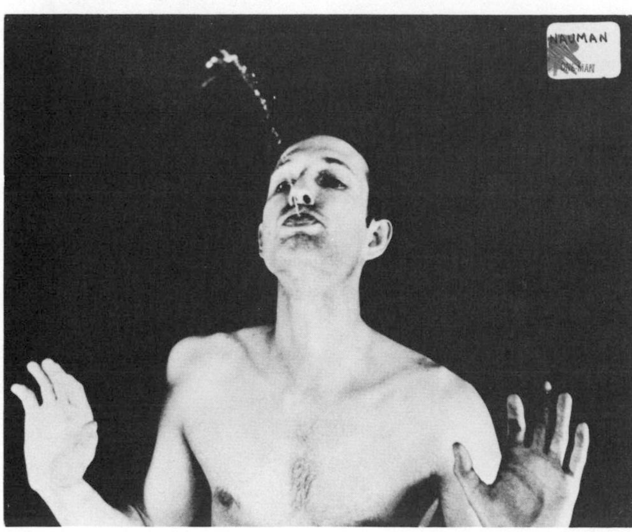

Bruce Nauman
Leo Castelli Gallery, New York
March

40 Now California Painters
The Tampa Bay Art Center, Florida
April 8–May 14
Catalog with text by Henry T. Hopkins, Jan von Adlmann, Karl M. Nickel

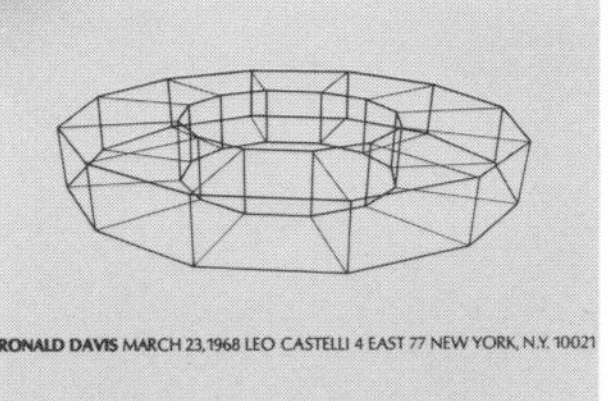

Ronald Davis
Leo Castelli Gallery, New York
March 23–

Documenta 4 (includes Bell, Davis, Hockney, Irwin, Kienholz, Nauman)
Kassel, West Germany
June 27–October 6

Bruce Nauman
Konrad Fischer Gallery, Düsseldorf, West Germany
July 10–August 8

Billy Al Bengston: Motel Dracula
San Francisco Museum of Art
September 1–November 2

California
Janie C. Lee Gallery, Dallas, Texas
October 15–November 15

David Hockney, Oeuvre Katalog–Graphik
Galerie Mikro, Berlin, West Germany
October
Catalog

John McLaughlin Retrospective Exhibition 1946–1967
Corcoran Gallery of Art, Washington, D.C.
November 16–January 5

Works from the 1960's by Edward Kienholz
Washington Gallery of Modern Art, Washington, D.C.
November 22–January 7

Sam Francis
Centre National d'Art Contemporain, Paris
December 10–January 12

Exhibitions in Los Angeles

Bruce Nauman
Nicholas Wilder Gallery
January 28–February 15

Joe Goode
Nicholas Wilder Gallery
January

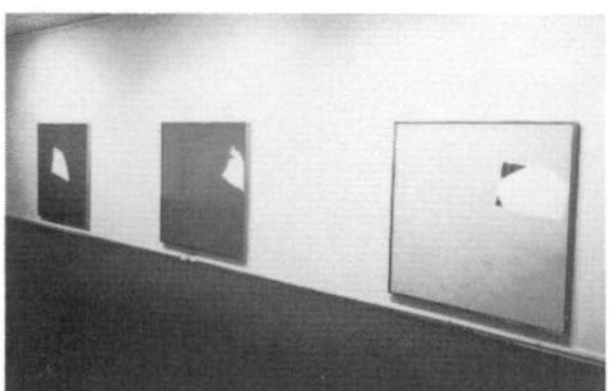

Frank J. Thomas

David Stuart

Erotic Art '69
David Stuart Galleries
February 7–March 4

Cy Twombley
Nicholas Wilder Gallery
March 4–22

Craig Kauffman
Irving Blum Gallery
March 11–

George Herms
Molly Barnes Gallery
March 17–April 11

New York: The Second Breakthrough, 1959–1964 (Dine, Johns, Lichtenstein, Louis, Noland, Oldenburg, Rauschenberg, Rosenquist, Stella, Warhol)
Art Gallery, University of California, Irvine
March–April
Catalog with text by Alan Solomon

Dan Flavin
Irving Blum Gallery
April 1–

LACMA

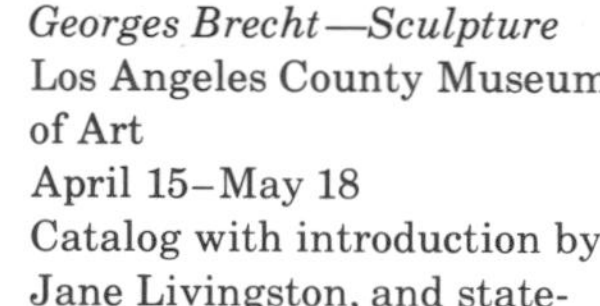

Georges Brecht—Sculpture
Los Angeles County Museum of Art
April 15–May 18
Catalog with introduction by Jane Livingston, and statements by the artist

Ronald Davis
Nicholas Wilder Gallery
April 15–May 3

Judy Gerowitz
Pasadena Art Museum
April 28–June 1

Kenneth Price
Riko Mizuno Gallery
April

New Paintings by Richard Diebenkorn
Los Angeles County Museum of Art
June 3–July 27
Brochure with text by Gail R. Scott

Richard Tuttle
Nicholas Wilder Gallery
June

The Appearing/Disappearing Object (Asher, Ruppersberg, Edge, Cooper, Baldessari, LeVa, Rudnick)
Newport Harbor Art Museum
May 5–June 28

Douglas Huebler
Eugenia Butler Gallery
Spring

1969

Edward Kienholz
Eugenia Butler Gallery
Summer

Ron Cooper
Ace Gallery
Summer

Al Ruppersberg
Eugenia Butler Gallery
Summer

Edward Moses
Riko Mizuno Gallery
Summer

LACMA

Willem de Kooning (retrospective)
Los Angeles County Museum of Art
July 29–September 14
Catalog with text by Thomas B. Hess
Organized by The Museum of Modern Art, New York

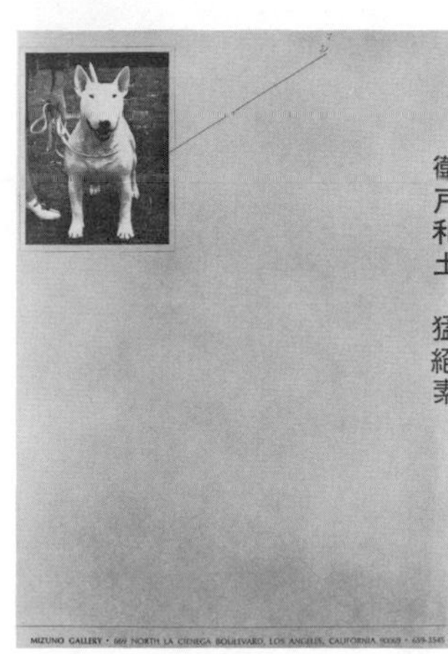

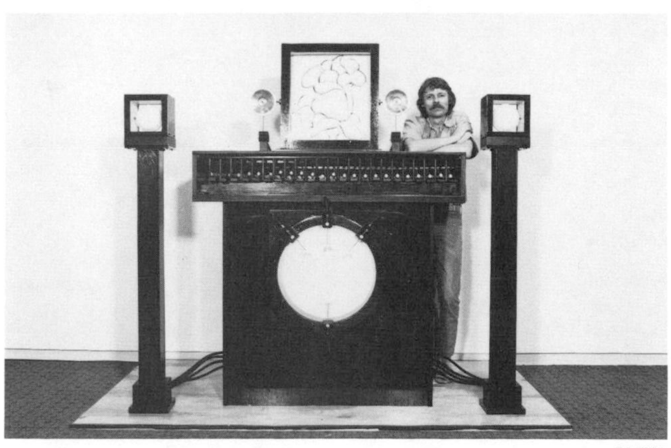

LACMA

Stephan von Huene: The Rosebud Annunciator
Los Angeles County Museum of Art
August 21–September 21
Brochure with text by Hal Glicksman

Recent Work by Robert Irwin
La Jolla Museum of Art
August 28–September 28

Artforum

Les Levine
Molly Barnes Gallery
October 14–November 14

Frank J. Thomas

Mel Bochner
Ace Gallery
September 2–October 6

Lee Mullican
UCLA Art Galleries
September 15–October 19
Catalog with introduction by Gordon Onslow-Ford

Lloyd Hamrol
Pomona College Art Gallery
Fall

Fifty Tantric Mystical Diagrams

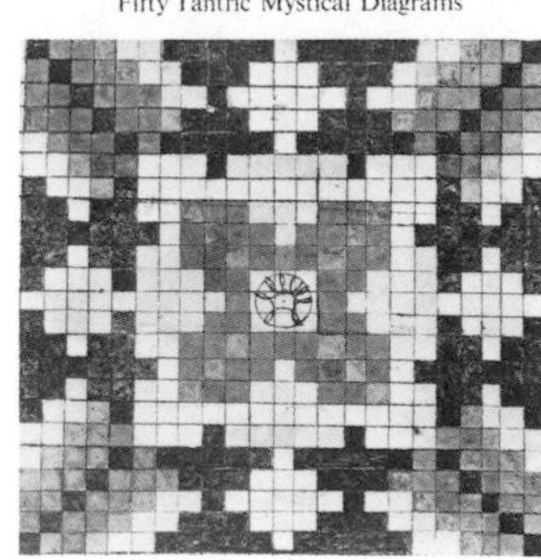

Fifty Tantric Mystical Diagrams
Los Angeles County Museum of Art
October 21–November 23
Brochure with text by Maurice Tuchman, Gail R. Scott, Pratapaditya Pal
Traveled to The Jewish Museum, New York

Tantric Works
Eugenia Butler Gallery
October 28–November 15

Frank Stella
Irving Blum Gallery
November 4–

Michael Asher
La Jolla Art Museum
November 7–December 31

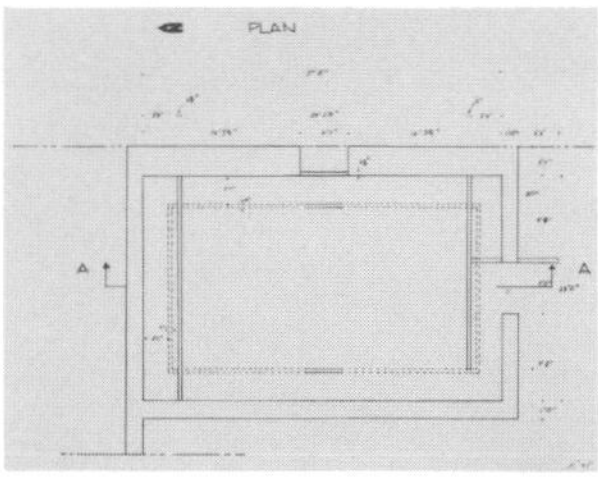

Maxwell Hendler
Eugenia Butler Gallery
November 18–December 6

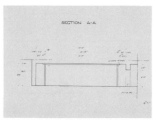

West Coast 1945–1969
Pasadena Art Museum
November 24–January 18
Catalog with introduction by John Coplans
Inaugural exhibition in new building; traveled to City Art Museum of St. Louis, Missouri; Art Gallery of Ontario, Toronto; Fort Worth Art Center Museum, Texas

Frank J. Thomas

Painting in New York 1944–1969
Pasadena Art Museum
November 24–January 11
Catalog with text by Alan Solomon

Eric Orr

Eric Orr—Sound Tunnel
Junior Arts Center, Barnsdall Park
November–May

Sam Francis: Paintings and Gouaches
Felix Landau Gallery
December 1–January 3

William T. Wiley: Monument to Black Ball Violence
Eugenia Butler Gallery
December 9–31

Vija Celmins
Riko Mizuno Gallery
December

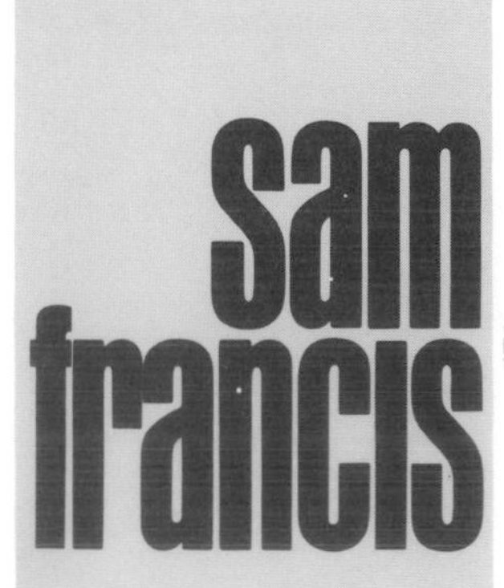

Exhibitions outside of Los Angeles

Three Modern Masters: Billy Al Bengston, Edward Ruscha, Frank Lloyd Wright
Gallery Reese Palley, San Francisco
March 24–April 19

When Attitude Becomes Form
(50 artists, includes Kienholz, Nauman)
Kunsthalle Bern, Switzerland
Spring

Robert Irwin—Douglas Wheeler
Fort Worth Art Center Museum, Texas
April 1–28
Catalog with foreword by Henry T. Hopkins, text by Jane Livingston
Organized by Fort Worth Art Center Museum in cooperation with Corcoran Gallery of Art, Washington, D.C.; Stedelijk Museum, Amsterdam

David Hockney
André Emmerich Gallery, New York
April 26–May 18

Anti-Illusion: Procedure/ Materials (includes Nauman)
Whitney Museum of American Art, New York
May 19–June 22

Bruce Nauman
Leo Castelli Gallery, New York
May 24–June 14

1969

Nine Young Artists, Theodoron Awards (includes Nauman)
The Solomon R. Guggenheim Museum, New York
May 24–June 29

14 Sculptors: The Industrial Edge (14 artists; includes Alexander, Bell, Kauffman, Valentine)
Organized by Walker Art Center, presented at Dayton's Auditorium, Minneapolis, Minnesota
May 29–June 21
Catalog with text by Barbara Rose, Christopher Finch, Martin Friedman

Pop Art Redefined (includes Berman, Goode, Hockney, Kienholz, Ruscha)
Hayward Gallery, London
July 3–September 3
Book by John Russell, Suzi Gablik; published by Thames and Hudson, London

22 California Artists
Phillis Kind Gallery, Chicago
Summer

Ronald Davis: Eight Paintings
Norman Mackenzie Art Gallery, University of Saskatchewan, Regina
September 12–October 19
Catalog with text by Terry Fenton

Kenneth Price Cups
Whitney Museum of American Art, New York
September 19–October 26

Human Concern/Personal Torment: The Grotesque in American Art (includes Kienholz)
Whitney Museum of American Art, New York
October 14–November 30
Catalog with text by Robert Doty

Three California Artists: Bengston, Moses, Ruscha
Multiples Gallery, New York
October

Richard Diebenkorn
Poindexter Gallery, New York
November 1–29

Billy Al Bengston
Utah Museum of Fine Arts, Salt Lake City
November 9–December 7

Kompas 4: West Coast USA
Stedelijk van Abbemuseum, Eindhoven, The Netherlands
November 21–January 4
Catalog with text by Jean Leering

Graphics: Six West Coast Artists (Bengston, Goode, Graham, Moses, Price, Ruscha)
Galleria Milano, Italy
December 10–January 7
By arrangement with Edizioni O

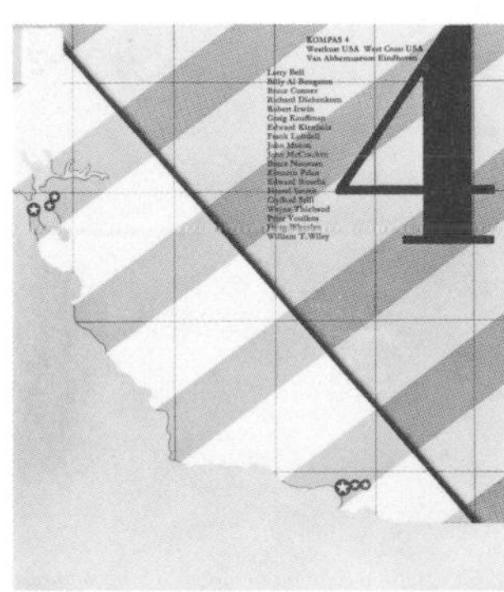

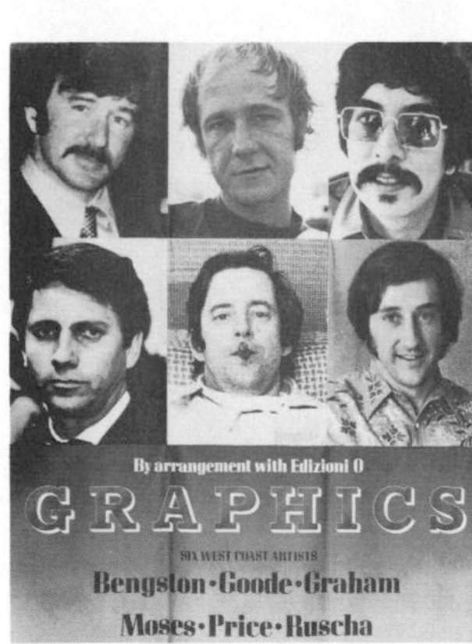

Spaces (includes Bell)
The Museum of Modern Art, New York
December 30–March 1

Bruce Nauman
Galerie Ileana Sonnabend, Paris
Winter

1970

Exhibitions in Los Angeles

Frank J. Thomas

Douglas Wheeler
Ace Gallery
January 2–31

John Cage
Pasadena Art Museum
January 25–March 1

Craig Kauffman
Pasadena Art Museum
January 27–March 1
Catalog with statement by the artist

king kong jello x-ray jello used jello sup
ersonic jello get it on jello disposable je
llo modern jello free jello stoned jello or
gan jello mouse jello am-fm jello formal
jello not now jello live jello monday jello
f.d.r. jello **craig kauffman** jello bubble gu
m jello go down jello jazz jello spoon jel
lo **pasadena art museum** jello five-star j
ello come jello pingpong jello muffin jell
o loud jello tiny rub jello **27 january – 1 m**
arch 1970 jello cuddle jello fish jello dirt
jello steel wool jello bug jello upstairs je
llo drop dead jello mean jello dance jell
o 8x8 jello holy cats jello picture me jell
o cough jello ddt jello lonesome jello for
mica jello blatent jello western jello hop
ping jello undone jello button-down jello
leather jello homeless jello starlet jello f
eather jello oh you kid jello **craig kauffm**
an jello one up jello empty jello sitting je
llo tv jello vietnam jello asphalt jello april
jello ghetto jello until jello oh jello **univers**
ity of california, irvine jello burn baby bu
rn jello ac/dc jello dig jello innocent jello
touch me jello **10 march – 5 april 1970** je
llo love me jello lace jello giggling jello
up jello endless jello sleeping jello brea
the jello finger jello tooth jello fertile jello

Richard Serra
Pasadena Art Museum
January 26–March 1
Catalog

Frank J. Thomas

Joseph Kosuth: Art as Idea/ Idea as Art
Pasadena Art Museum
January 27–March 1

Frank J. Thomas

Agnes Martin
Nicholas Wilder Gallery
January

Frank J. Thomas

Sam Francis
Los Angeles County Museum of Art
February 10–March 22
Brochure with text by Gail R. Scott

Color (Ronald Davis, Ellsworth Kelly, Morris Louis, Kenneth Noland, Jules Olitski, Frank Stella)
UCLA Art Galleries
February 16–March 22
Catalog with acknowledgements by Frederick S. Wight, texts by Charles Kessler, Jan Burland, Melinda Terbell, Richard N. Janick, Sue Ginsburg, Andrea Levin, Lynn Bailess, Carol Donnell, Sister Catherine Bock, Mary Ann Richardson

UCLA

John Baldessari
Eugenia Butler Gallery
February 17–March 7

Michael Todd
UCLA Art Galleries
March 9–April 5
Catalog with text by Thomas H. Garver, and statement by the artist

Frank J. Thomas

Bruce Nauman
Nicholas Wilder Gallery
March

Robert Morris
Irving Blum Gallery
Spring

Richard Artschwager
Eugenia Butler Gallery
Spring

Edward Moses
Riko Mizuno Gallery
Spring

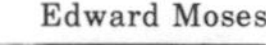

Edward Moses

DeWain Valentine
Pasadena Art Museum
May 11–July 5
Catalog with interview by John Coplans

Andy Warhol
Pasadena Art Museum
May 12–June 21
Catalog with text by John Coplans, Jonas Mekas, Calvin Tomkins
Traveled to Museum of Contemporary Art, Chicago

Dieter Rot: Staple Cheese (A Race)
Eugenia Butler Gallery
May

1970

JUDY GEROWITZ
hereby divests herself of all names imposed upon her through male social dominance and freely chooses her own name
JUDY CHICAGO

Robert Rauschenberg
Pasadena Art Museum
July 7–September 6

Barnett Newman
Pasadena Art Museum
July 30–August 30

David Hockney
Nicholas Wilder Gallery
September

Max Cole
Comara Gallery
October 5–24

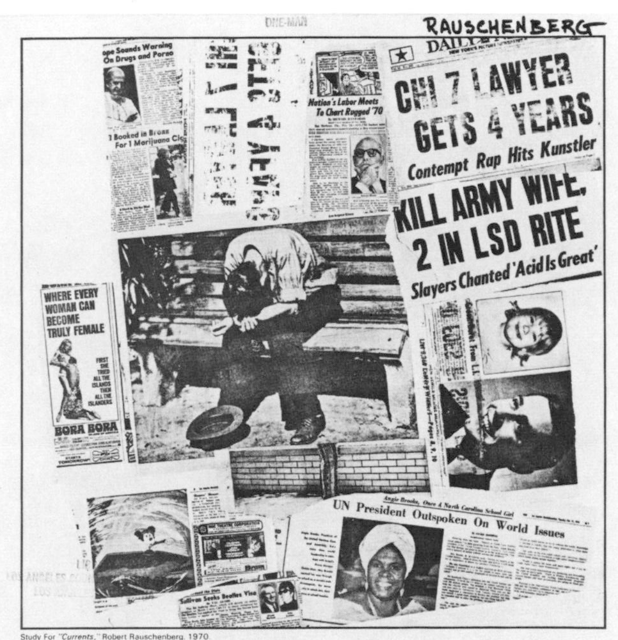

Study For "Currents," Robert Rauschenberg, 1970.

Frank J. Thomas

JUDY CHICAGO
JUDY CHICAGO Exhibition, Cal State Fullerton, Oct. 23 - Nov. 25
Preview 6 - 8 PM, Oct. 23, Faculty Club, Cal State Fullerton

Judy Chicago
California State University, Fullerton
October 23–November 25

Keith Sonnier
Ace Gallery
Fall

Richard Jackson
Eugenia Butler Gallery
Fall

Joe Goode
Nicholas Wilder Gallery
November 17–December 5

Sol LeWitt
Pasadena Art Museum
November 17–January 3
Catalog

The Cubist Epoch
Los Angeles County Museum of Art
December 17–February 21
Catalog with text by Douglas Cooper
Traveled to The Metropolitan Museum of Art, New York

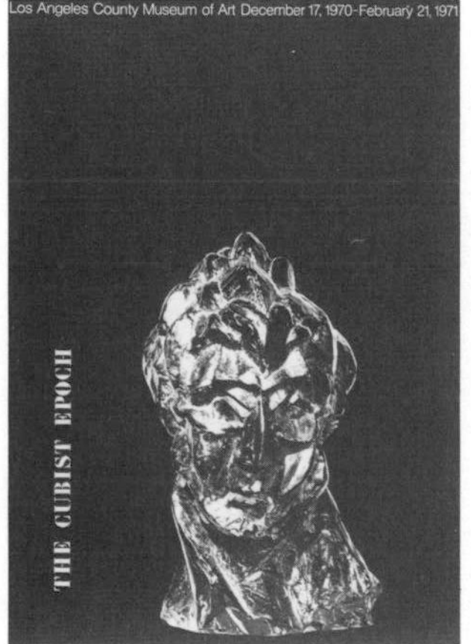

19 70

Exhibitions outside of Los Angeles

11 + 11 Tableaux (Kienholz)
Moderna Museet, Stockholm
January 17–March 1
Catalog with comments from interviews with K. G. Pontus Hultén
Traveled to Stedelijk Museum, Amsterdam; Städtische Kunsthalle, Düsseldorf; Musée d'Art Moderne, Paris; Kunsthaus Zurich, Switzerland; Institute of Contemporary Arts, London

Craig Kauffman
Pace Gallery, New York
March 21–April 8

Joe Goode
Galerie Neuendorf, Hamburg, West Germany
–April 20

Bell/Irwin/Wheeler
Tate Gallery, London
May 5–31

David Hockney, Katalog 31 1970
Kestner-Gesellschaft, Hannover,
West Germany
May 22–June 21

Pace Gallery, N.Y.

Looking West 1970 (74 artists)
Joslyn Art Museum, Omaha, Nebraska
October 18–November 29
Catalog with introduction by LeRoy Butler

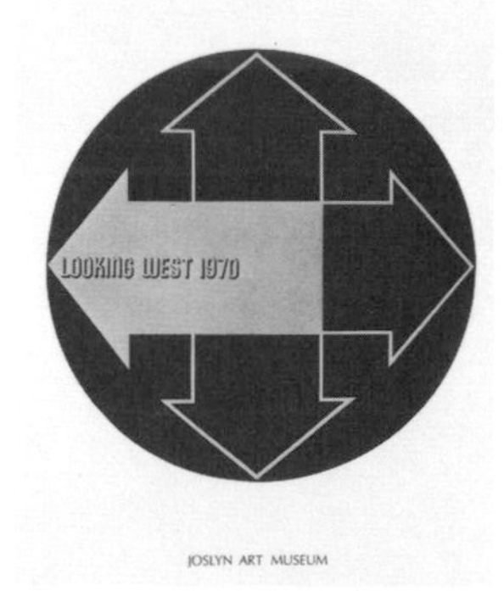

Jerry McMillen

Robert Irwin
The Museum of Modern Art, New York
October 24–February 16

A Decade of California Color (13 artists)
Pace Gallery, New York
November 7–December 2
Brochure

Edward Ruscha
Nigel Greenwood, London
Winter

In addition to the photographers whose images are credited, many individuals and institutions lent me visual materials for the chronology. I am grateful for the cooperation of Irving Blum, Virginia Dwan, The Frederick S. Wight Art Gallery of UCLA, Otis Art Institute of Parsons School of Design, Norton Simon Museum, Pomona College Art Galleries, *Artforum,* and many of the artists cited, who generously shared their resources. The Museum's Photography Department was responsible for photographing all of the posters and gallery announcements.

S.P.

Photographic Credits

Archives of American Art: p. 83 (lower).

Art in America: p. 32.

Larry Bell: p. 54 (upper and lower).

Billy Al Bengston: pp. 57 (left), 76, 86 (upper).

Charles Brittin: pp. 12 (left and right), 13 (left and right), 60.

The Brooklyn Museum, New York: p. 68 (lower).

Rudolph Burckhardt: p. 90.

Giorgio Colombo Fotografo: p. 49.

Ralph Crane, *Life Magazine,* © 1966 Time Inc.: p. 80 (lower).

Prudence Cuming Associates Ltd.: p. 26 (right), 75.

Dartmouth College Museum and Galleries, Hanover, New Hampshire: p. 96 (right).

Michael Denny: p. 58 (left).

Susan Einstein: p. 78.

Pat Faure: p. 77.

Sam Francis: pp. 69 (upper), 70.

Betty Freeman: p. 73 (lower left).

Gilman Paper Company: p. 91.

Joe Goode: p. 71 (lower).

Gianfranco Gorgont: p. 89 (left).

Richard M. Grant: p. 66 (lower).

Graves Art Gallery, Sheffield, England: p. 27 (middle left).

Dennis Hopper: pp. 57 (right), 63 (middle), 95 (upper).

Janss Foundation: p. 27 (middle right).

Robert Jaye: p. 63 (upper and lower).

John Kasmin: p. 73 (upper left).

Edward Kienholz: p. 80 (upper).

Mr. and Mrs. Gilbert H. Kinney: p. 68 (upper).

M. Knoedler & Co. Ltd., London: p. 43.

Los Angeles County Museum of Art: pp. 14 (left and right), 15 (right), 27 (upper left and right), 31, 37, 38, 39, 40, 42, 45, 47, 48, 50, 51, 55 (right), 56, 58 (right), 59, 61, 62 (upper and lower), 67, 72, 73 (upper and lower right), 74, 75 (lower), 79 (upper and lower), 81, 82, 84, 85 (upper), 87 (left and right), 93, 94 (left and right), 97, 100.

Margo Leavin Gallery, Los Angeles: p. 44.

Frances and Sydney Lewis: p. 96 (left).

Colin McRae: p. 41.

Museum of Fine Arts, Boston: p. 26 (left).

The Museum of Modern Art, New York: p. 46.

The Oakland Museum, California: p. 99 (left).

Kenneth Price: p. 92.

Robert Rowan: p. 85 (lower).

Edward Ruscha: p. 95 (lower).

The Santa Barbara Museum of Art, California: p. 99 (right).

Eric Schaal: p. 15 (left).

David Stuart Galleries, Los Angeles: p. 98.

Frank J. Thomas: pp. 30, 52, 55 (left), 64, 65 (upper and lower), 69 (lower), 88, 89 (right).

John Waggaman: pp. 66 (upper), 83 (upper), 86 (upper).

Walker Art Center, Minneapolis, Minnesota: pp. 27 (lower), 33.

Board of Supervisors, County of Los Angeles, 1981

Los Angeles County Museum of Art

Board of Trustees, Fiscal 1980–81